The Psychology of Prejudice and Discrimination

The Psychology of Prejudice and Discrimination

VOLUME 2
ETHNICITY AND MULTIRACIAL IDENTITY

Edited by
Jean Lau Chin

Foreword by
Joseph E. Trimble

PRAEGER PERSPECTIVES

Race and Ethnicity in Psychology
Jean Lau Chin, John D. Robinson, and Victor De La Cancela
Series Editors

Westport, Connecticut
London

Library of Congress Cataloging-in-Publication Data

The psychology of prejudice and discrimination / edited by Jean Lau Chin ; foreword by Joseph E. Trimble.

    p. cm.—(Race and ethnicity in psychology, ISSN 1543-2203)

    Includes bibliographical references and index.

    ISBN 0-275-98234-3 (set : alk. paper)—ISBN 0-275-98235-1 (v. 1 : alk. paper)—ISBN 0-275-98236-X (v. 2 : alk. paper)—ISBN 0-275-98237-8 (v. 3 : alk. paper)—ISBN 0-275-98238-6 (v. 4 : alk. paper) 1. Prejudices—United States. I. Chin, Jean Lau. II. Series.

BF575.P9P79 2004

303.3'85'0973—dc22   2004042289

British Library Cataloguing in Publication Data is available.

Library of Congress Catalog Card Number: 2004042289
ISBN: 0-275-98234-3 (set)
       0-275-98235-1 (Vol. 1)
       0-275-98236-X (Vol. 2)
       0-275-98237-8 (Vol. 3)
       0-275-98238-6 (Vol. 4)
ISSN: 1543-2203

First published in 2004

Praeger Publishers, 88 Post Road West, Westport, CT 06881
An imprint of Greenwood Publishing Group, Inc.
www.praeger.com

Printed in the United States of America

The paper used in this book complies with the Permanent Paper Standard issued by the National Information Standards Organization (Z39.48-1984).

10 9 8 7 6 5 4 3 2

Contents

Foreword

Civilized men have gained notable mastery over energy, matter, and inanimate nature generally and are rapidly learning to control physical suffering and premature death. But, by contrast, we appear to be living in the Stone Age so far as our handling of human relations is concerned.

(Gordon W. Allport, 1954, p. ix)

Although written over fifty years ago, the haunting words of the eminent social psychologist Gordon W. Allport may ring true today. His intent then was to clarify the various elements of the enormously complex topic of prejudice. Since the writing of his now well-cited and highly regarded text on prejudice, social and behavioral scientists have made great strides in furthering our knowledge of the field. Since 1950, for example, thousands of books, journal articles, and book chapters have been devoted to studying prejudice and discrimination. Professor Allport would be somewhat pleased with the numbers because that was partly his expectation when he said, "So great is the ferment of investigation and theory in this area that in one sense our account will soon be dated. New experiments will supersede old, and formulations of various theories will be improved" (1954, p. xiii). But has there been that much improvement that we have moved away from a Stone Age understanding of human relations to a higher level of sophistication? The question begs for an answer, but that can wait until later.

Let me back up for a moment to explore another line of thought and inquiry that bears directly on the significance and importance of this wonderful set of books on the psychology of prejudice and discrimination. For as long as I can remember, I have been deeply interested in the origins of, motives in, and attitudes about genocide and ethnocide; as a young child I did not use those horrific terms, as I did not know them then. But I did know about their implied destructive implications from stories passed along by sensitive teachers, ancestors, and elders. The deep social psychological meaning of the constructs later became an intense interest of mine as a graduate student in the turbulent 1960s, an era filled with challenges and protestations of anything regarding civil rights, discrimination, racism, sexism, and prejudice. During that era I threw my mind and spirit into the study of Allport's writings on prejudice—not merely to study them, but to explore every nuance of his scholarly works to expand the depth of my understanding and expecting to come away with fewer questions and more answers. I was not disappointed in my exploration. I was baffled, though, because I recognized more so just how complicated it was to prevent and eradicate prejudice and discrimination.

As I write these thoughts, I am reminded of a sign that was once posted over the porch roof of an old restaurant and tavern in a rural South Dakota community adjacent to an American Indian reservation. The sign was hand-painted in white letters on a long slat of weathered wood; it was written in the Lakota language, and the English translation read, "No dogs or Indians allowed." The store was and is still owned by non-Indians. The offensive, derogatory sign is no longer there—likely torn down years ago by angry protestors from the nearby reservation. While the sign is gone, the attitude and intent of the message still linger in and around the rustic building, except that it is more insidious, pernicious, and guileful now. The prevailing prejudicial and loathsome attitude is a reflection of many of the residents of the small town. Many of the town's residents tolerate Native Americans because they dependent on them economically, but their bigoted and closed-minded convictions are unwilling to accept Native Americans as equals and provide them with freedom of movement and expression.

The wretched, mean-spirited, pernicious attitudes present in that rural South Dakota town symbolize the prevailing changes in attitudes and behavior across North America—the blatant signs are gone, but in many places and for many individuals the prejudicial attitudes persist, sometimes in sly and subtle forms. On other occasions they are overt and repulsive. Chapters in these volumes summarize and explore the social and psychological motives and reasoning behind the persistence of prejudicial attitudes and discriminatory practices. They go beyond the conclusions drawn by Professor Allport and other early writers on the topic and take us into domains represented by those who have experienced prejudice and discrimination firsthand, as did their ancestors. Indeed, a voice not included in early studies on prejudice and discrimination is intensified and deepened as more and more ethnic groups and women are represented in the social and behavioral sciences than in years gone by.

Stories and anecdotes, too, recounted by the rising groups of diverse scholars and researchers, lend a new authenticity to the literature. Some of the accounts provide a different perspective on historical events involving racial hatred that provide more thorough descriptions of the details and perspectives. Revisionist historical approaches have a place in the study of prejudice and discrimination because for so long the authentic voices of the victims were muffled and muted. For example, as a consequence of European contact, many Native American communities continue to experience individual and community trauma, a "wound to the soul of Native American people that is felt in agonizing proportions to this day" (Duran & Duran, 1995, p. 27). The cumulative trauma has been fueled by centuries of incurable diseases, massacres, forced relocation, unemployment, economic despair, poverty, forced removal of children to boarding schools, abuse, racism, loss of traditional lands, unscrupulous land mongering, betrayal, broken treaties—the list goes on. Brave Heart and DeBruyn (1998) and Duran and Duran (1995) maintain that postcolonial "historical and intergenerational trauma" has left a long trail of unresolved grief and a "soul wound" in Native American communities that contribute to high levels of social and individual problems such as alcoholism, suicide, homicide, domestic violence, child abuse, and negative career ideation. The presence of Native American scholars contributed a voice that was suppressed for decades because some feared the consequences if these scholars told their stories. The stories and accounts of past racial events and their corresponding trauma also were not told because there were few visible ethnic scholars available.

Decades ago the topics of prejudice and discrimination largely emphasized race and, more specifically, the racial experiences of black Americans. Over the years the topic has expanded to include the experiences of other ethnic groups, women, the elderly, those with disabilities, those with nonheterosexual orientations, and those with mixed ethnic heritages. The volumes edited by Jean Lau Chin expand the concepts of diversity and multiculturalism to add a broader, more inclusive dimension to the understanding of prejudice and discrimination. The addition of new voices to the field elevates public awareness to the sweeping effects of prejudice and discrimination and how they are deeply saturated throughout societies.

The amount of scholarly attention devoted to the study of prejudice and discrimination closely parallels the growth of ethnic diversity interests in psychology. Until about thirty years ago, psychology's mission appeared to be restricted to a limited population as references to blacks, Asian Americans, Native American and Alaska natives, Hispanics, Pacific Islanders, and Puerto Ricans were almost absent from the psychological literature; in fact, the words *culture* and *ethnic* were rarely used in psychological textbooks. The long absence of culture in the web of psychological inquiry did not go unnoticed. About three decades ago, ethnic minority and international psychologists began questioning what the American Psychological Association meant by its use of *human* and to whom the vast body of psychological knowledge applied. America's ethnic psychologists and those from other countries, as well as a small handful of North American psychologists, argued that American psychology did not include what constituted the world's population. They claimed that findings were biased, limited to studies involving college and university students and laboratory animals, and therefore not generalizable to all humans. Comprehensive literature reviews reinforced their accusations and observations.

Accusations of imperialism, cultural encapsulation, ethnocentrism, parochialism, and, in some circles of dissent, of "scientifically racist" studies, run the gamut of criticisms hurled at the field of psychology during that period. Robert Guthrie (1976), for example, writing in his strongly worded critique of psychology, *Even the Rat Was White*, argues that culture and context were not taken seriously in the history of psychological research. Given these conditions and the myopia of the profession, it is no small wonder that prejudice and discrimination were not given more widespread attention. The topic was not perceived as salient and important enough for extensive consideration. The four volumes in this set are a testament to the amount of change and emphasis that are focused on ethnicity, culture, and the topics of prejudice and discrimination.

The changing demographics in the United States call into question the relevance of a psychology that historically has not included ethnic and racial groups and that fostered a research agenda that was ethnocentric and bound by time and place. This can no longer be tolerated, as the rapid growth of ethnic minority groups in the United States amplifies the need for more attentiveness on the part of the social and behavioral sciences. Consider the population projections offered by the U.S. Bureau of the Census. By 2050, the U.S. population will reach over 400 million, about 47 percent larger than in 2000 (U.S. Bureau of the Census, 2001). The primary ethnic minority groups—specifically, Hispanics, blacks, Asian Americans, and Native American and Alaska Natives—will constitute almost 50 percent of the population in 2050. About 57 percent of the population under the age of eighteen, and 34 percent over the age of 65, will be ethnic minorities.

America never was and likely will not be a melting pot of different nationalities and ethnic groups for another century or two. As the mixture and size of ethnic groups increase, we are faced with the disturbing possibility that an increase in prejudice and discrimination will occur accordingly. Given this possibility, the topics covered in these volumes become even more worthy of serious consideration, especially the ones that emphasize prevention. Given the demographic changes and the topical changes that have occurred in the social and behavioral sciences, the extensive contents of these four volumes are a welcome addition to the field. Editor Jean Lau Chin and her long list of chapter authors are to be congratulated for their monumental effort. The volumes are packed with useful and wonderfully written material. Some is based on empirical findings, some on firsthand experiences. The blend of various writing styles and voice adds to the breadth of coverage of the topic. The many points of view provided by the contributors will help shape the direction of research and scholarly expression on a topic that has been around since the origins of humankind. We can hope that the contributions of these four volumes will move the field of human relations from a perceived Stone Age level of understanding to one where we believe we are moving closer to eliminating prejudice, discrimination, and the vile hatred they engender.

Joseph E. Trimble
Professor of Psychology
Western Washington University
Bellingham, WA
March 21, 2004

REFERENCES

Allport, G. W. (1954). *The nature of prejudice*. Garden City, NY: Doubleday.

Brave Heart, M. Y. H., & DeBruyn, L. (1998). The American Indian holocaust: Healing unresolved grief. *American Indian and Alaska Native Mental Health Research, 8*(2), 56–78.

Duran, E., & Duran, B. (1995). *Native American postcolonial psychology*. Albany, NY: State University of New York Press.

Guthrie, R. (1976). *Even the rat was white: A historical view of psychology*. New York: Harper & Row.

U.S. Bureau of the Census. (2001). *Census of the population: General population characteristics, 2000*. Washington, DC: Government Printing Office.

Introduction

Prejudice and discrimination are not new. The legacy of the Pilgrims and early pioneers suggested a homogenous, mainstream America. Our early emphasis on patriotism in the United States resulted in a false idealization of the melting pot myth. Prejudice and discrimination in American society were overt and permeated all levels of society, that is, legislation, government, education, and neighborhoods. In the 1960s, attempts to eradicate prejudice, discrimination, and racism were explicit—with an appeal to honor and value the diversity within different racial and ethnic groups. This soon extended to other dimensions of diversity, including gender, disability, and spirituality. However, long after the war to end slavery, the civil rights movement of the 1960s, desegregation in the schools, and the abolition of anti-Asian legislation—indeed, in the midst of growing public debate today regarding gay marriage—we still see the pernicious effects of prejudice and discrimination in U.S. society.

Prejudice and discrimination toward differences in race, ethnicity, gender, spirituality, and disability have had negative psychological consequences, and they continue in primarily covert forms. Bias and disparities still exist and result in inequity of services, opportunities, and practices in American society. Combating prejudice and discrimination in today's environment warrants some different strategies. We live in an environment of heightened anxiety due to war and terrorism. Thanks to technological advances in communication, travel, and the

Internet, news and information from all parts of the world are almost instantaneously brought to us. We live in a global economy with a narrowing of borders between countries and groups. Generations of immigrants have resulted in the U.S. population becoming so diverse that there may soon be no single majority group within most major cities. Technological advances have eliminated the biological advantage of males in strength and the biological "limitations" of women of childbearing age in the work environment. Yet, the more things change, the more they stay the same. Irrational and unjust perceptions of other people remain—more subtle, perhaps, but they remain.

This four-volume set, *The Psychology of Prejudice and Discrimination*, takes a fresh look at that issue that is embedded in today's global environment. Images, attitudes and perceptions that sustain prejudice and discrimination are more covert, but no less pernicious. What people say, believe, and do all reflect underlying bias. **We do not claim here to address every existing form of prejudice or discrimination, nor do we cite every possible group targeted today. What we offer are insights into a range from the most to least recognized, or openly discussed, forms of this injustice.** Each chapter offers new perspectives on standing issues, with practical information about how to cope with prejudice and discrimination. The "toolbox" at the end of each chapter suggests steps to be taken at different levels to combat prejudice and discrimination and to achieve change. At the individual level, self-reflection needs to occur by both the victims and perpetrators of discrimination. Practitioners, educators, and all who deliver services potentially impart a bias perpetuating prejudice and discrimination. At the systems level, communities and policymakers must join together and have the will to combat discrimination.

How does one remain "whole" or validate one's identity despite persistent assaults to self-esteem from prejudice and discrimination? How does one raise children or teach amid societal institutions that perpetuate bias? Culturally competent principles and practices are needed to provide a framework for managing diversity and valuing differences.

Volume 1, *Racism in America*, looks at stereotypes, racial bias, and race relations. How do we avoid internalizing racism or accepting negative messages about a group's ability and intrinsic worth? How do we address institutionalized racism that results in differential access to goods, service, and opportunities of society? Volume 2, *Ethnicity and Multiracial Identity*, looks at discrimination toward differences due to immigration, language, culture, and mixed race. Volume 3,

Bias Based on Gender and Sexual Orientation, looks at gender bias, women's issues, homophobia, and oppression of gay/lesbian lifestyles. Volume 4, *Disability, Religion, Physique, and Other Traits*, strives to examine less-spotlighted bias against other forms of difference, and begins the difficult dialogue that must take place if we are to eradicate prejudice and discrimination.

Written for today's people and environment, these volumes are rich with anecdotes, stories, examples, and research. These stories illustrate the emotional impact of prejudice and discrimination throughout history and as it still strikes people's lives today. While the chapters spotlight psychology, they interweave history, politics, legislation, social change, education, and more. These interdisciplinary views reflect the broad contexts of prejudice and discrimination that ultimately affect identity, life adjustment, and well-being for every one of us.

Please take with you the strategies for change offered in the toolbox at the end of each chapter. Change needs to occur at all levels: individual, practitioner/educator, and community. The intent of the toolboxes is to move us from the emotional to the scholarly to action and empowerment. They are intended to encourage and compel readers to begin individual change that will spur community and social action. With each person who reads these volumes, gains understanding, and finds the motivation or method to help make his or her small part of the world a more just and open-minded place, we have moved closer to making our goal a reality.

Jean Lau Chin

CHAPTER 1

Light, Bright, Damned Near White: Multiracial Identity

Stephanie Rose Bird

In a country whose cultural orientation is built around sharp divisions marked by the polar opposite colors black and white, people who combine these two groups have struggled to assert their identities. Black and white people are pitted against one another, portrayed as being in opposition visually and culturally. While the group generally called *biracial* is a complex territory to explore both psychologically and culturally, there are also long-standing groups, referred to historically as *triracial isolates*, whose heritage blends the two groups with the addition of various Native American nations. This chapter explores the historic and contemporary issues involved with triracial and biracial American ancestry. It will also examine such occurrences abroad, pointing to the "Stolen Generation" of Australia and the noble families of Europe.

Finally, this chapter will assist readers in their search for ancestry. Woven throughout are the psychological issues raised by the assertion of biracial or triracial identity, as opposed to homogenous cultural identification as black, white, or Native American. The prejudice from dominant racial groups because of homogenous identifications is discussed along with suggestions for healing and moving forward while keeping multiracial identity intact.

WHERE DOES TAN FIT IN THE AMERICAN RACIAL RAINBOW?

When I was growing up in the 1960s and 1970s, it was common to hear the chant "Light, Bright, Damned Near White" directed at people who were obviously of mixed heritage. The blunt ethnic-cultural description "black" did a fine job of eradicating use of the terms *quadroon*, *octoroon*, and *mulatto*, which had become divisive, yet such blanket terms could never erase the complexity of mixed heritage. In South America, mestees and mestizos are a blended racial group with a distinctive identity shaped by a confluence of cultural influences. Apart from anthropologists and other scholars, few Americans readily use the terms when discussing multiracial or multicultural groups.

In the second half of the twentieth century, a concerted effort was made in North America to characterize mixed-heritage people as simply white or black. Some individuals of mixed heritage readily adopt the crisp white or black racial tags. However, a new generation of "tan" people seeks accurate definitions of their complex identity. For these people, checking the "other" box on an application or census is not an option, as it excludes segments of their ancestral heritage—often a parent or grandparents.

Personal Insights

Like many other Americans, I always knew that I was African, Native American, and European by blood but knew I was black in the eyes of America. As an artist and writer, I have been candid and dogged in my exploration of race. I know that I am a mélange of many cultures, though I identify culturally and racially with being black while recognizing strong Native American and European influences.

When I began to write my memoir *A Walkabout Home*, I wanted to be quite candid about my ethnicity; after all, my entire memoir is an exploration of identity. My memoir explores my physical, spiritual, and metaphysical being. Through my grandmother and her sisters, I heard strange names like *Red Bone*, *Guinea*, and *Moor*—silently, I wondered if they were talking about themselves. Then too, Grandma frequently mentioned that when she was in New England, people thought she was of Portuguese descent. Quite naturally, I wanted to know whether I was indeed a "red bone," a cultural group name black people felt comfortable assigning based on appearance, or whether my family were descendants of the "Guineas." Looking through my family photographs, I noticed an array of skin colors from black to white, with many tan families in between. According to family legend, several groups opted out of black society entirely, creating for themselves a mythic ancestry as white "ethnics" instead.

TOO LIGHT TO BE BLACK, TOO DARK TO BE WHITE: THE WAY OF MY PEOPLE

Pop, Ma's dad, had an interesting story and a peculiar way about him. He was born in 1890 on a plantation, the son of the English-Irish master and a former African slave mother. While this is common family knowledge, it should be noted that such offspring raised as free children are an anomaly. I say he was peculiar because he was a true reflection of his father, who was white, more so than his African-descended mother. He never really saw himself as black; nevertheless, he knew he wasn't white, either. A proud colored Negro—still, though most of us had embraced the concept of blackness long ago. His manners had strong affinities toward the British Isles rather than sharing the casual impromptu nature of either white or black American culture. Intercultural as well as interracial, he was proper to a fault: a real old-fashioned gentleman and philosophical to boot. He had a never-ending stockpile of proverbs, and this was one of his distinctive Africanisms.

Then there was Dad's part of the family. As if we were counting down to the new year, lil' brother and I were spellbound by an excruciating anticipation when we visited Dad's family, as we would mark off the seventeen or so exits of the New Jersey turnpike and parkway that drew the line between north and south New Jersey. We headed to north Jersey or, more specifically, to East Orange. It wasn't the city itself that moved us. East Orange was experiencing the steep decline that has blighted many a black neighborhood. There was a dwindling police presence, with an increase in drug dealing, number running (street lottery), violent crime, and funeral homes. Still, we loved the place, not for what it was, but because it was our ancestral home. Almost all of our people on Dad's side of the family lived within a few miles of East Orange—Mom's as well.

My great-grandmother was a laundress. To some folks' ears, that may sound humble, almost shameful; but it was a decent, well-paying job for a woman of color during her times. It was not without its challenges, either, as the clientele tended to be upper-class white people from suburban West Orange, Short Hills, and Upper Montclair in north Jersey. Ironing and mending were her specialties. She was a brown-skinned woman with cottony soft hair and high cheekbones; her mother was part Native American. My father would recount memories of her strength, clarity, and wisdom; what a great cook she was and how very tough she was; but for us she was a warm, wise elder.

When we would arrive at Grandma's building, as soon as she'd buzz us in, the blend of aromas told us that she'd been much too busy glazing the clove-and-maraschino cherry-covered ham, watching over the bubbling macaroni and cheese casserole; chopping and then soaking the gritty collard, turnip, and mustard greens (she loved mixed greens); and buttering up the buttermilk rolls for church. Come to think of it, Great-Grandma brought the church right over to her daughter's place with her, being that her religious work was never quite finished.

The incongruity wasn't limited to mother (Great-Grandma) and daughter (Grandma). The first was holy, and the latter more interested in partying and fun after her hard days bustin' up the kids who taunted her and her fair-skinned, long-haired sisters, who were too light-skinned to even be called "yella": instead it was "whitey girls," "crackers," and "paddies." This was the daily chant, on their way to school, from people of their own race. Her rite of passage into adulthood led to days of washin' up after rich white folk as a live-in, not far off from the drudgery of slave days. Still, in the eyes of most, she was fortunate enough to have "good" steady work just like her mother. It was on a comfortable estate, so she didn't complain. Come to think of it, she never complained. Clearly, she had no time for the notion of the *tragic mulatto*. Her ease with herself set the tone for all of our get-togethers. Her laughter was genuine—drawn from the soul.

If I had to break Grandma down into bloodline fractions so popular during the days of old (octoroon, quadroon, mulatto), I'd say she was one quarter Bette Davis, one quarter Billy Holiday, one quarter Joan Crawford, one quarter Alberta Hunter, and 100 percent Oya of Wind and Rain. As a child, I was never as at peace as when I was snuggled up to Grandma under her overstuffed down comforter. Her room smelled of a mixture of lilacs and cedarwood. Tough and witty, she had long, silky, henna-red hair, with numerous shades of glorious red fingernail polish and lipstick to match. She embodied the wise woman: smart, seasoned, courageous, and sweet. A woman whose life came to a sharp edge—an edge she was very happy to bring you to the brink of, if you cared to listen.

My great-grandmother's brother was also an eccentric, high-end domestic. He had taken to Irish and Scottish garb, and the last time I saw him he was in a wheelchair wearing tartan plaid and a fishermen's sweater. In his younger years, he had been a butler, with all the attending airs to match.

When I was growing up, it was a rude awakening to move from north to south New Jersey. You would think an interstate move down the turnpike would require only a minor adjustment. However, we moved from an almost entirely black neighborhood to a historically white, segregated society. This was in the late 1960s. I had not heard *nigger* uttered; but in south Jersey, it was a tag line readily assigned on playgrounds, in the classroom, and occasionally on the street.

Among my own people, I remember at a very early age being called yellow, the color of piss, 'Rican, and red bone. Some of the girls said I had hair like a baby doll's, and I rather liked that, as it didn't sound malicious. As they were also black, it did highlight me as somehow being "other."

In short, I guess I am the descendant of "house niggers" granted a position because of their mixed heritage. I see no need to compensate or feel shameful. That is just how things were, and I cannot and will not turn my back on my ancestors or the opportunities I enjoy that result from the sweat of their labor or their cultural identity. I remain curious about the rainbow, particularly the history of tan America, which remains something of a mystery. I also seek out role models who can remain tough, united, and inspirational in the face of both racism and colorism (which is typically prejudice afflicted from within one's ethnicity).

My search for identity led me on a meandering trail of research. I learned how to trace race online. I felt that this offered some objectivity that my relatives might lack. I was able to identify my relationship to the triracial isolate groups, with certainty based on my ancestor's homeland, customs, and surnames. I did the same with my Native American heritage and am working now on the European extractions. Indeed, as we shall see later, the Internet is a powerful research tool for anyone embarking on such a quest.

Separating fact from fiction can be tricky. Today, we can look at historical precedence, folklore, and geography to paint a fuller picture. Moreover, as we shall see in the conclusion, a plethora of genetic tests and innovative genealogical tools provide definitive answers when once ambiguity flourished.

Old World in the New World: Fact, Fiction, and Fantasy

Getting back to my grandmother and the Portuguese question touches on many fascinating elements of our history as Americans. Throughout early American history, the notion of being of Portuguese heritage was a rather common designation assigned to mixed-race people, as was the idea of having a Moorish or Turkish background. In many ways, identification with a foreign other masked the possibility of domestic admixtures with exoticism, giving such individuals some immunity from segregation, humiliating laws, and social exclusion.

No genetic connection between the Portuguese and my family exists as far as can be discerned. For others, a connection to the Portuguese, Turkish, or Moors, whether factual or mythic, afforded opportunities that would have been denied to triracial or biracial families with black, white, and Native American heritage. Obviously, numerous Americans descend from the Portuguese, Turks, and Moors. For some mixed-race people, though, the shroud afforded by a mythic ethnic identity enabled them to survive and prosper in early American society. It's no wonder my grandmother found the ethnicities assigned to her amusing, and yet in certain circumstances she was unwilling to deny such ancestry. This is the tightrope for social survival that many people walked.

Depending on the environment, the assumption of an Old World heritage proved useful to biracial and triracial Americans, as illuminated by court cases tried over 100 years ago. Here are a few historical notes from a famous court case regarding "Portuguese" (biracial) ambiguity as seen through the eyes of early Americans. The case was tried in Johnson County, Tennessee, in 1858. The documentation provides a glimpse into the way residents of the community readily embraced mixed families of purportedly foreign (Old World) origins, like the Perkins.

Joshua Perkins, born circa 1732 in Accomack County, Virginia, was the "mulatto" son of a white woman (Orders, 1731–1736). He owned land in Robeson County, North Carolina, in 1761; moved to Liberty County, South Carolina; and in 1785 moved to what later became Washington County, Tennessee (Philbeck). Succeeding generations of Perkins continued to marry either light-skinned blacks or whites of European descent, fading their African features. They were a prosperous family, owning a ferry, racehorses, and an iron ore mine. Members of this family ran the local schoolhouse and held official offices. Undercover, as an olive-skinned people with ties to Old World southern Europe, they reaped the benefits of societal acceptance. As the political winds changed abruptly, right before the Civil War in 1858 one of the Perkins was "accused" of being a Negro. He brought an unsuccessful lawsuit, accusing the defendant of slander.

Jacob F. Perkins, great-grandson of Joshua Perkins, brought an unsuccessful suit against one of his neighbors in the Circuit Court of Johnson County for slander because the neighbor called him a "free Negro" (Perkins File).

At least fifty people gave depositions or testified during his trial. Many of the deponents came from well-established families who had lived in North Carolina, South Carolina, or Tennessee for more than three generations. Only sixteen of the elder witnesses testified that he was a "Negro," describing him as follows:

> dark skinned man with sheep's wool and flat nose. (Deposition of Nancy Lipps)

> black man, hair nappy. . . . Some called Jacob (his son) a Portuguese and some a negro. (Deposition of John Nave)

> Knew old Jock (Joshua) in North Carolina on Peedee . . . right black or nearly so. Hair kinky . . . like a common negro. (Deposition of Abner Duncan)

However, several witnesses for Perkins testified that Joshua Perkins was something other than "Negro," and possibly Portuguese or Native American. They said little about his physical characteristics and those of his descendants. Instead, they argued that he could not have been a "Negro" because he was admired and trusted by the community. This raises an important issue that will be explored later, that "black" is not only a racial trait but also comes to describe the character of an individual:

> dark skinned man . . . resembled an Indian more than a negro. He was generally called a Portuguese. Living well. . . . Kept company with everybody. Kept race horses and John Watson rode them. (Deposition of Thomas Cook)

> mixed blooded and not white. His wife fair skinned. . . . They had the same privileges. (Deposition of Catherine Roller)

> Hair bushy & long—not kinky. Associated with white people . . . Associated with . . . the most respectable persons. Some would call them negroes and some Portuguese. (Deposition of John J. Wilson)

> He was known of the Portuguese race. . . . Four of his sons served in the Revolution. . . . Jacob and George drafted against Indians . . . they came from and kept a ferry in South Carolina. (Deposition of Anna Graves)

> They kept company with decent white people and had many visitors. (Deposition of Elizabeth Cook)

> I taught school at Perkins school house . . . they were Portuguese . . . associated with white peoples, clerked at elections and voted and had all privileges. (Deposition of David R. Kinnick) [Underlining added for emphasis]

The Perkins family lived in the hazy tan area of the rainbow. There was a societal agreement about their identity that approached legendary status. Many of those who testified had never even met the family but still felt certain of their identity. Rather than suspending racism and racial stereotype, the community adopted a myth of the Perkins's identity, allowing the status quo to be perpetuated. This was done by admitting mixed-race people into their society as variants of their own European heritage.

> I was well acquainted with Jacob Perkins (a second generation Perkins).
> A yellow man—said to be Portuguese. They do not look like negroes.
> I have been about his house a great deal and nursed for his wife. She
> was a little yellow and called the same race. Had blue eyes and black
> hair. Was visited by white folks. (Deposition of Mary Wilson)

Seventy-seven-year-old Daniel Stout asserted, "[n]ever heard him called a negro. People in those days said nothing about such things" (Deposition of Daniel Stout).

The Melungeon, Black Dutch, and "Gypsy"

I am not trying to suggest that white early Americans were generally an open-minded people to anyone who seemed of European descent. There is plenty of scholarly and genetic debate regarding the absorption of "undesirable" European cultures into various southern cultures in the United States. This adds further color to our discussion. In "Wayfaring stranger: The Black Dutch, German Gypsies or Chicanere and Their Relation to the Melungeon" (2000), Linda Griggs describes the Melungeon as an olive-complected, dark-eyed, dark-skinned people living in Appalachia. While some Melungeon claim Portuguese heritage, this ancestry is largely unsubstantiated. Melungeons are generally thought of as American admixtures of black, white, with some Native American referred to in anthropological terms as triracial isolates. This group is one of the largest and most active communities of contemporary triracial Americans. Melungeons are not quaint asides from early history; they are a lively culture online and off—as book authors, organizers, and educators. They are one of the fairest groups of triracial people, questioning the notion of whiteness in terms of race. The questions raised by Melungeon heritage delight, as a blessing, those who are open-minded, as they give entree to diverse American cultures. Melungeon background offends those who are comforted by an assumption of whiteness and the power it often affords.

Many Americans presumably of European ancestry suspect that they have ties to the Romany, Middle Eastern, or African-descended people. This idea arises from interpretation of family stories, physical features, inclinations, heirlooms, or photographs.

With the renaissance of Melungeon culture, old theories of their origins are revisited. One such theory asserted by Dr. Swan Burnett in *American Anthropologist* (1889) is that they are part Roma, commonly referred to as Gypsy. Black anthropologist Henry Burke recently reconsidered the Gypsies to be contributors to Melungeon ancestry. Another scholar, Myra Vanderpool Gormley, investigates the relationship of the so-called black Dutch to the Melungeon in the paper "In Search of the Black Dutch." *Black Dutch* is a term used by German Gypsies to describe themselves, as is the term *Chicanere* (Gormley, 1997). These people were absorbed into the Pennsylvania Dutch culture after being persecuted in Philadelphia during initial immigrations.

Eminent historian Henry W. Shoemaker, whose work came to prominence in the early twentieth century, is considered an authority on "black Dutch" culture. Shoemaker describes the black Dutch, or Dark Pennsylvania Mountain people, as of Near Eastern or aboriginal stock ("aboriginal" describes the original people of an area, and in this case they would be Native Americans; however, people commonly link the term *aboriginal* with the natives of Australia). In a lecture from 1924, he stated, "At least until the 1850s the men were of medium size, very slim and erect, with good features and large dark eyes. They wore their hair long; very little hair grew on their faces, but they tried to cultivate small side-burns." In a March 31, 1930, *Altoona Tribune* article he described "diverse Shekener girls and women . . . of astounding loveliness and their kinship to the so-called Pennsylvania German people, where strange, dark types predominate, was apparent. In fact the Pennsylvania German is but a more cosmopolitan scion of the She-kener . . . and all spring from the same Central and near Eastern polyglot that swarmed into Pennsylvania in the Eighteenth century of diverse origins" (1930). The Chicanere ranks decimated whenever a chance to settle down came into view; by these judicious marriages, their blood was in the veins of almost every "Pennsylvania Dutchman." According to Shoemaker, "the Pennsylvania Dutch boys and girls with their glorious dark eyes, wax-like complexions, wavy dark hair, and features of Araby, show the undying presence of forgotten Romany (Gypsy) forebears" (1930).

Shoemaker reports on the results of intermarriage between the Pennsylvania Dutch and people of Romany heritage, "giving an added dark strain to the already swarthy Pennsylvania German type, fused as it has been from South German, Huguenot, Esopus Spaniard, Hebrew, Swiss, Waldensian, Greek and Indian, the type of the true Pennsylvanian, Tauranian. . ." (1300 Words, 1930).

For those who are beginning to trace black Dutch ancestry, Griggs provides a list of established characteristics in her article "Wayfaring Stranger":

An Anatolian bump, a donut shaped protuberance on the back of the skull

Shovel teeth, which are curved across the back rather than straight and end in a ridge at the gum line (commonly found in Native Americans as well)

History of Familial Mediterranean Fever, an inherited rheumatic disease ethnically restricted to non-Ashkenazi Jews, Armenians, Arabs and Turks.

Ritualized cleanliness regulations

Common Names of the black Dutch: Smith, Mullinses, Mullens, Mullen, Schwartz, Boswell, and Kaiser (2000).

The Turks and the Moors

According to journalists Khalid Duran and Daniel Piper in "Faces of American Islam" (2002), Muslim immigrants came to North America as early as 1501, as slaves from Africa. How many Muslim slaves came in total is up for debate, but scholar Allan D. Austin (2002) estimates that there were about 40,000 brought to what is now the United States. Sylviane Diouf (2002), another expert in this area, puts the numbers higher, estimating between 2.25 million and 3 million in North and South America. While the Muslims from diverse countries were liked by the slave owners, those owners did not support Islamic beliefs. By the 1860s, importation of Muslim slaves ended.

The slaves who were brought over were concentrated along the southeastern United States, particularly North Carolina—a fate they shared with non-Muslim slaves from Africa. The Melungeons of Appalachia and the Cumberland Plateau who live in remote areas from Virginia to Kentucky may well have Muslim, Middle Eastern ancestry.

Two groups of triracial isolates—the Moors and the Turks of Sumter County, South Carolina—are believed to be related to Middle Eastern Islamic slaves. In fact, although the American South is thought of in terms of "white" and "black," South Carolina was a multiethnic, multicultural society, all the way back to the colonial era.

The "Free Moors" are believed to be the descendants of Muslims sold into slavery in the Middle East. The "Turks" of Sumter County are reputedly the descendants of pirates, or escapees from pirates, according to General Thomas Sumter, who settled in the area. These families also are often reluctant to discuss what they know of their heritage, fearing the stigma attached to an Islamic background in the Bible Belt or an association with slavery and pirates. Nevertheless, the groups remain cohesive and an essential part of the fabric of the Carolinian culture.

Just as with the Perkins family previously described, racial tensions that arose prior to the Civil War brought suffering and humiliation to the Melungeon people, the Turks, and the Moors. Today, all of these groups are coming out of the dusty annals of American history, demonstrating the vitality and unique contributions of their cultures.

THE BLACKFOOT QUESTION

My grandmother would also get a big kick out of saying we were Blackfoot because of our "nigger toes," but would never go into any real details. Many blacks who have family stories that include a Native American ancestor will point to the Blackfoot as the possible tribal identification. My research has confirmed that it would be rare but not impossible for blacks to be related to the Blackfoot.

The Blackfoot were referred to as such because of their distinctive black moccasins, not because they were darker-skinned. The Blackfoot people are thought to have been always concentrated in the Dakotas, whereas the majority of black Americans were found in the southern states, but there are no hard and fast rules for either group. Still, some freed black slaves did resettle in the West, and a few may have mixed with the Blackfoot. While it is little noted, numerous biracials (black/ Native Americans) were forced to resettle in the West along with full-blooded Native Americans on the Trail of Tears. There is a possibility of some cultural blending occurring from the Trail of Tears migration. Support is thin in this area; however, there are numerous black Native American groups who could assist one doing such a search. One of the most prominent black Native American organizations is the Black Indians Intertribal Native American Association (BIINAA), led by Chief Jerry Monroe Eagle Feather.

"BLACK, WHITE, AND RED ALL OVER": AMERICAN HISTORY

While the term *Five Civilized Tribes* casts aspersion on tribes outside this group, the term is widely used, so I will employ it here though

I don't agree with it. Genealogical documentation connects blacks definitively to the so-called five civilized tribal groups: Cherokee, Choctaw, Chickasaw, Creek, and Seminole. Historically there have been additional admixtures, with the most prominent being the Chickahominy, Gingaskin, Mattapony, Nansemond, Nanticoke, Nottaway, Pamunkey Rappahannocks, Saponi, Weanock, and Werowocomo people.

The Nanticoke, who still live in Canada, are a dark-skinned tribe of African and Native American descent. In the *Ebony* magazine article "Black Indians Hit Jackpot in Casino Bonanza" (June 1995), author Kevin Chappell reports on a similar tribe of black Native Americans in America.

According to Chappell (1995), the Mashantucket Pequot tribe of Connecticut owns the most profitable casino in the world. In 2003, they took in $800 million. It is this fact that has brought them international public attention. Confusion arises for the public, who harbor preconceptions of what "Native American" means and what it looks like. The Mashantucket have about 318 members, half of whom could pass for black. Their Foxwood Resort Casino is located in a sedate community in southeastern Connecticut called Ledyard. Remote location aside, they have raised the eyebrows of Donald Trump, who calls them "Michael Jordan Indians" because they seem to him to be blacks and not Native Americans.

While the tribe's members enjoy relative comfort because of their successful business venture today, they were nearly annihilated 350 years ago. The Pequots were massacred 300 years ago and enslaved along with Africans with whom they had intermarried. By the 1970s, this group was a shadow of its former self, with only two half-sister members to represent the tribe. Two is indeed a small number for a nation; the sisters were feisty and held fast to the 216 acres of Pequot land. Gradually, descendants returned to the reservation and the numbers were replenished.

Currently, the Pequot are not only successful as a sound culture with a solid economic standing, but they are also a model for diversity in a pluralistic America. Dark-skinned and light-skinned members may suggest an African or European heritage, but the tribe is united as Pequot people, a rainbow tribe. This group with lengthy American roots and a venerable history teaches important lessons to contemporary Americans. The resilience of the Pequot proves that connection to a place and a common history creates a bond more important than physical characteristics.

THE RACIAL TRIANGLE

As far back as the 1600s, people of African origin were marrying into the Native American community. Virginia DeMarce (1992), an expert on the topic, points out that the east coast 'Gingaskins were intermarrying into both the black and white communities. Both whites and blacks are known to have married the Nottoway, according to the census of 1808, taken by tribal leaders.

Among some of the larger groups that have arisen among the triracial isolates come those from clearly defined geographical locations, often within particular counties, as illustrated here:

Brass Ankles, Red Legs, Marlboro, Turks, Blues of South Carolina.

Cecil Indians, Guineas, Guinea Niggers, West Hill Indians of Maryland and West Virginia.

Haliwas of Halifax and Warren counties in North Carolina.

Issues of Amherst and Rockingham County, Virginia.

Jackson Whites of New York and New Jersey.

Lumbees, formerly called *Croatans*, of Robeson County, Virginia; North Carolina, and upper South Carolina.

Melungeons of Tennessee, and Kentucky (southern Appalachia).

Ramapo Mountain People, formerly the Jackson Whites.

Red Bones of South Carolina and Louisiana. (Walton-Raji, 1993)

Members of some of the larger established Native American tribes married into the black and white races, but groups such as the Catawbas are not considered to be triracial; rather, they are a single tribe. The Brass Ankles of South Carolina are a well-known large group of triracials. They are thought to have developed from the offspring of enslaved Native Americans and Africans—as each group was held in slavery around the same time, with an additional infusion of blood from Irish servants of southern plantations. The derogatory name *Brass Ankles* is derived from the fact that the people were either slaves or servants. Brass Ankles are believed to have small amounts of Native American and African ancestry and to be primarily of Irish descent.

The term *Cajan* may throw some people who could take it for an alternative spelling of *Cajun* (of Louisiana). The Cajan group was founded when a Jamaican man married a biracial (black/white) woman.

The Cajans married in with the Red Bones and "colored" Creoles, expanding their numbers and genetic pool.

Some specific surname patterns appear in the triracial communities. DeMarce (1992) cautions researchers not to hastily conclude that, just because the name is the same, that a relationship exists. Yet on the other hand, she acknowledges that a specific pattern of name dispersal in a limited population may truly indicate which groups are affiliated with others, indicating a connection to the triracial isolates for those searching for such a connection.

What's in a Name

There are niggers who are as white as I am, but the taint of blood is there and we always exclude it. "How do you know it is there?" asked Dr. Gresham. "Oh, there are tricks of blood which always betray them. My eyes are more practiced than yours. I can always tell them." (Harper)

Apart from geography, surnames are among the most important indicators of triracial identity. Some of the naming patterns within each group are as follows:

Brass Ankles: Shavers, Chavers, Chavis

Cajan/Alabama Creole: Chastang

Lumbee: Locklear, Oxendine

Melungeon/Florida Dead Lake People: Mullins, Goins, Collins, Sexton, Gipson, Gibson, Hatfield

Turk: Oxendine, Benenhaley (Nassau, 1993)

Now, I'm sure that those of you who watch television are familiar with Heather Locklear, who began her rise in the 1980s with a starring role in the popular television show *Dynasty*. She has gone on to be highly visible in *Melrose Place* and *Spin City*. She seems to be the quintessential Caucasian with blond hair (perhaps from the bottle she touts on television commercials) and hazel eyes. A more complex picture arises as the result of her name, *Locklear*.

Locklear is a Tuscarora name that means "hold fast." Locklear's paternal line descends from the triracial isolate groups. This may not be as clear as the nose on her European-appearing face but proven by her traditional Tuscarora name and her family's geographic origin—the lands of the Lumbee (Nassau, 1993).

Another name that may stand out of the groups listed above who are fans of American legend is the name *Hatfield*. Indeed, the

Hatfields are the long-feuding half of the Hatfields and McCoys. They are also a triracial isolate family linked to the Melungeon people (Nassau, 1993).

Surnames apart, you may wonder why the groups are called *triracial isolates*. Generally, it is thought that the name arises from the fact that the groups intermarried, isolating their ancestry from that of others. Indeed, having grown up among several of these groups in Southern New Jersey, I observed firsthand the fact that while they might socialize with people who identified with other racial groups, marriage outside the group was strongly discouraged.

My aunt married into a triracial family. Some of the members of the group identified strongly as Native American and some even lived on reservations. There was outrage at the fact that one of their members would marry my relative, even though both were well into middle age. Eventually, a few of the family members acquiesced, accepting my aunt as their own, but many remained distanced and some no longer considered my uncle to be a member of their own family.

Geography also plays a role. Many of the groups were established in remote regions of the country with difficult terrains. Some areas where the groups settled, as noted by the information above, include mountainous areas, lowlands, and swamps as well as rural areas well away from industrialized cities.

Sidebar: Biracial Royals Challenge Common Conceptions

The idea of a strong history of biracial and triracial Americans is well established. When we want to make a racial distinction between white and black, we typically point to Europe when speaking of the white race. Examination of the royal court of sixteenth-century Italy challenges this commonly held notion, for it is there that the first biracial head of state was born.

Allesandro de Medici was a powerful figure during the early Italian Renaissance. His father was Cardinal Giulio de Medici, who later became Pope Clement VII, also nephew of Lorenzo the Magnificent. While Allesandro was born the child of a black serving woman, since his father was a member of the elder line of the Medicis, he rose to power though technically a bastard. His children Giulio and Giulia took great pride in their Medici ancestry. The two were not only welcomed into Italian society, but also married titled individuals.

Today, many noble families of Europe can trace their ancestry back to Alessandro de Medici, the biracial duke of Florence. Scholar Mario de Valdes y Cocom illustrates that these royal families with African descendants are not only living in Italy but are in several other countries as well. The PBS special *Blurring Racial Boundaries* also highlights England's Queen Charlotte, wife of King George III, as someone who descended from the black Portuguese royal family of Margarita de Castro y Sousa. Here, bloodline is found in six different lines of European royals.

While some people labor under the impression that to be biracial is not to have a history, the lessons of Alessandro de Medici and Queen Charlotte suggest otherwise. The history of the two and all of their descendents demonstrates that not only do biracial people have a history but an illustrious and influential one at that (de Valdes y Cocom, 1998).

The Lumbee

Census readings from later years indicate that other groups, such as those with Lumbee surnames and those of other triracial groups, were listed simply as free people of color. Biracial and triracial people were included among these groups. As far back as the 1750s, a reference was made to a small group of Lumbees, about fifty families at that time, who were known to have members of mixed blood. Today the Lumbee are a large and vibrant group of over 40,000, still centered in Robeson County, North Carolina. They are the largest triracial group in the United States and are vigorously fighting legislation and bureaucracy, both mainstream American and Native American, to be considered a 100 percent Native American group.

The Lumbee have a venerable history. They cite acculturation and assimilation as contributing factors to lost languages and lost traditions. Here is a brief timeline:

12,000 B.C.: Native Americans settled areas of southeast North Carolina occupied today by the Lumbee.

1714: "Lost Colony" theory first asserted. Sir Walter Raleigh left colonists in what was then Roanoke, Virginia to get supplies from England. When he returned, the colonists were gone. Purportedly only an inscription in a tree remained. It was suggested that the English had gone to Croatan Island and integrated with the Manteo, an indigenous group.

1885: Group first called Croatan Indians.

1887: Funding was given to Croatan school.

1891: Stephen B. Week wrote an article in *Papers of the American Historical Association* with documentation, maps, and historical accounts of the Croatan or Lumbee people, descended from the colonists at Roanoke.

1911: Croatan name changed to Indians of Robeson County.

1913: Name changed again to Cherokee of Robeson County.

1953: Name changed to Lumbee Indians, as many lived near Lumbee River.

1956: Federal law recognized tribe as Lumbee.

It should also be noted that the Lumbee integrated with the Tuscarora people, a smaller group in the county. There are in fact eighteen counties and adjoining areas where the Lumbee live. These include Pembroke, Red Banks, Maxton, Moss Neck, Wakulla, and Rennert.

The Lumbee defy categorization, and they don't have a specific look, so they cannot be stereotyped. A Lumbee can be as fair as Heather Locklear or appear to be solely of African descent. Genetically, they are considered the most "Indian" (or Native American) of all triracial American groups. They not only blended with the Tascarora people but also the Halteras tribe of Algonguin, Cheraw, and other Siouan people, runaway slaves, free people of color (biracials), and renegade or outlaw whites.

There are prominent figures who are Lumbee, including professors, museum curators, administrators, executives, physicians, ministers, and artists. Lumbee people founded the first "Indian"-owned bank. They also have their own newspaper, called *Carolina Indian Voice*. The Lumbee are very active in the arts.

A curious characteristic that the Lumbee profess of themselves is "meanness." Meanness refers to their fierce pride in being Native American. Lumbee sensitivity to insult and a readiness to react to it, sometimes violently defending themselves, leads to the connection with the term *meanness* as well. They are a very cohesive unit, unwilling to bow down to stereotype or categorization dispensed by American legislative acts or even the Bureau of Indian affairs. The Lumbee are known to have very large families, which contribute to their large numbers. If they were to be considered officially a tribe, they would be the ninth largest.

THE LOST GENERATION—UNDERSTANDING
THE PAST TO LEARN TO LIVE IN THE PRESENT

> The social construction of race and racism is dependent on the general
> acceptance of rigid racial boundaries and racial classification systems.
> Proponents of racial segregation have always understood that interracial
> relationships and the children they produce eventually undermine racism
> by challenging the assumption of monolithic, fixed, and inherently
> incompatible races. The clear demarcation of races, which is an essential
> cornerstone of the social construction of race, is weakened by the exis-
> tence and recognition of widespread racial mixing. Consequently, those
> who favor racial separatism and believe in the concept of race are most
> likely to strongly oppose interracial relationships. (Payne, 1998, p. 153)

From afar, it is reasonable to presume that mixed-race people historically had advantages over monoracial people, particularly those of
Native American or black heritage, who could then escape the stigma
of belonging entirely to either group. Though the heritage may have
been mixed, society worked rather vigorously to assign people to groups
to fit their own desires. In early America, many mixed-race people were
deemed "free people of color," and there were "freed men" as well who
were descended from Africa. There were countless intercultural stresses
and disputes resulting from the nebulous boundaries caused by such
terminology, law or not.

Free blacks were also in danger of having their children stolen and
sold into slavery. In his Revolutionary War pension application on March
7, 1834, Drury Tann declared in Southampton County, Virginia, Court:

> [H]e was stolen from his parents as a boy by strangers, who were carrying
> him to sell him into Slavery, and had gotten with him and other stolen
> property as far as the Mountains on their way, that his parents made
> complaint to a Mr. Tanner Alford who was Then a magistrate in
> the county of Wake State of North Carolina to get me back from Those
> who had stolen me and he did pursue the Rogues & overtook Them at
> the mountains and took me from Them. ("Revolutionary War," 1834)

An advertisement in the April 10, 1770, issue of the *North Carolina
Gazette* of New Bern describes how the Driggers family was victimized
in Craven County, North Carolina:

> [B]roke into the house . . . under the care of Ann Driggus, a free negro
> woman, two men in disguise, with marks on their faces, and clubs in
> their hands, beat and wounded her terribly and carried away four of
> her children. (Fouts, 1770, pp. 65–66)

John Scott, "freeborn Negro," testified in Berkeley County, South Carolina, on January 17, 1754 that three men, Joseph Deevit, William Deevit, and Zachariah Martin

> entered by force, the house of his daughter, Amy Hawley, and carried her off, with her six children, and he thinks they are taking them north to sell as slaves. (Scott, 1754)

One of the children was recovered in Orange County, North Carolina, where the county court appointed Thomas Chavis to return the child to South Carolina on March 12, 1754 (Haun).

Stealing free blacks and selling them into slavery in another state was legal in North Carolina until 1779. The law did give a thin veil of protection to blacks and "coloreds." In 1793, the murderer of John James of Northampton County was committed to jail, according to the March 20, 1793 issue of the *North Carolina Journal*:

> Last night Harris Allen, who was committed for the murder of John James, a free mulatto, of Northampton County, made his escape from the gaol of this town. He is a remarkable tall man, and had on a short round jacket. (Fouts, 1793)

When families are broken, the damage that occurs to them and to their communities is hard to estimate. One of the most egregious infractions on the rights of biracial children ended in the late twentieth century in Australia. Geographically far away from the rest of this discussion, the story of the "Stolen Generation" of Australia is nevertheless instructive.

For 100 years, from 1870 to 1970, mixed-race Aborigines and Torres Strait Islander people of Australia were confiscated like illegal contraband, then placed into group homes similar in spirit to internment camps. Many of these centers were religious outposts operated by Catholic nuns. The government of Australia oversaw the program and planned to selectively breed mixed-race children so that their offspring would become increasingly white.

There were "training programs" to *civilize* the natives and those of mixed race; training prepared the mixed-race children to work as housekeepers, maids, and other service jobs for white Australians. The avid collection of biracial children broke many Australian Aboriginal homes, upsetting the unity of entire communities. Desperate to keep the children in their rightful homes, mothers and grandmothers sometimes placed the children over open fires to darken their skin or rubbed charcoal over their bodies. Some lived in exile in the roughest parts of the outback to keep others from noticing their biracial appearance.

Today, survivors and their families seek official apologies from the government, and some are seeking reparations. While many Aboriginal and Torres Strait Islanders now have their own land or countries, those taken from their homes still suffer disproportionately. For example, high percentages of the Stolen Generation suffer from depression. Some resort to lives of crime: 90 percent of incarcerated Aborigines in Victoria are members of the Stolen Generation. Poverty is pervasive in these populations, as are lack of higher education and the opportunity it affords. Poor role models and lack of contact with real family make it more difficult for the Stolen Generation to raise their own families. Lack of self-esteem, feelings of unworthiness, suicidal tendencies, violence, juvenile delinquency, alcohol and drug abuse, and personality disorders have high incidence in this group (Bringing them home report).

There are important lessons to be learned from the Stolen Generation:

- A child, no matter how diverse her background may be, still identifies most strongly with her parents and the community in which she grows up.
- People of mixed heritage cannot be forced to become fully one race or another if they are of mixed heritage.
- Racial identification is best decided by the individual and the parents.
- When a society, government, or agency assigns race or cultural orientation to mixed-race children, there are numerous negative psychological and sociological implications that afflict individuals and the community at large.

As part of a recovery program, concerted efforts are being made to offer therapy, some of it including Aboriginal ritual and ceremony, to help the Stolen Generation heal. Government agencies are attempting to help these mixed-race descendents of Australian Aborigines trace their genealogy and reunite with their traditional family communities in Aboriginal country (Bringing them home report).

Contemporary Biracial and Triracial Identity

The upbeat conclusion to this chapter would be to summarize the events of the past and then highlight the positive changes observed in contemporary culture. As you read, I'm sure that whatever cultural or ethnic heritage you embody, you can recall misconceptions that arose because of stereotypes. To explore contemporary biracial and triracial identity, I will turn the floor to the arts, because artists in their myriad disciplines are well suited to reflecting our societal mores while also helping us glimpse the future.

Many people become exclusive themselves, isolating the other parts of their known ethnic identity so that they can belong to a group. For some, this is a political act. In the anthology *Half and Half: Writers on Growing Up Biracial and Bicultural,* a variety of writers share personal reflections on nearly every conceivable type of ethnic or cultural mix. In the autobiographical article "The Mulatto Millennium," Danzy Senna laments what she calls "mulatto fever":

> But, with all due respect to the multicultural movement, I cannot tell a lie. I was a black girl. Not your ordinary black girl, if such a thing exists, but rather, born to a black-Mexican father, and a face that harkens to Andalusia, not Africa. I was born in 1970, when "black" described a people bonded not by shared complexion or hair texture but by a shared history. (Senna, 1998, p. 15)

Senna points to the one-drop rule, which suggested that any portion of African heritage made one "black" and retorts, "You told us all along that we had to call ourselves black because of this so-called one drop. Now, that we don't have to anymore, we choose to. Because black is beautiful. Because black is not a burden, but a privilege" (1998, p. 15). Senna, who is herself biracial and bicultural, expresses disdain for those who identify as mulatto. She cites the book title by populist Jim Hightowers, *There's Nothing in the Middle of the Road but Yellow Stripes and Dead Armadillos,* as a metaphor for the "mulatto" mentality (1998).

Conceptual artist, philosopher, and writer Adrian Piper has a long-standing interest in identity. Piper, who went to prep school and Ivy League colleges, uses her formidable wit and analytic skills to bring racial stereotyping to the attention of Americans. Piper is black, yet her skin is so fair and her physical features so classically European that she is frequently challenged by both black and white cultures concerning her identity. Many people seem to challenge her assertion of blackness, digging for an ulterior motive. Piper is proud to be black. While some of her ancestors have long since melted into white society, her branch of the family is proud to be black Americans.

In many ways, Piper is a role model for biracial, triracial, and light-skinned blacks. She is unflinching in her examination of her family, her self, and the reactions to both in our society. Influenced by conceptual artists, minimalism, performance, the "art as life" movement, and the philosophy of Immanuel Kant, Piper encourages viewers to transcend subconscious assessments of racial identity and urges them, sometimes through embarrassing confrontations, to change racist attitudes.

In the article "Passing for White, Passing for Black," Piper recounts the pain incurred when a distinguished professor said, "Ms. Piper, you're about as black as I am." She calls the accusation typical but admits that more often it comes from blacks. Her family was one of the remaining middle-class, light-skinned black families left in Harlem when she was growing up, as the others had moved to the suburbs. The remaining people were working-class, according to Piper. They called her "pale-face" or "Clorox baby" quite regularly. She recounts many painful memories incurred at the hands of her people and reports how demoralizing and alienating the exchanges made her feel. She uses words like *humiliation, betrayal, identity tests*, and *anger* frequently, in describing how her neighbors in Harlem treated her and how the antagonistic relationships made her feel.

At times, Piper seems to feel guilty that she is not darker-skinned, but as an intellectual, she realizes this is a futile and demoralizing emotion. She reports the desire to become more detached, to forgive, and to feel helpless; and that exaggerated fantasies of aggressors (white or black) diminish their own responsibility to be humane toward others. Rejection seems to have toughened her attitude toward upper-class whites and working-class blacks. While she realizes that historically light-skinned blacks have received preferential treatment, better jobs, and a higher education, she is firmly grounded in the here and now. Indeed, Ms. Piper has found that she thrives in the tan area, where character, personality, and deeds outweigh appearance and geographic origin. Her armor of self-worth is strengthened by calmly challenging the conventional thoughts of others; this is reinforced by her commitment to family and personal history.

In his paper "Getting beyond race: The changing American culture," Richard Payne eloquently describes the changing demographic of race:

> At the end of the twentieth century, major changes that have recently occurred in American society offer hope for the realization of better race relations in the twenty-first century. These include the dynamic force of generational replacement, the shifting of the demographic landscape, the growth of a strong black middle class, the enlistment of large numbers of racial minorities in the U.S. military, and the gradual erosion of racial boundaries resulting from increasing rates of interracial marriages and transracial adoptions. These changes make it difficult to maintain the status quo in relation to race.

Generational replacement and demographic changes weaken the foundations on which race is socially constructed, each successive generation of Americans becomes more tolerant and supportive of racial integration and equality. Greater access to education, increased interaction among individuals from different racial backgrounds, and society's growing intolerance of racist attitudes and behaviors consolidate this trend. The influx of immigrants also helps weaken racial boundaries by complicating the concept of race and racial categorization. (1998)

There is so much ignorance, stereotyping, and shame preventing us from understanding who we really are and how we are related to various groups. The Human Genome Project has beautifully documented the genetic commonalities that exist in all humans, yet many lay people have not yet integrated this information into their consciousness. It is my hope as a healer that this chapter will be a gift designed to demonstrate clearly and concisely the venerable history of triracial and biracial mixes in the United States from the seventeenth century to the present.

This chapter concludes with a practical application. Readers are equipped with the necessary tools to track their personal relationships to biracial and triracial cultures of North America. Organizations listed offer community, support, sharing, and information. This is my gift to readers and to my immediate family—I am married to an Englishman, and our children are as mixed as I am. Mixed-race children feel especially burdened, since their ultimate goal as they move toward adulthood is to define their sense of "self" in relation to others. The challenge is to accept a multicultural background as a blessing, recognizing that it is a reality for many people, not a social construct like race. Understanding the history of racial mixing and blended cultures allows this identity to be contextualized along with other cultural backgrounds. Ultimately, hybrid ethnicity is normal—especially with its lengthy history and the large numbers of members—not an oddity, shameful secret, or curse.

Race has caused an enormous rift in our society. Enjoying the connections implicit in being human is assisted by understanding the complexity of our multiracial heritage. By understanding our connections, perhaps the mistrust and dislike of "other" can evolve into better understanding, trust, acceptance, and as a nation, we can be healed. "Light, Bright, Damned Near White" is for America, for the triracial and biracial community; and most of all, it is written for the mental health and well-being of our children. This is a tool for parents, families,

Toolbox for Change

For	Images/perceptions	Strategies for change
Biracial	I am alone.	**Discover: Ancestry and genealogy**
Triracial	I do not belong to any	There are numerous resources for tracing genealogy; it has
Cross-cultural	group.	become a contemporary passion. Online, there are many
Intercultural	Isolation is the natural	quick and relatively easy ways to get started with
Multicultural	outcome for mixed	understanding your background and ancestors, including
Interracial	children.	www.ancestry.com and www.genealogy.com
Transracial adoptees	There is no way to figure	These sites contain resources that help you trace relatives, living
Cross-cultural	out what groups you	and deceased, through surnames. There are also a wide
adoptees	belong to.	variety of surname collectives and e-groups.
Adoptees	No group would find me	
Curious	as a member. My	**Test: DNA**
	background is too	
	complicated.	Testing DNA has allowed understanding seldom available
	My origins are obscured by	before, particularly for those who have been adopted or who
	the past; I can never	have scarce genealogical records. The tests have limitations, as
	change this fact.	the types of readings provided reflect genes adopted, though
		there are probably others that were not passed down. The
		other problem with the tests is that they give a picture based
		on all males or all females, but not both; for example, if you
		are female you can trace your matrilineal line. The reason is
		that the Y chromosome is passed from father to son, virtually
		unchanged. In the female reading, the mitochondrial DNA

used reflects the maternal line. The tests are still valuable and a great starting point if there is no other adequate resource available. These genealogically driven tests include the following:

Family Tree DNA

Oxford Ancestors

Relative Genetics

Genetree

DNA print genomics—This uses autosomal genetic markers called SNPS (like DNA) and produces a racial profile rather than information about ancestry.

| Person with Native American along with other ancestry. | As a mixed-blood, half-breed, or whatever other derogatory term people attribute to my heritage, I could never belong to any solid group of Native American people, officially or even informally. People would laugh at me if I went to a pow wow or other tribal event. | **Information is a powerful tool: Native American and black Indian groups**

The Bureau of Indian Affairs (BIA) still adheres to blood quantum as a way to gain membership and affiliation with certain Native nations.
A card called Certificate of Degree of Indian Blood (CDIB) is required for entrance to most tribes.
Black Indians and Intertribal Association (BIINAA), associated with the website www.blackIndians.com, exists as a less formal collective of people with biracial and triracial ancestry. |

continued

Toolbox for Change (continued)

For	Images/perceptions	Strategies for change
	I know I am part Native American but I cannot prove it. Native Americans are isolationists and cultural elitists. They do not embrace outsiders.	BIINAA does not have the strict adherence to blood quantum or paperwork required by the above-mentioned associations. Full-blood, half-blood, and mixed Native Americans' names are listed on a wide array of documents called *rolls*. These rolls were utilized for official reorganization, allotment of land, and certain privileges in the late 1800s through the 1900s. Though not definitive, the rolls are an excellent preliminary way to establish a relationship to specific American Nations. Some of these lists are accessible free of charge from the Internet, while others require registration and payment of a fee. Here is a listing of a few: **1817: Reservation Roll**—Applicants for tract of land in the East, searchable by surname. **1871–1835 Emigration Roll**—Permitted emigration to Arkansas by the Cherokee. **1830: Armstrong Roll**—Records the Dancing Rabbit Creek treaty with the Choctaw. **1889: McKennon Roll**—Records Choctaw of Mississippi, Louisiana, and Alabama. **1890: Wallace Roll**—Lists Cherokee freedmen. **1889–1914: Index to Final Roll**—Also called the **Dawes Roll**, permits tracing of Native American ancestry by surname.

1909: Guion Miller Roll—Records Eastern Cherokee.
1954: Ute Roll—Records full-blood Ute tribe of Utah.

Proactive organizations, associations, and conferences, as well as magazines, now exist to enrich the multiracial, triracial, biracial, and transracial adopted communities.

Virtual community: Building community online

Blogs: Passive and active participation. Blogs are unique contemporary forms of Internet communication based on the concept of the daily journal. Blogs permit passive participation as a reader, while many encourage active participation by permitting written comments. To build community that caters to your specific concerns, you should consider starting your own blog. Some active Internet blogs to use as a model or read include the following:

A mixed blog
www.multiracial.com/blog

My parents feel a part of a single racial group, but I feel pulled in numerous directions culturally.

I guess I feel all of the elements of my ancestry. I want to meet others like me, explore, communicate, question and share.

I do not look white, black, Indian, Asian, or Latino. There are not any people for me to relate to or fit in with.

I need to get used to living in cultural isolation, but it is depressing.
I do not want to be alone.
I wonder where I can go for help. Maybe I should adopt a false persona— pretend to belong to an exotic culture I do not really belong to just to fit in.
I'm tired of feeling alone, yet I fear rejection.
I have so many thoughts in my head, I feel like

27

continued

Toolbox for Change (continued)

For	Images/perceptions	Strategies for change
I am from a mixed background. I would explore the complexity of my culture but only in a safe space.	I am going to explode if I do not talk with someone, but there is not anyone around here who would understand.	
I have been adopted into a white family but I am biracial.	No one talks about this kind of stuff around here. It is best to keep these feelings inside.	
I live in a very rural area.		
I live in conservative suburbs.		
I am seeking spiritual guidance.	I wonder if there are unique churches or faiths that support my multiracial, multicultural, intercultural, or biracial identity.	**Turn it over to a higher power: Interfaith and multiracial spirituality**
I want to make connections with others like me through organized religion.		Church and temples afford a wonderful opportunity for building community and support. The following denominations were either founded on interfaith, intercultural, and multicultural perspectives, or support or encourage them:

28

Bahá'í—One of the world's youngest and one of its steadily growing religions. The message of the founder, Bahá u'lláh, is that divisions of race, class, creed, and nation need to be broken down and done away with. The Bahá'í believe that humanity is one single race. There are five million adherents across the globe, including 2,100 ethnic, racial, and tribal groups.

Unitarianism—A noncreed faith inspired by Judeo-Christianity. Open to all.

Buddhism—Many westerners are finding answers to combat racism through Buddhism because it emphasizes the interior (spiritual side) rather than outside appearances and material positions.

Get involved: Join and participate in multiethnic organizations.
Association of Multiethnic Americans
PO Box 341304, Los Angeles, CA 90034-1304. According to their web site (www.ameasite.org), AMEA seeks to educate and advocate on behalf of multiethnic individuals and families while helping to eradicate discrimination against them.

Someone who likes helping others:
Advocate
Organizer
Leader
Mentor
Motivator

I have talked things out, read a lot, and even attended conferences. Now I'm ready to act as a mentor and advocate for those from my background.

continued

Toolbox for Change (continued)

For	Images/perceptions	Strategies for change
Author Speaker		AMEA provides valuable health information through its bone marrow database resources. **MAVIN Foundation** 600 First Ave., Suite 600, Seattle, WA 98104. MAVIN has a magazine and a local support group, hosts national conferences on the mixed race experience, and provides information on bone marrow transfer sources for mixed-race people. It is beginning a scholarship, internship, and international training program. **Melungeon Heritage Association** Reading list for educators, parents, and practitioners available on this triracial culture. P.O. Box 4020, Wise, VA 24293. **American Society of Folklore**—Learn about the diverse populations in the United States and the world so that your vision will not be limited to black and white. This group encourages participation, has an annual conference, and produces an academic quarterly, *Journal of American Folklore.* Contact AFS Executive Director: Timothy Lloyd, Mershon Center, Ohio State University, 1501 Neil Ave. Columbus, OH 43201-2602. Email Lloyd.100@osu.edu

| A non-Australian, non-aboriginal person:
Healer
Attorney
Civil rights activist | It is sad about what happened to the Australian Aborigines and Torres Strait Islanders. But I live too far away to do anything to help. | **Journey of Healing** project: Council for Aboriginal Reconciliation
www.reconciliation.org.au
Forgotten History Foundation
www.forgottenhistory.org
"Australia's stolen generation: Genocide a forced assimilation of the aboriginal peoples." (article)
Case studies (statistics and results of what happened)
Case studies and statistics
Bringing them home: The report, from the Reconciliation and Social Justice Library, Council for Aboriginal Reconciliation |
| Practitioners/ Educators:
Psychologist
Counselor
Religious leader
Teacher
Professor
Therapist
Social Worker
Physician
Librarian
Writer
Public speaker | This biracial, triracial, multiracial, transadoptee stuff is too complex. I do not know enough to advise or offer an opinion, even though my client/student/confidant desires help. I should just stick to the areas of my expertise and ignore the obviously troubling issues I see. | **Read, learn, write: Publications**
These are excellent resources: provocative and open to your articles and papers as well.
AMEA Networking News c/o Connie Hannah, 833 Mt. Pleasant RD, Chesapeake, VA 23320. AMEA published a comprehensive multiracial child resource book.
Root, M. P. P., & Kelley, M. (Ed.). *Identity and development: Multiracial heritages.*
Bible, J. (1994). *Melungeon: Yesterday and today.* Self-published. |

continued

Toolbox for Change (continued)

For	Images/perceptions	Strategies for change
Interviewer Researcher Healer	Based on what I know, I will just assign this obviously mixed-race person to the group she bears the most resemblance to.	DeMarce, V. E. (1992). Verry slitly mixt: tri-racial isolates families of the upper south, a genealogical study. *National Genealogical Society, 80*(1).
I date someone from a different culture; I want to learn what I can now about blended families and communities.	It is best to stick to your own kind.	**Call in or subscribe, get some advice, stay up-to-date, or reach out.** *Interracial/Intercultural Pride* 2625 Alcatraz, Suite 369, Berkeley, CA 94705-2702. Phone: 510-923-9513.
I want to date and meet more people of different backgrounds.	No one from a different culture would ever be romantically interested in me.	*Interrace: The Source for Interracial Living* P.O. Box 15566, Beverly Hills, CA 90209. *Interracial Voice* (No longer published, but back issues of this lively magazine are still available.)
I am white. I am black. I am Native American. I am Latino. I am Asian. I am a Pacific Islander. I am a little of everything. I grew up in a racist family or community.	I want to reach out to people from other cultures romantically, but I am afraid that maybe some kind of racism or stereotyping exists in my subconscious. People from a different culture will automatically assume I am the enemy.	*MAVIN Magazine* (see organizations) *New People: The Journal for the Human Race* P.O. Box 47490, Oak Park, MI 48237. *Society for Interracial Families Newsletter* 23399 Evergreen, Suite 2222, Southfield, MI 48075. *Standards—The International Journal of Multicultural Studies* Email standards@colorado.edu for more information on this e-journal.

I am open-minded and ready to get over racial division and cultural animosity.

I am ready to make a difference.
I want to learn through doing.
I thirst for knowledge.

Race is too big a topic to overcome or even to discuss with people from different types of ancestry.
People will be suspicious of me, and I don't want to have to prove myself.
I'll be viewed as a phony or a fake.

There probably isn't really anything out there specifically geared toward my needs and interests.
We don't really have a past as mixed people, do we?

Adrian Piper/The Arts
Exhibition Catalog, Adrian Piper, Fine Art Gallery, University of Maryland, Baltimore County.
Heartney, E. (2001). Blacks, whites and other mythic beings [on Adrian Piper's work]. *Art in America.*

The Power to Change Permits Evolution
It is hard work to change ingrained patterns of recognition that lead to stereotyping, yet change is vital to healing and evolution. Following are listings of various ways that you can enhance the capacity to understand the complexity of multiracial, biracial, and multiethnic identity through research, study, and direct engagement.

Badejo, D. L., & Christian, M. *Understand history: For scholars, students and the general public.*
Christian, M. (2000). *Multiracial identity: An international perspective.* New York: Macmillan.
Byrd, C. M. (2002). *Beyond race: The Bhagavad-Gita in black and white.* XLIBRIS [ebook].

continued

33

Toolbox for Change (continued)

For	Images/perceptions	Strategies for change
		ISBN: 1-4010-4390-9 (Trade Paperback)
		ISBN: 1-4010-4391-7 (Hardback)
		Cose, E. (1997). *Color blind: seeing beyond race in a race obsessed world.* New York: Harper Collins.
		Hunter, K. (1969). *Walk towards the sunset* [play]. First staged in Sneedville, TN.
		Kennedy, B. (1997). *The Melungeons: The resurrection of a proud people* (Rev. ed.). Macon, GA: Mercer University Press.
		McBride, J. (1997). *The color of water: a black man's tribute to his white mother.* New York: Riverhead Publisher.
		Page, C. (1997). *Showing my color: Impolite essays on race and identity.* New York: Perennial.
		Pollitzer, W. (1972). The physical and genetics of marginal people of the south eastern United States. *American Anthropologist, 74,* 719–734.
		Root, M. P. P. (1995). *The multiracial experience.* Thousand Oaks, CA: Sage Publications.
		Simon, R. (2000). *Adoption across borders: Serving the children of transracial and intercountry adoptions.* Langam, MD: Rowman and Littlefield.
		Spickard, P. (1989). *Mixed blood: Intermarriage and ethnic identity in 20th century America.* Madison, WI: University of Wisconsin Press.

Thernstrom, S. (Ed.). (1980). *Harvard encyclopedia of American ethnic groups.* Cambridge, MA: Belknap Press, Harvard University Press.

Gain a Historical Perspective: Research Papers

DeMarce, V. (1992). Verry slitly mixt: Tri-racial isolate families of the upper South. *National Genealogical Society Quarterly 80*(1).

Dromgoole, W. A. (1890). Land of the Melungeons. *Nashville Sunday American, 10.*

Learn: For Educators and Parents (Books and Videos)

Root, M. P. P., & Kelley, M. (Eds.). *Multiracial child resource book.*

Wardle, F. "Tomorrow's Children." A column in *New People.* By the Center for the Study of Biracial Children (CSBC), 2300 South Krameria St., Denver, Colorado.

Interracial/Intercultural Pride offers the video *Serving biracial and multiethnic children and their families.*

Center for the Study of Biracial Children (research facility). See www.csbc.com/

MAVIN Foundation and Association of Multiethnic Americans (www.ameasite.org/)

continued

Toolbox for Change (continued)

For	Images/perceptions	Strategies for change
		Provides comprehensive reading list for educators, parents (all ages), and practitioners. (See organizations for contact information.)
I am ready to become more fully engaged. I have read, discussed the issues, and belong to a powerful organization.	I don't want to put my foot into my mouth by insulting anyone. Maybe I'm not all the way prepared, but how does one know when is the right time to act?	**Study: College Level Courses on Multiracial Identity People of Mixed Racial Descent** Annual undergraduate level course, University of California–Berkeley. Prof. Robert Allen. **Multiracial, Multiethnic People: The Law and Society** Law course, Golden Gate University's School of Law in San Francisco. Prof. Carlos A. Fernandez-Gray. **Multi-Ethnic Identity and Communities** University of Michigan–Ann Arbor. Instructor Karen Downing. **Other Than Other: The Legitimacy of a Multiracial, Multiethnic Identity** By Prof. Carlos A. Fernandez-Gray, guest lecturer at various universities. **Listen, Observe, Accept** The key to accepting the intricacy of multiracial and multiethnic identity is to listen and accept rather than thrust onto others opinions based on stereotypes.

friends, and the large body of professionals involved with shaping the outlook of the upcoming generations to move forward.

REFERENCES

Austin, A. D. (2002). Faces of American Islam. *Policy Review.* Heritage Foundation.

Bringing them home: The report. Reconciliation and Social Justice Library, Council for Aboriginal Reconciliation, Forgotten History Foundation. Available from: www.forgottenhistory.org

Burnett, S. (1889). *American Anthropologist.*

Chappell, K. (1995, June). Black Indians hit jackpot in casino bonanza. *Ebony,* 46.

DeMarce, V. E. (1992, March). Verry slitly mixt: Tri-racial isolates families of the upper South, a genealogical study. *National Genealogical Society, 80*(1).

Deposition of Abner Duncan, 86 years old. The Perkins File.

Deposition of Anna Graves, 77 years old. The Perkins File.

Deposition of Catherine Roller, 80 years old. The Perkins File.

Deposition of Daniel Stout.

Deposition of David R. Kinnick, aged 77. The Perkins File.

Deposition of Elizabeth Cook, about 71. The Perkins File.

Deposition of John J. Wilson, about 70 years old. The Perkins File.

Deposition of John Nave, 88 years old. The Perkins File.

Deposition of Mary Wilson. The Perkins File.

Deposition of Nancy Lipps. The Perkins File.

Deposition of Thomas Cook, 75 years old. The Perkins File.

Diouf, S. (2002). Faces of American Islam. *Policy Review.* Heritage Foundation.

Duran, K., & Piper, D. (2002). Faces of American Islam. *Policy Review.* Heritage Foundation.

Fouts. (1793). *North Carolina Journal, 1,* 205.

Fouts. (1770). *North Carolina Gazette, 1,* 65–66.

Gormley, M. V. (1997). In search of the black Dutch. *American Genealogy Magazine, 12*(1).

Griggs, L. (2000). *Wayfaring stranger: Black Dutch, German Gypsies or Chicanere and their relation to the Melungeon.* (Author).

Harper, E. W. Excerpt from *Iola Leroy or Shadows Lifted.*

Haun. *Orange County Court minutes.* Vol. 1, pp. 70–71.

Nassau, M. E. (1993). *Melungeons and other Mestee groups.* Wise, VA: Author.

Orders, 1731–1736, 133.

Payne, R. J. (1998). *Getting beyond race: The changing American culture.* Boulder, CO: Westview Press.

Perkins File in the T. A. R. Nelson Papers in the Calvin M. McClung Collection at the East Tennessee Historical Center.

Philbeck. Bladen County Land Entries, no. 1210.

Piper, A. Passing for white, passing for black. *Transition*, Issue 58.

Revolutionary War pension application on March 7, 1834, by Drury Tann.

Senna, D. (1998). The mulatto millennium. In C. C. O'Hern (Eds.), *Half and half: Writers on growing up biracial and bicultural*. New York: Pantheon Books.

Shoemaker, H. W. (1930). *1300 Words*. cPA Mts.

Shoemaker, H. W. (1930, March 31). *Altoona Tribune*.

Testimony of John Scott, "freeborn Negro," in Berkeley County, South Carolina, on January 17, 1754.

Valdes y Cocom, M. de (1998). *Blurring racial boundaries* [Television broadcast]. PBS.

Walton-Raji, A. (1993). *Black Indian genealogy research*. Westminster, MD: Heritage Books.

CHAPTER 2

Asian Americans in the Workplace: Facing Prejudice and Discrimination in Multiple Contexts

Debra M. Kawahara
Jaye Jang Van Kirk

Sue is a thirty-year-old, second-generation Korean American woman who currently works for a large aerospace corporation in California. She earned a bachelor of science degree with honors in electrical engineering from the University of California–Los Angeles and has been working as an engineer for this company since graduating seven years ago. Prior to this position, she worked part-time writing computer programs for the U.S. Navy for approximately one year. Sue prides herself on being a hardworking, diligent, conscientious worker and will go the extra mile to get the job done, even if that means staying all night to complete projects for a deadline. Her current boss commented that he can always count on her to get the work done and that he can basically delegate work to her without needing to supervise it. However, Sue has become increasingly aware that other coworkers do not always do their fair share. Yet, they tend to be given more credit and sometimes promoted to project leader, even though Sue believes that her contributions are more significant.

After a recent incident when she felt that she was overlooked once again for project leader, Sue made an active attempt to figure out whether there was something she was doing that prevented her advancement in the department or whether there was something else happening. She approached her boss to get feedback about her work. Her boss stated that he was very satisfied with her work and that she was a fine employee. She then asked what she could do to be promoted to the next level. He answered with a rather general statement about continuing her high quality of work and that it would eventually lead to a project leader position. He encouraged her to speak with those who had been recently promoted to find out what their strategies for promotion were, and he thanked her for informing him of her career goals.

Given her boss's advice, Sue talked to other co-workers who had been promoted. She found that the information was very general, like the information her boss had given her, except for one thing. One of her female co-workers shared her opinion of how Sue was viewed by others. In the department, Sue was known to have the technical qualifications and expertise needed to be a project leader, but did not share her thoughts or ideas during project meetings. Sue reflected back to her co-worker that her attempts to vocalize her thoughts were often ignored, forgotten, dismissed, or that others took credit for them. The co-worker further pointed out that her relationships with others in the department were more formal, cordial, and civil; but lacked closeness or friendliness. Sue recognized that she rarely spent time outside of work with her co-workers informally and that there was a clear separation between her work life and her home life. Much of her personal time was spent with her family and activities in the Korean American community.

While many people assume that one's background, efforts, and dedication are the primary factors used for evaluation, personal and social interactions also play a role in one's likelihood of success. Being comfortable participating in social activities and developing social networks are not only critical to one's success, but can also influence one's satisfaction with work.

MAKING LIFE DECISIONS: CULTURE, FAMILY, OR THE SELF

A twenty-year-old Asian American female, Chloe desires to attend medical school. Her enthusiasm in pursuing her goals is tempered by the fact that her parents have clearly expressed their desire for her to go into another profession like pharmacy, because it can be quickly achieved, enable her to have a family, and is a profession that is valued and respected within the Asian community. While she is making her way through school as an undergraduate, she is feeling torn about what career path to follow. The weight of her family's preference is strong on her decision. Should she obtain her degree in pharmacy, a field that does not fuel her passion, or should she pursue medicine at the risk of her parents' disapproval? Such a dilemma in a young woman's dreams—to be supported by our cultural expectations that we all can fulfill the "American Dream" to become anything that we want with hard work; or to comply, as the Asian culture expects, to a parent's wishes—can be difficult to negotiate. The ultimate decision will clearly never be Chloe's own because she understands her role in the context of her family. So for Asians and Asian Americans, full autonomy and independence from parental influence may not be options because they are not parts of the context of their cultural values. The strength of the connection to one's cultural values and one's family shapes many decisions.

While obtaining their college educations, Asian Americans may confront difficult decisions that could ultimately affect their career paths. Should they complete a degree to satisfy their parents, by going into a profession that is valued for its status and prestige (for example, medicine or engineering), or pursue their passion in an unrelated area? Not only is obtaining an education mandatory, the strong push to complete the degree in a respectable time interval in a particular subject area is also well understood by Asian Americans.

Bicultural Efficacy: Managing Two Cultures

Both Sue and Chloe are being pulled by belief systems and cultural expectations away from their Asian family cultures and western social culture concurrently. The manner in which each woman handles her situation will depend on how she is able to negotiate her two cultural worlds successfully. The presence of two such worlds is often referred to as biculturalism, meaning that both women have two internalized cultures that guide their thoughts, perceptions, and feelings (LaFromboise, Coleman, & Gerton, 1993; Phinney & Devich-Navarro, 1997). Whether these women are able to do this effectively will depend on their bicultural efficacy. *Bicultural efficacy* is defined as the ability to develop and maintain interpersonal relations within two groups without relinquishing one's cultural identity (LaFromboise et al., 1993). In such situations, it is believed that the person's bicultural competence will assist her or him in building and maintaining support networks in the different contexts while also providing support when either group rejects the person or when the person is developing competence in one group.

In these two examples, the women are faced with the task of developing competency in a majority cultural setting while maintaining their cultural connections. Ideally, the bicultural individual develops the skills and abilities to be competent in a second culture without losing that same competence in the culture of origin. Ultimately, successful bicultural individuals have a sense of psychological well-being as well as mastery in their social, work, and family environments.

All of us hope that we can make positive contributions to the world and that we can have the freedom and opportunity to explore how those goals can be achieved. The reality of the professional and social worlds, however, often sets limits on a person's opportunities. While significant strides have been made in providing individuals from underrepresented groups more opportunities to advance professionally and socially, there still remain many challenges that prohibit individuals from taking part fully in some opportunities in society (Hwang, Francesco, & Kessler, 2003; Kunkel & Burleson, 1998; Stewart, Germain, & Jackson, 1992). More people have gained appreciation of the importance of sensitivity to diversity issues. However, translating verbal support into action requires additional amounts of commitment and understanding.

The focus of this chapter is to identify some of the limitations that affect one's ability to make the kind of contributions desired. Some may be related to ethnic/cultural factors, and others may reflect the sociocultural context of the environment. Part of success is an awareness of what one brings to a situation (beliefs, values, ethnicity, gender, etc.) as well as ability to assess the expectations of the situation. It is hoped that with an increased awareness of the factors that may limit one's opportunities, the individual will be able to more consciously employ strategies that bring the positive contributions desired.

Another intent of this chapter is to provide information about what to anticipate based on the specific circumstance and how the person may handle any challenges that arise from ethnic/cultural differences. Attention to one's preferred style of interaction among the expectations and demands of the setting or context is often key to developing appropriate coping strategies. In addition, the chapter will also address the importance of providing opportunities that enable people to collaborate with one another as equals so that they can see how their combined talents can effectively achieve mutually shared goals and interests.

WHY KNOWING WHERE YOU ARE MATTERS IN HOW TO ACT: BEING CULTURALLY AWARE

In addition to ethnic heritage ties, there are experiential contexts that have shaped one's impressions and perceptions of what life is and what it can be. Asian Americans whose life experiences have been in the context of a large Asian community may have little appreciation for the differences that they encounter when their lives transplant them into environments where the social, cultural, and ethnic demographics are significantly different. Their preferred and automatic assumptions and modes of functioning used to operate in everyday life will now be tested in different contexts. When moving to a new environment where the demographics change from being racially/ethnically homogeneous to racially/ethnically diverse, these Asian Americans are often unaware of a shift in the context of their status and the resultant impact of how they are now perceived by others. They also may not be cognizant of the importance of being more sensitive to how different social contexts influence how they are perceived.

Understanding how their status can shift from one circumstance to another will be beneficial in guiding their actions so that they are suitable for each situation. Within the context of a new environment, they are now encountering demands from new circumstances that may be affecting their comfort and success in this new environment. It is their degree of assimilation that will be an important part of their ability to gain acceptance and success. The task then for the newly transplanted bicultural individual is to become aware of the shifting demands of the various sociocultural environments of which they are a part. Many bicultural individuals already have some awareness of how their behaviors and demeanors shift between their home lives and their professional or social lives. Successful navigation between two cultures may require one to know when to express more self-assertion, verbal expression, and social engagement with others. Importantly, it is not only the awareness of when to shift, but also what behavioral shifts are most appropriate for particular circumstances that help the individual avoid inappropriate "cultural carryover."

BEING ASIAN: THE VIEW FROM THE INSIDE AND OUTSIDE: APPEARANCES CAN BE DECEIVING

Another aspect of this stage of development is the emerging awareness of the differences between Asians and Asian Americans. At an individual level, young adults may begin realizing that how others perceive them differs from how they perceive themselves. An external attribution that Asian Americans may encounter based on physical appearance is that of "immigrant." While the generic term "Asian" may be used to classify all Asians, the Asian American often self-identifies as an American with an Asian ethnic background. Additionally, persistent comments that often cue Asian Americans that others perceive them differently include comments such as, "Where were you born?" "You speak English well," "How long have you lived here?" or "No, really, where are you from?" There are then some aspects of each culture that clearly make Asians and Asian Americans different from one another while other aspects of an Asian heritage serve as a common basis of both cultures. Therein lie some of the difficulties that bicultural Asian Americans face in being able to clearly understand what is expected of them in particular circumstances. Additionally, the more subtle cultural differences that exist between Asian immigrants and Asian Americans may not be immediately apparent to them, and it also may not be clear why these differences may be relevant to the challenges that they are experiencing in their own lives. So, when others group Asians together without understanding differences in values, customs, language, and level of assimilation, Asian Americans may be exasperated to find a lack of sensitivity to what they perceive as distinct differences among the various Asian ethnic groups. These examples and other occurrences are reminders of how Asian Americans straddle two cultural worlds.

LANGUAGE CONNECTIONS TO CULTURE

For second- and third-generation Asian Americans, the inability to speak their ancestors' language can be yet another point of separation between their ethnic background and belonging to American culture. Proficiency in the language of one's own ethnic heritage is often noted by family members, while comments about one's English fluency is a constant reminder of how one is perceived differently by the outside world. Such stereotypical expectations and comments about one's command of English often are incongruent with the Asian American's self-perception, because in the minds of Asian Americans, he or she is American. When such instances are repeated over and over again, they also remind Asian Americans of how they are perceived differently in different cultural contexts.

These two examples illustrate some of the issues that Asian Americans encounter daily. Often, diligence, dependability, and conscientiousness are desirable traits that are often associated with admirable work ethics. Being subdued and formal with strong family connections and cohesiveness is also associated with being Asian. What many people may be less aware of that is particularly relevant to this topic is how living in a bicultural world affects one's daily interactions. In work and social settings, being viewed worthy of higher-status positions and having respect and credibility can be hard-fought achievements. Thus, understanding the interaction between one's behaviors and another person's perceptions is critical to seeing a person's talents and abilities and providing that individual with opportunities to demonstrate his or her potential.

The Importance of Being Aware of Stereotyping

Cultural Values and Preferred Styles of Interacting

Asian identity is framed within a set of sociocultural influences that are expressed in subtle and overt ways in everyday interactions. The physical manifestations of being Asian often result in other people responding to society's perceptions of the stereotypical Asian. Descriptions such as "quiet," "model minority," "exceptional," "passive," and "deferent" can perpetuate limited images of Asians' abilities that do not adequately reflect the breadth of Asian cultures. Common assumptions also include the belief that anyone with Asian physical characteristics is foreign-born. Each of these examples represents a constant reminder for Asian Americans that they are perceived differently by society. Awareness of noticeable differences in people's reactions based on these stereotypes often convey the challenges of knowing how to express the appropriate behaviors for particular social circumstances (home, school, work, etc.). For Asian Americans, awareness of the different demands of white and Asian cultures can prelude the development of a bicultural identity. For Asian Americans, the fluid expression of identity is tied to what situational circumstances they are currently in. For some, the contrast of social demands is quite apparent. In the context of culture and family, Asians and women can behave in ways often described as collective, where interdependency, cooperation, and a sense of obligation to one's community are emphasized (Kunkel & Burleson, 1998; Sue & Sue, 2003; Uba, 1994). There is little expression of the self in the context of one's

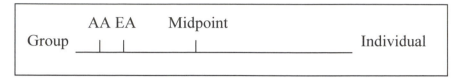

Figure 2.1. Bipolar continuum for group/individual values: Asian Americans (AA) and European Americans (EA)
Source: From Kawahara (2003).

family or community. Moreover, there is a tendency to behave in ways that show respect for elders or other authority figures that is expressed by passivity and deference (Atkinson, Whiteley, & Gim, 1990; Wong & Ujimoto, 1998). While achieving autonomy may be critical in developing the kind of self-assertion skills that are often highly valued in work or academic settings, the benefits of having strong connections to family and culture are important buffers to stressors encountered in life (Lee, 1997; Mallinckrodt & Leong, 1992). Moving beyond the Asian community and family then requires a shift in behavior to assertiveness and independence.

Cultural sensitivity is necessary for both Asian Americans and for individuals working with individuals from an Asian background. Understanding an individual's values and responses to circumstances often requires thoughtful consideration. Accurate interpretation of an individual's preferred style of social interaction may be context-dependent, according to researcher Yoshito Kawahara (2003). Kawahara's research very revealingly demonstrates that Asian Americans and whites are not that different in orientation in the "group versus individual" continuum. The commonly held belief is that Asians tend to be group-oriented while whites are individualistic. Kawahara contended that, for both groups, cultural values possessed a situational component that was expressed in work and social settings. Moreover, his research found that whites were also group-oriented and that the difference between the two populations was that Asian Americans tended to express these values to a greater degree, as shown in Figure 2.1. Careful attention to the context of a person's behaviors is important in understanding what they are trying to express.

It should be emphasized that attending to expressions and behaviors in a given context is important, since careful attention to cues from the sociocultural environment can be useful in knowing how to respond most appropriately. Attention to the context is essential because it also pertains to cultural sensitivity for individual expression. In addition, it is important that people be aware of unintentionally judging someone else's actions using their own value standards. Cultural sensitivity should be viewed as a dynamic process that is especially of great consequence for bicultural individuals.

THE CONTEXT OF YOUR BEHAVIORS MATTERS TO YOUR SUCCESS

Awareness of one's own cultural values can be important in understanding one's expectations of how individuals will interact and be treated in a work or social setting. Similarly, awareness of another person's cultural values can help in anticipating how the other person will view, interpret, and interact behaviors. For example, Asian Americans may express their respect for authority in work or social settings by expressing a passive and deferent demeanor. How might these behaviors be interpreted? These behaviors are not necessarily universally translatable across situations, especially in different cultural contexts, so the behaviors may not be interpreted as a sign of respect. If one is not aware that deference and passivity express respect rather than lack of initiative or understanding, he or she could easily misinterpret the meaning of the behaviors (in white circumstances). Therefore, cultural sensitivity to accurate interpretation and avoidance of cultural biases should be maintained. Regarding the expression of one's preferred style of social interaction, the tendencies toward deference and passivity can make it significantly more difficult for an Asian American to engage in social interactions requiring oral communication and assertiveness, especially with authority figures, because such overt expressions have not been a part of the cultural messages and expectations that the person is familiar with.

In Table 2.1, Kawahara (2003) summarizes cultural values differences between Asian Americans and whites that are often expressed in social and work settings. Awareness of how these values are expressed can be key in providing people with opportunities to contribute their individual talents in ways that they feel most comfortable. In group versus person-oriented values, the emphasis is on collaborative functioning versus the influence of the individual. For collectivist versus individualist values, a person's focus includes consideration of others rather than for self. Interdependence emphasizes mutual support, whereas independence focuses on what can be achieved through individual efforts. These first three values show significant changes according to the situation. Cooperation emphasizes a common goal and

Table 2.1
Opposing values of Asian Americans and European Americans in work/social settings

Asian American	European American
Group oriented	Person oriented
Collectivist	Individualist
Interdependent	Independent
Cooperative	Competitive
Harmony	Mastery
Duty and obligation	Free will/Personal rights
Formal	Informal
Self-discipline	Spontaneous
Pessimism	Optimism
Situation-centered	Person-centered
Indirect/Nonassertive	Directive and assertive

Source: Kawahara, 2003.

unity of efforts, while competitiveness emphasizes achievement through opposition and antagonism. Harmony expresses acting in synchrony and within the context of the circumstance, while mastery seeks direction and power over circumstances. Duty and obligation refer to actions based on responsibility and accountability to others, and free will/ personal rights refer to actions based on individual desires. Formal approaches emphasize prescribed protocol, while informal approaches emphasize familiar and more casual strategies. Self-discipline approaches tasks through restraint, effort, planning, and organization; while spontaneous approaches take advantage of the immediate and unstructured nature of some circumstances. Pessimism expresses doubt, concern, and negativity; and optimism emphasizes confidence and hopefulness in what can be. Individuals who are situation-centered are responsive to the individuals and circumstances that guide their choice of responses, while person-centered options focus more on the perceptions and impacts on the individuals. Those who have an indirect/nonassertive approach to communication tend to address issues in a nonconfrontational, passive demeanor; while those who are directive and assertive are more likely to speak openly, freely, and specifically to issues.

These values point to differences. However, they should not be viewed as definitive characterizations of Asian Americans and whites because "stereotypes diminish and divide" (Kawahara, 2003). What can happen is that dominant groups may use stereotypes to discount and dehumanize others where those others' differences are viewed as deficits rather than alternative yet viable perspectives or approaches. One must be cautioned about how values can act in "subtle, insidious and nonverbal ways" to discount the abilities and contribution of others (Kawahara, 2003).

The advantage of being bicultural is having the flexibility of utilizing one's talents and abilities according to the needs of the situation. One's insights and contributions enhance the likelihood that more people will understand a message because of the common perspective that one shares. The ability to bridge cultures is a valuable tool in this increasingly globalized society. Learning to navigate both worlds effectively by incorporating regular use of strategy shifting may enhance one's ability to accomplish one's goals.

The information in this chapter is intended to provide insights about the internal and external factors that may influence one's ability to fulfill set goals. The previous recommendations were intended to assist in gaining increased awareness to the "internal" aspect of what can influence the dynamics of a situation (for example, individual style and cultural history). Expressing oneself in ways that are harmonious with the environment is an attainable skill. There may be, however, circumstances that are external to the person and beyond one's control (such as intolerant colleagues, and unwelcoming work and social environment). Changing one's self to the extent that one no longer feels comfortable can create psychological and emotional stress as much as being in a hostile environment can. Maintaining a sense of well-being and preserving one's integrity, self-worth, and self-confidence are essential, as are recognizing when a situation is actually harmful and damaging to one's physical and mental health. The next section addresses situations that Asian Americans may face due to prejudice and discrimination from others, and addresses possible, proactive steps that a person can take to deal with such situations.

ELIMINATING POSSIBLE MANIFESTATIONS AS A PROACTIVE POSITION: IDENTIFYING PREJUDICE AND DISCRIMINATION

There are various forms of prejudice and discrimination that occur. Some are blatant and can be identified readily. Others are more invisible, insidious, and subtle; and it is harder for the person to pinpoint what exactly is happening. The subtle forms are more difficult to detect, yet they can be the most discriminatory in practice. The following section describes some forms of prejudice and discrimination to hopefully help the reader identify if and when a situation arises.

Racial Slurs

These include name-calling, derogatory racial terms or epithets, stereotyped imitations with accompanying accents and facial expressions, jokes, and/or cartoons. For example, a complaint filed with the Equal Employment Opportunity Commission reported a Japanese American employee of a freeway service patrol company being called "Nazi Jap," "retarded Jap," "chink," and "gook" by the company owner and other employees.

Blatant Stereotyping

Stereotyping is another form of prejudice and discrimination. The stereotypes of Asians and Asian Americans are imposed on the Asian American individual, even when the individual may not even embody those stereotypic characteristics. This can become even more prominent if the person is the only Asian American in the organization, because the variability among different people is not available to disaffirm the stereotypes. The other result is that people who are using the stereotypes will look for more evidence to confirm the stereotypes and ignore evidence that counters them. Thus, the stereotypes become even more strongly believed and perceived.

Unfavorable Educational Returns and Lower Wages

Although Asian Americans are often seen as the model for success and referred to by the stereotype of the "model minority," statistics have found that there are strong inequities in educational attainment and occupational status. According to the Federal Glass Ceiling Commission Report in 1999, different studies have found over and over again that Asian Americans are not only overrepresented in science and technical fields and underrepresented as managers, but that the payoff for educational attainment is less than it is for whites (Woo, 2000). For example, Asian males in the West with four or more years of education earned less than their white male counterparts.

Not Getting Promoted

Asian Americans often feel barriers to advancement, such as promotion from a professional and/or technical position to a higher-level administrative position. Basically, promotions are blocked. This all-too-familiar scenario can be seen in the example of Sue at the beginning of the chapter. Many whites expect that Asian Americans will quietly accept these decisions and continue to work hard for the company. However, most people want the same work incentives that other workers have, and Asian Americans are no different. When promotions are seen as being unfairly given to those who are less qualified or that there is differential treatment based on race and/or gender, a worker may become dissatisfied and disillusioned about work, thereby impacting his or her productivity and performance.

Tracking

Another form of discrimination is to give or place Asian Americans into less-desirable, less-career-advancing work assignments or opportunities. This would be similar to segregating or channeling Asian Americans into certain career positions or paths by virtue of the work experience that is allowed or available to them.

Differential Treatment

Related to tracking is differential treatment based on race. This is often more noticeable when the person is the only employee from the racial group, and the differential treatment can be blatant and direct or subtle and indirect. A direct example would be the avoidance of social contact with the employee, while a subtle one would be the lack of inclusion in informal outings such as lunch or gatherings held outside of the office.

Different Standards of Evaluation

These can happen when the standards for evaluation are rather general and not specifically detailed out for all to understand. Insidious forms of institutional prejudice and discrimination can be implemented by making the standards elusive and changeable. For example, suppose the qualifications for a management position are outlined in the job description and include technical expertise and years of experience. Yet, other qualities such as interpersonal skills and business connections are also considered for the position, but not listed on the job posting. The result is that the unlisted qualities eliminate certain candidates from the pool based on perceptions of the hiring committee and/or lack of opportunity or training.

Unrealistic and Unreasonable Expectations

These can come in the form of being given an overabundance of work that is unreasonable for one person to complete or is beyond the person's position and expertise. By doing this, the person is set up to fail and thereby represent the incompetence and inadequacies of that group. This can be related to stereotypes and serve to further confirm them.

Doing a Job Too Well

On the other extreme, Asian Americans can be mistreated when they excel at work. Mistreatment can include a resistance to their expertise, penalization for excelling in their work or working diligently, and interference with their performance. This can become an issue when another becomes jealous or may not want to see an Asian American succeed. For example, a successful Asian American female found herself being harassed by her newly appointed white male boss when he recognized that she had much power and influence on the staff. He slowly began to restrict her work and isolate her from the other staff persons. As the situation escalated, he began leaving her out of important meetings and communications and then writing her up for insubordination.

Intimidation, Threats, and Actions

Intimidation, threats, and actual actions are the most extreme and obvious forms of prejudice and discrimination. These can include threats of physical harm to the person or someone the person knows, property damage, continued harassment and emotional abuse, stalking and/or spying, tampering with or destroying the person's work, intimidation through public humiliation, and the presence/use of weapons.

INDIVIDUAL RESPONSES TO PREJUDICE AND DISCRIMINATION

Experiencing severe and stressful discrimination can lead to both physical and psychological consequences. The toll on the person's functioning can be overwhelming and devastating, affecting the person's whole life. This is because the prejudicial and/or discriminatory events are often perceived as unfairly attacking the very core of what these people believe or embody. These incidences, when combined with the perceptions of being under attack, can be compared to living in a war zone, and symptoms similar to being in combat or held hostage can manifest.

In work situations, it is often reported that the employee initially believes that the organization will adhere to the policies of harassment and/or discrimination, so the employee still believes that the right thing will be done and justice will prevail. However, this assumption is often shattered when the policies and rules are not upheld or it is perceived that the organization is protecting the harasser/discriminator to avoid a problem, conflict, and/or litigation. A minimization or dismissal of the complaint only increases the employee's sense of isolation, violation, and wrongdoing.

As the employee continues to endure the situation, a heightened sense of vulnerability and fear is elicited in the employee. The knowledge of not having the organization's support to intervene, along with the daily encounters with the perpetrator, only increase the employee's need to protect himself or herself from any further harassment or abuse. This vulnerability and fear can generalize so that the employee can look and be paranoid and suspicious of everyone and everything. This heightened awareness can be physically and emotionally draining and even impact the employee's performance and personal life.

Another aspect that is brought into question is one's work identity. Often the employee's competencies, abilities, and/or work ethic are personally challenged. As the incidences increase in conflict and hostility, the employee's self-confidence often is shaken and he/she will question whether it is worth staying in the field. However, this employee is caught in a difficult situation. Staying in the position means enduring more physiological and psychological stress and its consequential effects. Leaving the position or completely shifting into another field means a personal, professional, and financial loss. It can cause feelings of hopelessness and anger for having to be put into this position or having to make this decision.

Maria Root, an expert psychologist on racial and ethnic harassment in the workplace, has compiled a list of ten common symptoms suffered by individuals who have sought therapy or been evaluated as a result of racial and ethnic harassment in the workplace (Root, 2001, 2004).

Anxiety

This may include excess worrying over the situation, restlessness, tension, a feeling of edginess, irritability, muscle tension, having difficulty concentrating or focusing, and somatic/physical complaints. Anxiety can be heightened if the person anticipates a meeting or interaction with the perpetrator.

Paranoia

Paranoia is persistent suspicion not just about the motives of the perpetrator(s); it generalizes to the motives of others as well. This is further compounded by worrying about what others think about one in terms of his/her integrity, work, and handling of the situation and how one is being portrayed by others' incorrect or inaccurate information. As a result, the employee may isolate from or avoid contact with others for fear that such contact may cause more damage to his reputation or that the interactions will be used against him as evidence for the perpetrator.

Depression

Some common features of depression include, but are not limited to, sadness or feeling down and blue; crying or tearfulness; increased irritability; decrease in tolerance for stress and discomfort; loss of pleasure or interest in activities; functioning less efficiently than usual at work and home; difficulty concentrating or thinking clearly and making decisions; thinking negatively about oneself and one's future; and feeling unmotivated and responsive to rewards and praise. In general, there is a sense of going through the motions, with a lack of fulfillment or satisfaction in one's life that was there before the whole situation occurred.

Sleep Disturbance

Root (2001, 2004) separates this symptom from depression because it is often one of the initial symptoms seen. Sleep difficulties can be found in falling asleep, staying asleep, and in the amount of sleep. Because of the anxiety and restlessness, the person may wake up several times a night or sleep only two or three hours a night. On the other extreme, the person may sleep an excessive amount (such as nine to eleven hours a day) because of the extra energy needed to deal with the situation or to escape thinking about the situation.

Loss of Confidence

A lack of confidence in being able to evaluate and trust people makes it difficult to interact with others. In most situations, interacting with others, whether they are co-workers or actual consumers, is often compromised because the employee tends to be distant and guarded, resulting in others becoming more distant and guarded in their interactions. Furthermore, as the employee's relationships become less connected, the employee may lose confidence in being able to establish and maintain close relationships with others.

Feelings of Worthlessness

The feelings of worthlessness involve the devaluing of one's abilities, competencies, or value in the work environment. These are especially difficult if one derived much esteem and pride from one's work, profession, and career prior to the harassment experience. One outcome may be that the person really questions whether she had and still has anything to offer, or whether all she worked hard for was for nothing.

Intrusive Cognitions

Like others who have experienced traumatic events, the person could have involuntary or recurrent thoughts, images, and/or replays regarding the harasser or the work situation. These thoughts or replays can interfere with the employee's ability to work or perform and can engender significant distress and anxiety. Even when sleeping, the thoughts or images can appear, and suddenly the person is experiencing the same fear, distress, and arousal that were present in real-life. The energy expended on the thoughts, images, and/or replays as well as the emotions associated with them often exhausts the person, further hampering the person's ability to work and manage the situation.

Helplessness

Often when the situation initially occurs, the employee takes steps to change the situation. When the employee's actions make no impact or even cause more duress, he can feel helpless. This only confirms that nothing that the employee does will change the situation. If he has to remain in this position for a prolonged time, he can feel trapped, further exacerbating the anxiety, depression, and feelings of worthlessness. In addition, the employee can feel helpless in protecting or salvaging his reputation, especially if the harasser/persecutor holds a more powerful or influential position in the organization.

Loss of Drive

With all of the events happening, it is not surprising that the person loses a sense of purpose and motivation to continue to work. This can even continue after leaving the situation or after the situation is resolved. The person may feel exhausted from the experience for perhaps months or years, and it takes some time to recover and heal physically, mentally, emotionally, and spiritually. A once-ambitious and driven person can find that the goals once desired are set lower or even abandoned. A change in the line of work can even occur because of how disheartening and disillusioning the experience has been. Questions like "What for?" or "Why work so hard when in the end no one really cares how hard you work?" can also surface.

False Positives

This is the process where the traits and characteristics of the harasser/persecutor become generalized to others who have similar traits and characteristics, so that reactions similar to those felt against the harasser/persecutor are triggered. These reactions are a natural coping mechanism that helps the person protect herself from further harm. For example, the victim may become anxious or mistrust someone who is of the same race as the original harasser/persecutor. Because the incident has become so ingrained as life-threatening, it elevates the person to a fight or flight response. Root (2001) found that the response is more severe for those who have not experienced significant racial or ethnic discrimination than for persons who have dealt with severe racism and/or discrimination.

TIPS AND STRATEGIES TO COMBAT PREJUDICE AND DISCRIMINATION

Cultural Awareness and Knowledge of Self

One main point of this chapter is to highlight the need for persons, especially those from diverse backgrounds, to have awareness of their own cultural values and belief systems as well as an ability to identify others' values and belief systems. By identifying and assessing when these values and beliefs are compatible or incompatible with the situation, the person will be better able to adjust or shift his thoughts and behaviors to be effective in a specific circumstance. This is particularly important when the individual moves into an environment that is significantly different from his own worldview or perspective. Ideally, this bicultural individual has the adeptness and skills to move between situations smoothly without relinquishing his cultural identity, thereby becoming culturally competent in various settings and situations.

Mentoring

Isolation can result from being the only or one of the few Asian Americans in a situation, whether that is at work, school, or in a social group. Finding a means to remain connected to people who can support, sustain, and encourage one's efforts becomes critical. Much has been written on how success is achieved. One of the most influential factors is having a mentor. Mentors can serve several purposes.

Support and Guidance

They can be important in providing a supportive and guiding influence in another person's development. Oftentimes when she is going through something, having someone who has "been through it" can provide important clues to surviving the "process."

Resources

They can direct you to resources that can be of assistance and ease the path. Such support can make an important difference in how easy or difficult an experience can be for an individual.

Role Modeling

Identifying mentors who have similar interests and/or are of the same gender or ethnicity can be helpful because they can serve as role models of success. They understand the challenges and stressors of the situation and what needs to be done, and they can validate the experience of being alone and isolated.

Someone to Confide In

Mentors are people who can be trusted and confided in. All of us have gone through difficult times in our lives, and a mentor who is willing to hear concerns, anxieties, and fears without harsh criticism or judgment can help one become more confident in one's decisions. A mentor can serve as a sounding board for decisions and can offer advice while also allowing one to test the boundaries. A good mentor will trust the mentee's judgment and allow the mentee to make his own decisions.

Opportunities

Mentors can also provide mentees with links to opportunities. Their networks of people and resources can be important in opening more doors and providing important sources of information.

Have Multiple Mentors

Many people are under the assumption that they should have a single mentor. However, it is more beneficial to have several mentors. It is important to develop relationships with several people who can serve as mentors for different needs. Each person has unique strengths that can be important in different aspects of one's development.

Participating in Various Organizations

Making efforts to participate in organizations that serve your interests (gender, ethnic/cultural, professional, religious) can be an important part of successful survival in an environment that is not optimal. Both professional and specific interest groups should be sought. Each can provide different networks, opportunities, experiences, and forms of support for success. Professional and academic programs often have advocate groups that can serve as important springboards for information and resources. Many have specific groups who understand and help with experiences and can provide additional resources or contact persons so that one can begin building a network of support to assist in one's academic and professional development. The individuals within each of these organizations understand many of the issues faced because they too have faced similar challenges. Many people within these organizations are very willing to speak about their experience, can answer questions and concerns, or can direct you to additional resources. In becoming an active part of these organizations, one can find important connections to people who can help through various challenges. Importantly, their shared knowledge and experiences can help others achieve their goals while helping them avoid learned mistakes.

Setting Boundaries and Limits

There are inherent challenges associated with being the only "fill in the blank" at work, school, or a social setting. Being the sole representative of one's ethnic/cultural group can place many demands and expectations on this individual. A major expectation and/or responsibility may be to assist others who are following in the same path. In addition, this person is often asked to participate in task forces and committees addressing racial and diversity issues. These requests are often in addition to the normal and required activities assigned to the person. When this occurs, one must carefully weigh where one's energy and political/social influence are devoted. The person may feel determined to become involved in programs to enhance the diversity of representation as one of the most salient aspects of his or her contribution to social change. However, with this decision, the person is making a choice to expend some of his or her talents and energy on social and political issues at the expense of academic or professional development. This decision is critical not only for one's future, but for others who follow. Some people choose to accomplish the tasks simultaneously while others approach the tasks by achieving one goal first and then devoting their energy to fulfilling the second goal. It is important to prioritize the demands and expectations of the situation as well as the kinds of contributions that one can make without jeopardizing one's position. Then the individual should set realistic goals and achieve them by considering how the community can best be served without compromising his or her own goals.

Some Recommendations When the Situation Is More Severe

Asking for Help and Guidance

Some Asians and Asian Americans believe that asking for help will be seen as a weakness or that imposing on those who are higher in the system is unacceptable. However, receiving aid, guidance, or mentoring is a critical tool for anyone. It is especially crucial when someone is in a racist and/or sexist environment and prejudice and discrimination are occurring. These connections can provide information and support for dealing with both individual and organizational issues. In addition, both internal as well as external support should be sought. The internal support network will be helpful in advising how to delicately negotiate the organizational dynamics and politics as well as rally support for you within the organization. Externally, people can give you emotional support and advice without being constrained by their organizational positions. This allows them to be open and free to speak about the individual(s) involved without jeopardizing their reputation.

Document, Document, Document

As soon as you suspect something is happening, start documenting everything, including previous incidences and any events leading up and contributing to the negative work environment. This should include any incident that occurs, with the time, date, and persons involved; any conversations, meetings, or consultations that you have regarding an event, situation, person, or organization; and any feelings or outcomes resulting from the situation, such as illnesses, treatment, and therapy. You can send documentations to your e-mail address so that the date and time of the documentation are recorded. Further, keep all written correspondences as further evidence.

Consider Another Position and Organization

Although society discourages "giving up" and looks down upon not being able to resolve one's problems head on, the toll of choosing to stay in a work environment that is discriminatory, hostile, and/or degrading cannot be minimized. Working in such an environment can negatively impact one's physical, mental, emotional, and spiritual health and well-being. The impact can also have far-reaching consequences in terms of one's personal life and relationships.

For most people, work is a means to being able to live one's life. If the quality of a person's life is impaired by a disruptive and harmful work environment, then the person needs to question whether it is worth staying in the position. At that point, the person has three choices: (1) stay and cope with the discrimination; (2) seek another company that treats her better; and (3) consider options outside the company, such as filing a complaint with the Equal Employment Opportunity Commission (EEOC) or pursuing a lawsuit.

When confronted with discrimination, many employees choose to find a new position. It has to be remembered that a work environment that is nurturing, supportive, and fair will probably be more conducive toward your career advancement as well as your own sanity, further increasing your level of satisfaction and fulfillment at work.

Toolbox for Change

Strategies for combating prejudice and discrimination

Gain cultural awareness of self and others.
Gain the ability to identify and assess values and belief systems.
Find multiple mentors.
Participate in both professional and cultural organizations.
Set boundaries and limits on one's time and activities.
When the situation is severe:

1. Ask for help and advice.
2. Document all incidents and communications.
3. Consider another position and organization.
4. Know your rights and the laws that are on your side.

Know Your Rights and the Laws on Your Side

People often feel helpless and overwhelmed when racism is occurring in the workplace. It is at these times that people need to be aware of the federal employment laws that do not tolerate prejudice and that penalize companies for discrimination. The most significant antidiscrimination law covering the workplace is Title VII of the federal Civil Rights Act of 1964. Under this law, workplace discrimination based on race, skin color, religious orientation, or national origin is illegal and subject to punishment. The EEOC bears the responsibility of administering and enforcing this law. In cases where discrimination is found, the EEOC can provide remedies under Title VII such as reinstatement and promotion, recovery of wages and losses, money damages, and payment of attorney's fees.

However, although the EEOC's caseload increased by nearly 40 percent from 1990 to 1998, it is believed that Asian Americans still underreport prejudicial and discriminatory cases even though they experience it as much as other minorities do (Repa, 2002; www.catalystwomen.org). Filing a report may cause conflict and dissonance for some Asian Americans. The notion of harmony and avoiding conflict could possibly influence some to not file a complaint. Again, this is a personal decision that must be made by the person.

Another alternative to filing a complaint or lawsuit is mediation. This is less expensive, quicker, and generally more satisfying to the parties. Those who want or need to fix a workplace relationship generally use mediation more than those who have filed a complaint or have been fired. In mediation, the conflicting parties hire a third party who is objective. The mediator's job is to listen to all sides of the dispute and then help the parties come to a mutually acceptable working arrangement. If you are interested in mediation, you should check with your human resources department to see whether these services are acceptable.

REFERENCES

Advancing Asian women in the workplace: What managers need to know. Retrieved October 15, 2003, from www.catalyst.women.org/research/work.htm

Atkinson, D. R., Whiteley, S., & Gim, R. H. (1990). Asian-American acculturation and preferences for help providers. *Journal of College Student Development, 31,* 31–161.

Federal Glass Ceiling Commission. (1999). *Good for business: Making full use of the nation's human capital.* Washington, DC: U.S. Government Printing Office.

Hwang, A., Francesco, A. M., & Kessler, E. (2003). The relationship between individualism-collectivism, face, and feedback and learning processes in Hong Kong, Singapore, and the United States. *Journal of Cross-Cultural Psychology, 34*(1), 72–91.

Kawahara, Y. (2003, April). *Culture-based values of European Americans and Asian Americans.* Paper presented at the Crossing Boundaries: Coalition Building, Community Formation, and Activism at the West and the Pacific Regional Association for Asian American Studies Conference, Pomona, CA.

Kunkel, A. W., & Burleson, B. R. (1998). Social support and the emotional lives of men and women: An assessment of the different cultures perspective. In D. J. Canary & K. Dindra (Eds.), *Sex differences and similarities in communication: Critical essays and empirical investigations of sex and gender in interaction.* Mahwah, NJ: Lawrence Erlbaum Associates.

LaFromboise, T., Coleman, H., & Gerton, J. (1993). Psychological impact of biculturalism: Evidence and theory. *Psychological Bulletin, 114,* 395–412.

Lee, E. (1997). Overview: The assessment and treatment of Asian American families. In E. Lee (Ed.), *Working with Asian Americans: A guide for clinicians.* New York: Guilford Press.

Mallinckrodt, B., & Leong, F. T. (1992). International graduate students, stress, and social support. *Journal of College Student Development, 33,* 71–78.

Phinney, J., & Devich-Navarro, M. (1997). Variations in bicultural identification among African American and Mexican American adolescents. *Journal of Research on Adolescence, 7,* 918–927.

Repa, B. K. (2002). *Your rights in the workplace*. Berkeley, CA: Nolo Press.

Root, M. P. P. (2001). Racial and ethnic origins harassment in the workplace: Evaluation issues and symptomatology. In D. B. Pope-Davis, H. L. K. Coleman, W. M. Liu, & R. L. Toporek (Eds.), *Handbook of multicultural competencies in counseling psychology*. Thousand Oaks, CA: SAGE Publications.

Root, M. P. P. (2004). The consequences of racial and ethnic origins harassment in the workplace: Conceptualization and assessment. In K. Barrett, & W. H. George (Eds.), *Race, culture, psychology, and law*. Thousand Oaks, CA: SAGE Publications, Inc.

Stewart, R. J., Germain, S., & Jackson, J. D. (1992). Alienation and interactional style: A style of successful Anglo, Asian, and Hispanic university students. *Journal of College Student Development, 33*, 149–156.

Sue, D. W., & Sue, D. (2003). *Counseling the culturally diverse: Theory and practice* (4th ed.). New York: John Wiley & Sons.

Uba, L. (1994). *Asian Americans: Personality patterns, identity, and mental health*. New York: Guilford Press.

Wong, P. T. P., & Ujimoto, K. V. (1998). The elderly: Their stress, coping, and mental health. In L. Lee, & N. W. S. Zane (Eds.), *Handbook of Asian American psychology*. Thousand Oaks, CA: SAGE Publications.

Woo, D. (2000). *Glass ceilings and Asian Americans: The new face of workplace barriers*. Walnut Creek, CA: Altamira Press.

CHAPTER 3

Colonialism Revisited: The Hawaiian Experience

Ann S. Yabusaki
Kenichi K. Yabusaki

History can be thought of as a collection of stories. It can be a story of a people, event, experience, or observation; written from the eyes of the beholder, it is always subjective. It is in this spirit that we share the story of colonialism in Hawai'i. In telling our story, we mean no disrespect to the Hawaiian or any other culture. For us, the story of colonialism in Hawai'i is ongoing and more than a clash of cultures; it is a story of a nation fighting for its soul, reclaiming the freedom to be: to live, govern, and define itself.

Oppression manifests itself in many forms. On the continental United States, people tend to focus on the destructive forces of racism, sexism, homophobia, separation of abilities and disabilities, ageism, and many other "isms." In Hawai'i, the focus tends to be on the oppressions of colonialism. Military intimidation and racism, tools of the colonizer, are used to dispossess a people of their land, psyche, and souls. Comas-Diaz, Lykes, and Alarcon (1998) describe similar practices in Guatemala, Peru, and Puerto Rico.

Colonization is a violent process, and decolonization sometimes can be equally violent. As we observe and participate in protests against the military in Hawai'i, we are swept in a sea of emotion: a deep love of the spirit of the *aina*, or land, the ocean, and the sky. As the stewards of the land, entrusted by their gods, sages, and ancestors, the Hawaiian people protest the desecration of their land. As participant-observers of this energy, we ask, "How does a nation with over 2,000 years of history heal from colonization? How does a nation reclaim its soul?"

ALONG CAME A COLONIALIST: DEFINING COLONIALISM

Colonialism is defined by Random House Webster's Dictionary (2001, p. 263) as "the system or policy by which a nation seeks to extend or retain its authority over other peoples or territories." Others describe colonialism as "the specific form of cultural exploitation that developed with the expansion of Europe over the last 400 years" (Ashcroft, Griffith, & Tiffin, 2000, p. 45). Underlying the practice of colonialism is the ideology of imperialism or the idea of conquest and expansion. In later years, colonialism became coterminous with industrialization or the development of a modern capitalist system of economic exchange. Colonies were established to provide raw materials and labor for the ". . . economies of the colonial powers. It also meant that the relation between the colonizer and colonized was locked into a rigid hierarchy of difference deeply resistant to fair and equitable exchanges, whether economic, cultural or social" (Ashcroft et al., 2000, p. 46). Speaking of race relations in colonized countries, Ashcroft et al. note, "In the colonies where the subject people were of a different race, or where minority indigenous peoples existed, the ideology of race was also a crucial part of the construction and naturalization of an unequal form of intercultural relations . . . the idea of the colonial world became one of a people intrinsically inferior, not just outside history and civilization, but genetically predetermined to inferiority" (2000, pp. 46–47). Hence, racism is intricately woven into the practice of colonization.

Another way of defining colonialism is through the eyes of the colonized. A good friend, Poka, told us the following story involving the Kanaks, who are considered the pagan people of what is today known as New Caledonia, now colonized by the French.

One day a Kanak was sitting on his porch when he saw a Frenchman walking on the path toward him. As the Frenchman approached, the Kanak greeted him, and on this hot day, invited him into his home to relax and have some refreshment. The Frenchman obliged and after relaxing and enjoying the food and drink, asked, "How much do I owe you for your wonderful hospitality?"

The Kanak found this question strange and replied, "You don't owe me anything. It is our custom to share what we have."

The Frenchman was puzzled but delighted with the idea of sharing. The next day, he brought two friends to the Kanak's home to show them the wonderful custom of these people. When they arrived, no one was home. Recalling what the Kanak had said, the Frenchman invited his friends into the home and helped themselves to food and drink. The Kanak returned shortly and, to his surprise, found the Frenchmen helping themselves to food and drink in his kitchen. The Kanak was puzzled and thought, "What a strange custom to enter uninvited into someone's home and eat their food."

The Frenchmen greeted the Kanak as if he were an old friend and invited him to drink and eat with them. They then asked if they could see where he and his wife slept. Again the Kanak was puzzled, and now concerned. "What a strange custom to make such an intrusive request," he thought. Not knowing how to decline gracefully, he reluctantly showed them the rest of his home and led them to the sleeping quarters.

One of the Frenchmen then said, "We really like this place; you've made it so comfortable! We'd like to move in and sleep here."

The Kanak, now highly agitated, asked the Frenchmen, "If you move into our home, where will my wife and I sleep?"

"Oh, you can sleep in the kitchen, or better yet, on the porch."

The Kanak had had enough. Raising his fists he yelled, "Get out of my house!"

The Frenchman, trying to placate his new friend, said, "Now, now. . . . You don't have to resort to violence. Let's be civilized about this matter. In fact, let's take a vote."

A BRIEF HISTORY

The following story of the history of Hawai'i is taken primarily from *A Native Daughter* by Haunani-Kay Trask (1993), a Native Hawaiian[1] and scholar of Hawaiian studies.

Born of Papahanaumoku (earth mother) and Wakea (father sky), the islands or *moku* came to be. Out of the beloved islands came *taro*, child of Papa and Wakea; and from *taro* came the chiefs and people of Hawai'i. The genealogy of the Hawaiian people comes from the earth, sky, and cosmos. *Malama 'aina* means to care for the land and implies a reciprocal interdependence. For example, older siblings are expected to tend to the younger ones; they in turn love and honor older siblings. As stewards of the land, the people are responsible for earth, their mother. Mother earth nurtures and cares for the people and they, in turn, must protect and ensure her life.

In 1778, Captain James Cook stumbled onto the shores of
Hawai'i. Here he met a culture and society that had established
itself over 2,000 years before with a sophisticated and highly sensitive
attunement to the spirit of all things and love for the world they had
inhabited. He brought capitalism, western individualism, Christianity,
and a worldview that, to many Hawaiians, was antithetical to theirs.

> My people had been dispossessed of our religion, our moral order, our
> form of chiefly government, many of our cultural practices, and our
> lands and waters. Introduced diseases, from syphilis and gonorrhea
> to tuberculosis, small pox, measles, leprosy and typhoid fever killed
> Hawaiians by the hundred of thousands, reducing our Native population
> (from an estimated one million at contact) to less than 40,000 by 1890.
> (Trask, 1993, p. 7)

Americans arrived after the British and dominated the sandalwood
trade by 1820. In a scourging critique of American imperialism, Trask
(1993) suggests that Calvinist missionaries arrived shortly and intro-
duced religious doctrines that were as destructive as their diseases.
The collapsing Hawaiian population proved to be fertile ground for
the missionaries as they preached the demise of the Hawaiians as
the "will of a Christian God" (Trask, 1993, p. 7). Many native people
converted, believing in the Christian promise of life everlasting.

Religious and economic forces pressured the chiefs and king for
land. In 1842, at the height of the whaling industry, President John
Tyler declared in the Tyler doctrine that Hawai'i was in the "U.S.
sphere of influence" and off-limits to European powers. The U.S.
House Committee on Foreign Affairs replied to the Tyler doctrine
with a statement suggesting that "Americans should acknowledge their
own interests" (in Hawai'i) as a "virtual right of conquest" (Trask,
1993, p. 8).

By the middle of the nineteenth century, Hawaiian chiefs could no
longer stop private ownership of land by the foreigners. In 1843, King
Kamehameha III, under pressure from his *haole* (white foreigner)
advisors, allowed for the division and private ownership of land. "Traditional lands were quickly transferred to foreign ownership and bur-
geoning sugar plantations. By 1888, three-quarters of all arable land
was controlled by the *haole*" (Trask, 1993, p. 8).

The 1850s were a struggle between plantation owners vying for
U.S. annexation of Hawai'i to avoid U.S. sugar tariffs and using
military intimidation, and a monarchy attempting to maintain its
sovereignty. King Kamehameha III opposed annexation and refused to

sign treaties of annexation. Prince Alexander Liholiho, who succeeded Kamehameha III in 1854, proposed a policy of sovereignty with reciprocity. He hoped to decrease the high sugar tariffs paid to the United States, make Hawaiian sugar competitive with that of the Philippines and other foreign markets, and recognize Hawaiian sovereignty. The reciprocity treaty died in the U.S. Senate.

Liholiho was succeeded by his brother, Prince Lot as Kamehameha V, in 1863. Kamehameha V continued to pursue a reciprocity treaty to protect Hawaiian independence. Meanwhile, the American minister to Hawai'i, James McBride, wanted a U.S. warship permanently stationed in the Honolulu harbor to protect American interests. He suggested that a port at Honolulu be ceded to the United States as a condition of the reciprocity treaty. In 1866, the U.S.S. *Lackawanna* was assigned to the islands for an indefinite period. Shortly afterward, newspapers such as the *New York Times* wrote (1868), "There is no question we are bound within a short time to become the great commercial, and controlling, and civilizing power of the Pacific" (in Trask, 1993, p. 10). The concept of Manifest Destiny was clearly entrenched within the American psyche.

The biggest push toward annexation of Hawai'i came from sugar planters in Hawai'i. Heated debates erupted about reciprocity, annexation, and the Hawaiian right to self-govern. In 1869, Henry Pierce, minister to Hawai'i, urged the cessation of Pearl River Lagoon (now called Pearl Harbor) as a naval station in exchange for a reciprocity treaty. Reciprocity, he reasoned, would be a step toward annexation.

In 1872, Kamehameha V died and William Lunalilo, greatly loved by his people, succeeded to the thrown. Lunalilo reluctantly negotiated a reciprocity treaty and allowed the Pearl River Lagoon to be ceded to the United States. U.S. General John McAllister Schofield, a major figure in Hawaiian military history, testified in Congress: "The Hawaiian Islands constitute the only natural outpost to defenses of the Pacific coast. . . . The time has come when we must secure forever the desired control over those islands or let them pass into other hands" (Trask, 1993, p. 11).

Lunalilo reversed his decision when the native public loudly protested the cession of Hawaiian land. Hawaiians knew that they, like the American Indians, would be treated with racism and little respect because of their skin color. They had witnessed their kings, Liholiho and Prince Lot, ejected from trains during a visit to the United States because of their skin color. Newspapers argued that Hawaiians would be slaves under annexation (Trask, 1993).

Fewer than thirteen months after assuming the throne, Lunalilo died of tuberculosis. Debates continued to rage in the Hawaiian nation about annexation and the presence and interference of the U.S. military. Protests increased in the towns of Honolulu and Lahaina, Maui, along with concerns about alcohol and prostitution. Peace-keeping, however, masked the true reason for a military presence. The military presence was there to protect American economic interests, and when disturbances threatened the sugar industry, the military intervened.

The U.S. military intervened in the election for the throne between the pro-American King Kalakaua and the pro-British Queen Emma. After a brief skirmish, King Kalakaua prevailed, assumed the throne, and, in 1875, signed a reciprocity treaty with the United States. Sugar exports jumped from an unprecedented 17 million pounds in 1875 to 115 million pounds in 1883. Americans now owned twenty-five of the thirty-two sugar plantations that dominated the Hawaiian economy.

An economic crisis in the 1880s left Kalakaua's government in debt. People called for a solution to the budget. In 1887, Kalakaua was forced to cede Pearl River Lagoon to the United States and adopt a new constitution in exchange for duty-free sugar. The new constitution essentially gave the power of the legislature to the missionary descendants and gave the right to vote to foreigners willing to swear allegiance to the new government.

Between 1877 and 1890, 55,000 new immigrants, mostly Asians, entered Hawai'i. At the same time, the native population was halved and the *haole* population soared. By 1890, the Hawaiians were 45 percent and *haole* and Asians were 55 percent of the population. These numbers alarmed the native people, as they foresaw and feared the loss of their nation.

Queen Lili'uokalani succeeded her brother, King Kalakaua, in 1891. Determined to return Hawai'i to her people, she designed a more democratic constitution, one that removed the property ownership requirement for voters (many Hawaiians did not own land) and conferred the privilege to vote only to subjects of the kingdom. Foreigners would not be allowed to vote. Alarmed, businessmen and foreign supporters immediately organized, formed a "Committee of Safety," and enlisted the help of U.S. Minister John L. Stevens to block this move toward sovereignty. Minister Stevens agreed to land the U.S. Marines and recognize the "Provisional Government" (the Committee of Safety) as representing the people of Hawai'i.

Faced with military force and perhaps the loss of life, Lili'uokalani ceded her authority not to the provisional government but to the United States on January 17, 1893.

She wrote to Sanford B. Dole, descendant of missionaries and newly chosen head of the provisional government:

> I yield to the superior force of the United States of America, whose minister . . . has caused United States troops to be landed at Honolulu. . . . Now to avoid any collision of armed forces and perhaps the loss of life, I do under this protest, and impelled by said force, yield my authority until such time as the Government of the United States shall, upon the facts being presented to it, undo the action of its representatives and reinstate me in the authority which I claim as the constitutional sovereign of the Hawaiian Islands. (Trask, 1993, p. 17)

On February 1, 1893, Minister Stevens raised the American flag over Hawai'i. President Grover Cleveland, deeply concerned over the events in Hawai'i, withdrew legislation for annexation of Hawai'i from the U.S. Senate on March 4. On March 29, James Blount, commissioned by Cleveland to investigate the overthrow of the Hawaiian government, ordered the troops back to their ships and lowered the American flag.

After four months of research, Blount submitted a scathing report of the conspiracy of the provisional government and Minister Stevens to illegally overthrow the Hawaiian government. Cleveland carefully reviewed the document, and in a lengthy explanation to Congress, explained why he would never submit an annexation treaty to them. Thus, the issue of harm and need for reparation was brought to the American government. Unfortunately, Cleveland was not reelected president, and Queen Lili'uokalani was never restored to the thrown.

In 1894, Hawai'i became the Republic of Hawai'i, and it was annexed in 1898. In 1959, it became a state of the Union. Most Native Hawaiians stayed away from the polls in protest of the illegal overthrow of their government.

Another view of the above history comes from the Native Hawaiian Study Commission (1983). This report was commissioned by U.S. President Ronald Reagan to explore the history of the United States in Hawai'i:

> Vol. 1 of the Report was written by the non-Native members . . . and predictably *denies* complicity of the United States in the overthrow of the Hawaiian government in 1893, and the forced annexation of Hawai'i in 1898. Vol. 2 of the Report was written by the Native Hawaiian

members of the Commission and argues for both restitution and self-government for Native Hawaiians based upon the U.S. role in overthrowing the Hawaiian government and forcibly incorporating Hawai'i into the United States in 1959. (Trask, 1993, p. 72)

Clearly, history depends on who writes it. History presented from the inside out is often suppressed by the victors. It takes time to uncover and distill the stories of the oppressed; but it is the voice of the oppressed that makes the ordinary extraordinary and behavior understandable. To understand the psychology of a people, we must hear and receive their stories through their ears, eyes, feelings, beliefs, values, and meaning. It is through their voices and hearts that we begin to understand and appreciate more deeply the people and events in Hawai'i.

IS "DAMN *HAOLE*" A RACIST REMARK?

In 1998, we attended a forum sponsored by a local church in Honolulu entitled "Racism—is there a problem in Hawai'i?" The forum was organized by a *haole* pastor. The pastor opened the forum by sharing his experience of walking out of a store in the small town of Wai'manalo on O'ahu and being called "damn *haole*" by a local, longtime resident of Hawai'i. The pastor was offended and felt that this was a racist remark. He convened this forum to discuss how white people were perceived in Hawai'i.

During the discussion, the pastor's wife, a white woman and high school teacher, commented, "If your children would come to class on time and take school seriously, they would be successful (in this culture)." This remark sparked a heated discussion with representatives from the Office of Hawaiian Affairs, representatives of other Hawaiian groups, and local white community members. By the end of the forum, the whites were describing Hawaiian and Samoan children as lazy, and the Hawaiians and locals were accusing the whites of colonialism. The issue of racism was never addressed or resolved.

Haunani-Kay Trask, a Native Hawaiian professor and director of the Center for Hawaiian Studies at the University of Hawai'i, has spoken extensively about the genocide of her people. The colonization and illegal overthrow of the Hawaiian nation by the United States does not endear the *haole* to the Hawaiians. The consciousness of dominance is so keen and sensitive that many *haoles* are bewildered by what they would call racism. They do not realize that it is a privilege to experience the subtle and not-so-subtle anger of those whose cultures were—and continue to be—oppressed, exploited, and denigrated. Courage and trust are required by the oppressor in order to participate in a deeply passionate and often angry discussion on colonialism.

We left the forum with deep sadness. We had witnessed a continuation of colonialism by people like the pastor's wife who, with the best intentions, judged and denigrated the worldview of another. Is racism a problem in Hawai'i. Why was it only now, in 1998, being addressed? Racism is inherent to colonialism: it is used to justify behavior. The issue in Hawai'i focuses on the broader issue of colonialism, and racism *per se* is rarely addressed. Although the Hawaiian people were raped by the motives of colonialism, they have not forgotten their identity as a people and nation. Reminders of colonialism run deep in the minds and hearts of the Hawaiian people, and "damn *haole*" is not necessarily a personal attack, but an attack against colonialism.

WHO IS HAWAIIAN, ANYWAY? THE HAWAIIAN RECOGNITION BILL

One of the most hotly debated issues facing Native Hawaiian people today is the Hawaiian Recognition Bill (HRB), better known as the Akaka Bill after one of its senior authors, Hawai'i's U.S. Senator Daniel Akaka. The HRB authorizes Congress to provide federal recognition of political status for Native Hawaiians, comparable to the status of Native American Indians. Native Hawaiian people would be recognized as an indigenous people with a special trust relationship with the United States and be entitled to self-determination as a sovereign political entity.

Without delving into the lengthy and officious wording of the HRB, conflict seems to arise from at least three issues. The first concerns the definition of "Native Hawaiian." The second concerns who determines what is Native Hawaiian. The third concerns the betrayal of a sacred trust between Hawai'i and the United States that was conferred by the United Nations.

According to the HRB, "Native Hawaiian" means the following:

> [A]n individual who is a member of the indigenous, native people of Hawaii who are the direct lineal descendants of the aboriginal, indigenous, native people who resided on or before January 1, 1893, in the islands that now comprise the State of Hawaii, and occupied and exercised sovereignty in the Hawaiian archipelago, including the area that now constitutes the State of Hawaii; and an individual who was a

Native Hawaiian eligible during 1921 for the programs authorized by the Hawaiian Homes Commission Act (42 Stat. 108, chapter 42) (including lineal descendants of that individual). (Senate Report 108-085, 2003)

There are approximately 400,000 Native Hawaiians in the United States, of whom 240,000 reside in Hawai'i. If one defines "Native Hawaiian" by the criteria proposed by the HRB, only about 20 percent of the total Native Hawaiian population will benefit. What happens to Native Hawaiians with blood lineage who do not fit within the guidelines of the HRB? How do we recognize—or do we recognize— those with no Hawaiian blood lineage but who were born and raised and are the fifth generation living in Hawai'i? Because there is no absolute way to define who is "Hawaiian," one solution may be for people to declare themselves Hawaiian by citizenship and relinquish any other citizenship (Laenui, 1997).

Many Native Hawaiian people object to the U.S. Congress defining who or what is a "Native Hawaiian." They ask, "Why can't we define who we are?" But the question then becomes, who are the "we" who define who we are? The discussion continues and rhetoric flies, but the passion for self-governance in some form lives on in spite of the differences among the people.

Finally, Title 25 of the U.S. Constitution, Section 71, states, "No Indian Nation or tribe within the territory of the Untied States shall be acknowledged or recognized as an independent nation." Proponents for the HRB who claim that passage of the Akaka bill would be a stepping stone to independence may be mistaken, because there is no legal or political precedent for independent nationhood. The United States is a federation of states that form a union. By definition, no state that is part of this federation (Hawai'i is currently part of this federation) may withdraw from the Union. If an independent Hawai'i were to become a nation-within-a-nation, Hawai'i might later have no right to withdraw and pursue its independence. Therefore, by supporting the HRB, those supporting the Hawaiian sovereignty movement may, in fact, be cutting their own throats (Agard, 2003).

MODELS OF HAWAIIAN SOVEREIGNTY

If Hawaiian sovereignty becomes a reality, then what model should be taken? Alternatives in the HRB include amending the existing federal law to call for the U.S. government to reconcile with Native Hawaiians by defining "reconciliation" as the government granting immediate federal recognition upon passage of the HRB, but not to label Hawai'i as a "domestic dependent nation." The relationship between Hawai'i and the United States must be carefully defined so as to keep the doors for independence open. Alternatives also call for an immediate vote to posthumously reinstate Queen Lili'uokalani and the lawful Hawaiian government as it existed before its illegal takeover by the United States in 1893. Concomitant with this reinstatement would be an election of delegates to a constitutional convention to revise and update the Queen's constitution and all other constitutions functioning under one umbrella (Agard, 2003).

In summary, one model suggests a nation-within-a-nation or an integration model similar to that of the Native American Indians. Another urges complete independence from the United States, restoring Hawaiian independence to preinvasion times. Finally, a third suggests an association that allows gradual transition away from the United States and ending with full independence.

The issues surrounding Hawaiian independence are a complex web of politics, deceit, double standards, motives, and interpretations of laws. We may have oversimplified the core issues and controversies surrounding Hawaiian sovereignty, but we also recognize that Hawaiian sovereignty might not be an issue if the Kingdom of Hawai'i had not been colonized in the first place. The deep emotional struggle for independence by Native Hawaiians is like a spirit on fire, with living examples in the eruptions and flows of lava on the Big Island of Hawai'i.

SHOULD THE PERPETRATOR BE THE JUDGE?

On November 23, 1993, the U.S. government, under international law, confessed to illegally gaining possession of Hawai'i by its actions in 1893 (the illegal overthrow of the Kingdom of Hawai'i), 1898 (the illegal and forced annexation of Hawai'i), and 1959 (the illegal statehood without the Native Hawaiian vote) (Laenui, 1997). When the United Nations (UN) was formed in 1945, leaders of nations gathered to sign a UN charter calling for self-governance of territories under colonial-style conditions. In 1946, the General Assembly placed the United States under a sacred trust "to develop self-government, to take due account of the political aspirations of the peoples, and to assist them in the progressive development of their free political institutions . . . with due respect for the cultures of the peoples concerned" ("Is Hawaii a State?" 2003). The United Nations assigned the United States to assist the territories of Alaska, Guam, American Samoa, the Virgin Islands, the Panama Canal Zone, Puerto Rico, and Hawai'i in gaining self-governance.

Over the years, the United Nations clarified the process of self-governance. Nations in sacred trust were to let the people of the territories choose how they would relate to the United Nations: integration as part of a larger nation, free association, or independence. This self-governance process was meant to break the chains of colonization between territories of colonizing nations. As a result, many African, Pacific, and Asian nations emerged from colonization (Laenui, 1997).

In Hawai'i, rather than permitting three choices, the United States permitted the populace to vote on only one: integration. In 1959, the people were asked to vote on the following: "Shall Hawai'i immediately be admitted into the Union as a State?" A yes vote placed Hawai'i as a state within the Union. A no vote resulted in continuing status of Hawai'i as a territory of the United States. The choices of free association and independence were never placed before the people. The people were never educated, and no one spoke about the right to these choices.

The United States reported to the United Nations in 1959 that Hawai'i had exercised its right to self-governance, and in doing so, elected to become a state. In turn, the United Nations removed Hawai'i from its list of territories subject to self-governance. "An intentional perversion of the truth was thus committed to induce the UN to deny Hawaii [the] fundamental right to self-determination" (Laenui, 1997, p. 2).

In a 2003 letter to the editor of the *Honolulu Advertiser*, Steve Tayama, a resident of Wai'manalo, asked whether the legal process to seek justice for a crime was to ask the accused to be the judge. Should the United States be ". . . the one to tell us if the illegal overthrow of the Kingdom of Hawaii—annexation without a treaty or statehood evolving from the illegal overthrow—is legal or not? Let us bring this issue to a neutral court. This is the recognized process to solve this kind of problem. This is why international organizations were formed" (Tayama, 2003).

Tayama's point is well taken. The United States has confessed to violations of international laws. Should the appeal for retribution and justice be directed to the U.S. Congress, an arm of the accused and perpetrator? Is this not a conflict of interest? A United Nations–appointed judiciary committee, excluding U.S. representation, may be a fairer solution to determine restitution and justice for Hawai'i.

CONTINUING FORMS OF COLONIALISM

The colonizer understands the importance of language. After nearly 2,000 years of being spoken, why would the Hawaiian language be banned in 1896 by the American-imposed government? In 1900, upon becoming a territory of the United States, "all schools, government operations and official transactions were thereafter conducted in English, despite the fact that most people, including non-Natives, still spoke Hawaiian at the turn of the century" (Trask, 1993, p. 188). The colonizer understands that language perpetuates a way of being, a way of life, a culture, and a worldview; and that a powerful way to suppress a people and their culture is to ban the use of their language. Desecration of language is part of hegemony or total domination by one nation over others (*Random House Webster's Dictionary*, 2001).

Language, then, is a key factor in decolonization. With the revitalization of the Hawaiian language, values, and ways of life, Hawaiians are moving toward decolonization. Speaking Hawaiian forces one to think in Hawaiian; and thinking in Hawaiian forces one to think about things Hawaiian and reclaim what it means to be Hawaiian.

Using *Hapa*

In 1995, a conference on biracial identity was held in northern California. Two individuals who were part of the Hawaiian sovereignty movement objected to the use of the Hawaiian word *hapa* as part of the name of an organization. The organization was accused of ". . . appropriating the word *hapa* from Native Hawaiians. [In using the term] . . . without any knowledge of the meaning of the word [and] . . . without permission [from Native Hawaiians] . . . it was claimed the organization . . . contributes to and furthers the oppression of native Hawaiian peoples" (Ropp, 1995, p. 7).

Hapa is a transliteration of the English *half.* In Hawai'i, if one were to call an individual *hapa*, most people would understand that the person was of mixed race; however, from the standpoint of the Hawaiian language, it is improper use. Proper use is to place a noun after the term *hapa*, as in *hapa haole*, *hapa* Japanese, etc. Misusing words or using words for one's convenience is disrespectful to the Hawaiian language and culture.

People within the organization replied, "This is not a new criticism. At many of the forums, people, especially Hawaiian nationalists, object to our use of the word *hapa*. We are highly conscious of the origins of the term, *hapa*, especially in its Hawaiian context. But on the Mainland, the word took on a different context from Hawaii and is more broadly applied to mean a person of mixed, especially mixed Asian race" (Ropp, 1995, p. 7).

Unfortunately, the organization continues to misuse the term *hapa*. Appropriating words, phrases, or gestures from a culture; changing meanings to suit themselves; and ignoring the deeper meanings, contexts, and significance of these words as ways of being, perpetuate the practice of colonialism. This practice will trigger reactions, and these reactions can best be understood in the contexts of colonization and decolonization.

What Does *HOV* Mean?

Recently, while driving on a freeway on O'ahu, we saw a sign that read *HOV Lane*. One of us, having been in the military, immediately translated HOV as "high-occupancy vehicle." For civilians, the HOV lane is equivalent to a carpool lane. The presence of these signs suggests a very subtle, but very distinct, presence of the military, and one can feel as though Hawai'i were under military rule.

The military has a strong presence in Hawaii. Today, there are more than forty U.S. military installations occupying more than 200,000 acres of land in Hawai'i. On O'ahu alone, approximately 25 percent of the island is occupied by the military. The Hawaiian Islands are strategically located for housing, training, and quick deployment of troops to almost anywhere in the world; however, emotions are mixed about their presence in Hawai'i.

Some people support the military in Hawai'i and feel protected from foreign enemies. Since the terrorist attacks on September 11, 2001, patriotism has run high. Some people argue that the military helps the economy because it creates jobs and income for the state. Those who oppose the military's presence and expansion argue that they have experienced great losses to their land and environment (including watersheds), culture, sacred archaeological sites, and much more. Overcrowding and land used for military training easily upset the fragile ecological balance of an island. They point out that the military has a poor history of restoring land to its pre-use condition. For example, the island of Kaho'olawe was used as a training and bombing site for the U.S. military beginning in World War II. On November 12, 2003, the island was officially returned to the state, giving people access to the land. Only 9 percent of the land, however, has been cleared of sub-subsurface ordnance, and 70 percent has been cleared of surface exploded and unexploded ordnance. The military declares that after spending 300 million dollars cleaning Kaho'olawe, it has no more funds and is withdrawing. Overjoyed, thousands of people attended the ceremonies at Iolani Palace on O'ahu to receive Kaho'olawe. Prayers, chants, songs and dance, and stones from all over Kaho'olawe were brought to the palace to be blessed and begin the healing.

Other lands occupied by the military have never been recovered or healed by the people of this state. Punalu'u and Waikane Valleys on O'ahu are examples of lands destroyed by the military. Training on the island of Hawai'i is destroying the *mana* or life force of the extinct sacred volcano Mauna Kea.

In October 2003, the U.S. Army presented a three-volume Stryker Brigade environmental impact statement for acquisition of more than 24,000 acres (23,000 acres on the island of Hawai'i and 1,400 additional acres at Schofield Barracks on O'ahu) to expand and accommodate approximately 310 new eight-wheeled, nineteen-ton Stryker combat vehicles. Public hearings were conducted throughout the state. Dozens of protestors were barred, and people wielding signs were arrested. Authorities feared that the sticks on which the signs were mounted would be used as clubs if violence erupted, but the signs were not mounted on sticks. Protestors said the arrests and banning of signs violated the First Amendment of the U.S. Constitution. Once inside the meeting hall at Turtle Bay Resort on O'ahu, many residents testified, "The land belongs to *Ke Akua* and we are the keepers, stewards and receivers of its bounty. If you *malama* [or take care of] the *aina* [or land], the *aina* will take care of you. Such a simple concept but one that the U.S. Army has not accepted and will probably ignore even if we ask you to embrace it" (Mattoon, 2003, p. 1). People worried whether the hearings were nothing more than formalities and that, eventually, the military would prevail.

What is the price, if any, of downsizing or eliminating the military from Hawai'i? Are an island nation, a culture, and fragile ecosystem expendable in the name of defending freedom? The mountains, ocean, and land answer through the hearts of the Hawaiian people.

A NATION RECLAIMING ITSELF

People heal themselves from the traumas of colonialism and hegemony in different ways. In spite of the dominance of colonialism and western politics, programs that teach and practice the traditions of the

Poe Hawai'i (ancient Hawaiians) continue to grow. Cultural immersion programs are slowly and tenuously growing: public schools teach in the Hawaiian language (Gavelek, 2003). Primary health, mental health, and substance abuse programs incorporate Hawaiian values and practices. Programs for youth increasingly use traditional rites of passage. Canoe trips and competition, working in the *kalo loi* (taro fields), pounding taro, restoring ancient fish ponds, and researching the *ahupua'a* (land divisions) are increasingly popular in school and after-school programs. Parenting programs incorporate the values of the Hawaiian people as a basis for practice. A Hawaiian studies program exists at the University of Hawai'i. For many, the experience and meaning of the *Poe Hawai'i* practices begin the healing process. The programs below illustrate some of these programs.

Ka'ala Farm

Under a dense growth of *Kiawe* trees and other vegetation near Wai'anae on the Leeward Coast of O'ahu, a hidden treasure was unearthed: a sophisticated irrigation system constructed by the ancient Hawaiians (*Poe Hawai'i*) that led to sunken *kalo* (taro) *loi* (fields). These *loi* were part of a large *ahupua'a* that extended from Mount Ka'ala to the sea. The area was named Ka'ala Farm.

The *ahupua'a* was a system of wedge-shaped land divisions stretching from the mountains to the ocean. Each had a free-flowing stream, and the various environments sustained plant, animal, or sea life that provided food, water, and materials for shelter. These resources were shared among the people of the *ahupua'a*. The *ahupua'a* was a sophisticated and sacred ecological system created by the *Poe Hawai'i*; it embodied the values of reciprocity and interdependence between people and between the people and land. Trask notes, ". . . there was no money, no idea or practice of surplus appropriation, value storing or payment deferral because there was no idea of financial profit from exchange" (1993, p. 5).

Children and adults come to Ka'ala Farm to learn the history and traditional practices of Hawai'i and to experience the meaning of the *ahupua'a*. *Kalo* is cultivated in ways taught by the elders, who, in turn, were taught by their ancestors. Because Native Hawaiians descended from the *kalo*, there is deep meaning and reverence to what is practiced and taught at Ka'ala Farm.

Land development for homes, shopping centers, businesses, and golf courses on the Leeward side of O'ahu has destroyed the natural flow of water from Mount Ka'ala. Water has been diverted from natural streams to these growing communities, and *kalo loi* no longer flourish in the area. In similar fashion, water on the Windward side of O'ahu is diverted for development, and *kalo loi* are quickly disappearing from the areas of Kahalu'u and Wai'ahole. Diverting the water endangers the streams and the surrounding ecosystems. The damage is irreparable, and the entire state of Hawai'i experiences a taro shortage. The very plant from which the Hawaiians are descended has succumbed to industrialization, whose roots are embedded in colonialism.

Our guides at Ka'ala Farm tell us that the effects of colonialism and westernization will eventually destroy western man's ability to be self-sufficient. They stress the self-sufficiency of the *Poe Hawai'i* to grow taro and other plants and harvest sea life just as their ancestors did thousands of years ago. We were invited to experience the *loi*. As we sank our bare feet into its muddy water, we felt a deep love and connection to the *aina*. *Malama aina* (caring for the land) cannot be explained; it has to be experienced.

The *Opelu* Project

Similar to the Native American Indians on the continental United States, Native Hawaiians experience some of the highest rates of poverty, ill health, birth deaths, and rates of incarceration. Ancient fish ponds of the *Poe Hawai'i* have been destroyed by commercial developments, such as resort hotels and golf courses.

The *Opelu* Project, a family aquaculture program in Wai'anae, O'ahu, combines modern technology with traditional Hawaiian values and practices to empower families and the chronically mentally disabled.

Pua'nani Burgess, who directed the *Opelu* Project for more than eighteen years, gave us a tour of the project and mediated the process. She explained to us that the *Poe Hawai'i* once harvested *opelu*, the mackerel scad, in their fish ponds. Mashed taro and sweet potato were used as chum to attract the schools of fish. The *Poe Hawai'i* were ingenious fishermen who could spot the dominant male fish, lure it into their fish ponds, and thus attract the rest of the *opelu* school. The *Poe Hawai'i* also practiced conservation. To ensure the return of fish schools, fishing for *opelu* was banned at certain times of the year.

The *Opelu* Project uses large plastic tanks to grow tilapia, a fast-growing warm-water fish of the cichlid family. Each tank is a self-sufficient system that supports photosynthetic microorganisms to oxygenate the water, which goes to an adjacent clarification tank that collects solid waste onto filters. The water is recirculated back to the main tank. Solid waste is removed from the filters, composted, and used as fertilizer. Each tank can yield up to 600 pounds of tilapia every six months. Fish are sold to the local community or fish markets to supplement a family's income. A certain percentage of the profits are used for repair and maintenance and to purchase more systems for other families. More recently, the chronically mentally disabled are being trained to maintain these aquaculture systems, embracing the philosophy that "work is medicine." Overall, families and individuals learn to work together and acquire skills using modern technology, while preserving the traditional values and practices of the past.

Alternative Healing Methods

Many programs addressing the health and mental health of the people include Hawaiian healing methods. Chants, legends, songs, and dance that tell the story of the Hawaiian nation and its people are heartfelt and healing for many. Several substance abuse prevention and treatment agencies incorporate the values of the Hawaiians as part of their curricula. *Kupuna*, or the elderly and wise people, are consulted and often participate in these programs. Meetings are opened with *pule* or prayers, new programs and buildings are opened with native blessings, and people gather to discuss ways of healing in a western world. Many culture-sensitive programs and services are considered unconventional, unproven, and therefore do not qualify for reimbursement by insurance companies. Hence the struggle to reclaim health—both mental and physical—is also a struggle for decolonization.

CONCLUSION

The relationship between the colonizer and the colonized is sometimes like being in the forest and not seeing the trees; that is, we are so entrenched in the mind-set of the colonizer or dominant culture that we fail to see its influences on our lives. We have attempted to convey this message using Hawai'i as an example of a nation and people colonized by the *haole*. In today's world as in the past, no human group or territory is immune to colonialism.

Colonization and its ramifications go far beyond the Hawaiian experience. Whether intentional or not, it is incumbent that one understand the cultural basis of all religious, political, and/or economic motives that lead to the decimation of another culture. Throughout our chapter we have implied that physical, mental, emotional, and spiritual health and well-being are intimately tied to the cultural, social, and political contexts of life. The meaning of colonialism is not absolute, as meanings are constructed by the interaction of the individual with the social and political orders.

For some, in the name of industrialization or progress, colonialism might be considered a virtue. However, no virtue can be separated from its defects. We have seen the destructive forces of colonialism in Hawai'i brought by religious indoctrination, racism, political and economic motives, and military force working in concert. We must ask, "How do we define progress?" and "Is a nation that has existed for centuries not progressive?"

Malcolm X once stated, "A race of people is like an individual man; until it uses its own talent, takes pride in its own history, expresses its own culture, affirms its own selfhood, it can never fulfill itself" (Gavelek, 2003, p. 20). These words echo through the hearts of many people living in Hawai'i. The resiliency and spirit of Hawai'i's people are reflected by those who struggle for sovereignty and independence, those who fight for their beloved *aina,* and those who fight to preserve the wisdom, customs, values, and traditions of their ancestors. Other nations and people who have been colonized share similar struggles and feelings.

As in psychotherapy, the client determines the agenda and solution; the therapist attempts to create a safe context for and bears witness to the story. Analogously, we must understand the context and meaning of the colonized or oppressed; and as colonizers, we must own our responsibilities and be mindful and sensitive to the process of decolonization.

Many Americans have not experienced the decimation by colonialism and hegemony of something that is equivalent to life itself. The vast diffusion and integration of western ideals have protected us from considering seriously the cultures of other peoples. The challenges of living in an interdependent world while embracing those who seek independence may seem paradoxical. The solutions will not be easy,

Toolbox for Change

1. We are guests in foreign lands.
2. As guests, we must be sensitive to our hosts.
3. As guests, we must be mindful of our intentions.
4. As guests, we must prevent iatrogenic practices.

and compromises will be inevitable. We cannot change the past; however, we can change ourselves.

NOTE

1. The term *Native Hawaiian* refers to people with Hawaiian blood or ancestry. *Hawaiian* sometimes refers to people who were born and raised in Hawai'i, but who have no indigenous blood or ancestry. In this chapter, *Native Hawaiian* is used to describe people who possess blood lineage to the indigenous people of Hawai'i.

REFERENCES

Agard, K. K. (2003). *Implications of federal recognition via the Akaka bill.* Retrieved November 2, 2003, from www.stopakaka.com/2003/implication.html

Ashcroft, B., Griffith, G., & Tiffin, H. (2000). *Post-colonial studies. The key concepts.* London and New York: Routledge.

Comas-Diaz, L., Lykes, M. B., & Alarcon, R. D. (1998). Ethnic conflict and the psychology of liberation in Guatemala, Peru, and Puerto Rico. *American Psychologist, 53*(7), 778–792.

Gavelek, F. (2003, Fall/Winter). 1 Mua! Use of Hawaiian is growing. *Pleasant Hawaii: The magazine of pleasant Hawaiian holidays.* Honolulu, HI: This Week Magazines.

Is Hawaii really a state of the union? (2003). Retrieved November 2, 2003, from www.hawaii-nation.org/statehood.html

Laenui, P. (1997). Hawaiian statehood revisited. *The Honolulu Weekly* [Electronic version]. Retrieved November 2, 2003, from www.opihi.com/sovereignty/statehood_revisited.htm

Mattoon, C. P. O. (2003, November 4). Testimony on the SBCT Draft Environmental Impact Statement at Turtle Bay Resort, Kahuku, Oahu, Hawaii.

Native Hawaiian Study Commission. (1983). Report on the culture, needs, and concerns of native Hawaiians (Vols. 1 and 2). Washington, DC: U.S. Government.

Random House Webster's College Dictionary. (2001). (2nd rev. ed.). New York: Random House.

Ropp, S. M. (1995). Editorial comment: HIF under attack, in *What's Hapa'ning.* Newsletter of the Hapa Issues Forum, p. 7.

Senate Report 108-085 (2003, June 27). *S.344 Native Hawaiian recognition bill as revised in markup by the Senate Select Committee on Indian Affairs, May 14, 2003, and reported to the Senate on June 27, 2003.* Retrieved on November 5, 2003, from www.angelfire.com/hi2/hawaiiansovereignty/AkakaS344Mark

Tayama, S. (2003, October 18). Commentary: International venues should settle the issue. *The Honolulu Advertiser*. Retrieved November 2, 2003, from the.honoluluadvertiser.com/article/2003/Oct/18/op/op08aletter

Trask, H.-K. (1993). *From a native daughter.* Monroe, ME: Common Courage Press.

CHAPTER 4

Sociohistorical Constructions of Race and Language: Impacting Biracial Identity

Matthew J. Taylor

Very often history is a means of denying the past. Denying the past is to refuse to recognize its integrity. To fit it, *force it* [italics added], function it, to suck out the spirit until it looks the way you think it should [Welcome to the world of being biracial].[1]
(Winterson, as cited in Root, 1992, p. 7)

Historically, race has been constructed within the American psyche as a dichotomous variable—an either-or proposition. Moreover, our construction and use of language have developed to mirror this reality, which ultimately aids in its perpetuation. Has this divergent approach to race outlived its usefulness and applicability? Is it realistic, given the face of today's changing demographic landscape? At present, there remain cultural and linguistic disconnects between the phenomenological experience of the biracial individual and the expectations of the dualistic society within which they reside. On the individual level, there are implications for psychosocial development (Hall, 2001; Root, 1995). More broadly speaking, what will develop from the resolution of this dilemma is a new paradigm impacting how the citizens of this country view race and racial identity. This paper explores the impact that the sociohistorical constructions of race and language have on the lives of biracial individuals. To this end, the author, who is biracial, will blend sociohistorical conceptions of race and linguistic philosophy with personal narrative components and conclude with implications for multiracial identity development.

WHO "WE" ARE

The most recent census data suggest rapidly increasing numbers of individuals identifying as multiracial. Census 2000 represented the first census in which respondents could mark two or more races. Almost 3 percent of the United States population, 6.8 million people, reported two or more races. New York City and Los Angeles, respectively, were identified as locales in which the largest numbers of multiracial individuals resided. Of particular note are the data that reveal that 40 percent of those with multiracial lineages are younger than eighteen years old (U.S. Census Bureau, 2001). It is these latter numbers that particularly provide evidence that there is a growing amount of diversity within our communities and our nation.

The Awakening: Introducing Myself

I am biracial. I am the product of the union of a man of black descent and a woman of German-American heritage. My skin is a composite of light brown and tan; or if you prefer, other descriptive color schemes are bisque, peru, wheat, pale goldenrod, and moccasin. Yes, my skin does visibly burn with extreme exposure to the sun. My hair is a perfectly proportioned blend of curls and straight components. My eyes are brown. My speech pattern is relatively nondescript, with a hint of an East Coast upbringing. Some are surprised to learn that I am biracial; others seem to have known all along.

SOCIOHISTORICAL CONCEPTIONS OF RACE: YOU ARE WHAT YOU LOOK LIKE

While the race-based social hierarchy in the United States can be traced back as far as colonization and the arrival of the Europeans to the shores of the Americas, the roots of this movement appear early in the eighteenth and nineteenth centuries with the works of Carolus Linnaeus and Charles Darwin. In his 1735 work *Systema Naturae*, Linnaeus presented his classification system for plants, animals, and minerals; while in 1859, Darwin offered *The Origin of Species*, which set forth his theory of natural selection ("survival of the fittest"). These biologically based scientific philosophies would soon find themselves coupled with the geopolitical conflicts that accompanied European colonization and the subsequent conquering of native peoples around the globe; and would be utilized to justify and explain these social, cultural, and military occurrences. Predicated upon notions of the "culturally superior" European colonizers and "savage and inferior" natives who were colonized, a Linnaean-type social classification developed for humans. This newly created social hierarchy relied heavily upon physical appearance (phenotype), something that undoubtedly separated the Europeans from many of the indigenous/colonized populations. Not only did racial appearance become an "outward mark of innate and permanent inferiority" (Snyder, 2001, p. 92), but it also symbolized the "death" experienced by many indigenous cultures, which were dubbed as inferior, and in the spirit of social Darwinism, subsequently replaced by a superior entity.

So began a recurring pattern of control and oppression based upon phenotype that would later come to be the sociological and psychological foundations of intergroup relations in the United States. Whether it was found in the extermination practices impacting Native Americans, the race-based sight system underlying the enslavement of blacks, the seizing of Spanish/Mexican land in what would later become the southwestern United States, or the legislated Chinese exclusion and forced internment of Japanese Americans, there was a "system of appearance" implemented that led to discrimination that benefited whites and maintained the social hierarchy (Omi & Winant, 1986; Root, 1992). From the early pseudobiological scientific construction of race, rooted in Linnaean and Darwinian thought, sprang a culturally driven hierarchical conception of race more rooted in social, economic, and political forces. As the social hierarchy continued to develop, race and its perceived overt appearance were not only used to distinguish the Europeans, with all of their "positive" traits and qualities, from all others; they also came to be the "markers" from which we could infer a host of innate characteristics, such as sexual behaviors and intelligence to one's proclivity to commit crimes. This social order, based on (Euro) cultural definitions of race, further revealed itself via individual expression in the form of interpersonal interactions and associated stereotypes. The elusive nature of this concept is the very human quality of relying upon the appearance of "the other" as an evolutionary tool to determine friend from foe, as well as a host of other characteristics. As noted before, sociohistorical conceptions of race are more rooted in social, economic, and political forces, yet on the day-to-day basis a simplified "sight system" is used to provide clues about others. The rigidity with which these socially defined notions of race were applied and stamped into the collective unconscious of society and firmly entrenched in its institutions is revealed by Allen (2001), who paraphrases Supreme Court comments from *Dred Scott v. Sanford* (1857) that state, "[A]ny white man, no matter how degraded, is socially superior to any African American, no matter how cultured and independent in means" (p. 361). The stage was thus set. The racial ideology of America is rooted in what Omi and Winant (1986) term "racial etiquette," which is a set of interpretive codes: codes of behavior, attitudes, values, and beliefs. These culturally defined codes offer meaning to physical characteristics, such that "black" in Philadelphia means something very different from "black" in São Paulo, Brazil. Yet, it is this overreliance on selected anatomical features as the basis of race that makes racial categories prone to error (Webster, as cited in Ferber, 1995). The arbitrary and ambiguous nature of the dualistic race-based dichotomy that developed within the United States was flawed from its onset, and this is no more apparent than when applied to biracial individuals.

Beginning in the seventeenth century, miscegenation (race-mixing) had been a constant in the United States, yet the social standing of the children resulting from these unions had been anything but constant. As the American slave system was formed, built almost exclusively upon physical appearance, and later expanded in its breadth, there came the need to prohibit interactions between the races, which further served to maintain white supremacy and social standing (Daniel, 1996). The result yielded legislation and social norms that ostensibly prohibited miscegenation, especially in the South, and considered biracial children to be black by the law of hypodescent, or the "one-drop" rule. Not only did this increase the number of slaves, especially as it was considered the master's "right" to use his female slaves sexually as a form of concubinage, but it also reinforced white privilege and protected white racial and cultural purity (Daniel, 1996). However, it must be noted that the social position of mixed-race individuals varied geographically as well as chronologically. Rockquemore and Brunsma (2002a) offer an excellent historical outline that details the alliance between biracial individuals and white society in some states, which shifted to white hostility and a subsequent alliance of biracial individuals with black society as the Civil War loomed and following its conclusion. Currently, the landscape within which racial/ethnic reference group biracial children fall is unclear. While the laws prohibiting interracial unions have all been declared unconstitutional

(Rockquemore & Brunsma, 2002a), in a *de facto* sense hypodescent still exists, as minority group societies continue to be more willing than the dominant culture to accept biracial individuals into their ranks.

The Awakening: What Are You?

For biracial individuals, the questions begin early. Earlier than we have the ability to truly understand their meaning. Earlier than we have the language required to supply adequate answers. I was four years old when an elderly woman called me a nigger as I played in front of my apartment building. From my teary-eyed mother, who realized that the blissful ignorance of my childhood was beginning to fade, I learned that this was a "not so nice word for black people." But my mother was white. Did that mean I was black? I did not understand. Pandora's Box of Racialization (American-style) had been opened for me.

THE SOCIOHISTORICAL CONSTRUCTION OF LANGUAGE AND HOW IT IMPACTS OUR VIEW OF THE WORLD AND THOSE IN IT: WHERE DOES BIRACIAL STATUS FIT?

As human societies create themselves and their world, language is culturally constructed and used to reflect the existence that is being played out (Vico, 1744). Language comprises structure and symbols that represent reality as it conveys cultural meaning, myths, and codes. As a system built upon inherited cultural values and bipolar positionals, language gives shape and meaning to experience and ultimately serves to remove any ambiguity from that experience. De Saussure believed that, similar to other socially learned constructs, "there were no pre-existing ideas and that nothing was distinct before the appearance of language" (1959, p. 112). This has direct implications for our current discussion, given the socially constructed and communicated notions of race that we are prone to absorb in childhood. Linguistic systems are created via arbitrary yet socially agreed-upon designations embedded within bidirectional relationships, as humans construct language; but they themselves are simultaneously constructed by it. In essence, language *thinks us*, as it guides our valued-laden cognitive processes; *orients us* with a cultural structure and framework; and *directs us* to develop culturally appropriate values, attitudes, belief, and behaviors (J. Parker, personal communication, September 22, 2003).

Language is related to the collection of race-based dichotomies that have developed from phenotypes (such as colonizer-savage; owner-slave; victim-criminal/potential criminal), and how we decipher their meanings. As a system of interdependent and related terms, the components of language find much of their value in the "simultaneous presence of the others [their antagonistic opposites]" (De Saussure, 1959, p. 114). Within this antithetical relationship, one entity cannot exist without the other, but particularly without the other being devalued; for instance, without evil, good ceases to have meaning; and without black, white takes on a different meaning. To the French philosopher Jacques Derrida (1997), it is the social and value-based constructions of language that result in artificially/culturally produced and defined dichotomies. He goes so far as to consider a rather contradictory relationship with the "other," such that on the one hand a person can only address and relate to the "other" to the extent that differences are highlighted; yet at the same time, the "different" are frequently excluded and prevented from "crossing over to 'our' border" (p. 106). This approach to linguistic production of "other as different" unconsciously requires the perception that they are lesser and inferior. These notions of language and how they may relate to biracial identity find substance in the fact that the law of hypodescent fiercely prevented individuals with "one drop" of racial "minority" blood from entering into the elite hierarchy of white society. The result was, and is, a cultural and linguistic disconnect between the phenomenological experience of the biracial individual and the expectations of society. Thus, it is through the combination of societal proscription, behavioral manifestations, and linguistic constructions that biracial individuals find themselves marginalized.

The Awakening: On the Complexities of Gumbo—I'm a Little of This and a Little of That

Can I define myself using terms that do not result in a comparative treatise of black and white culture? I would very much prefer to define myself in a way that does not concede to the national rhetoric of hypodescent, yet simultaneously accounts for the exclusionary reality of a life between black and white societies. More importantly, how do I relate myself to others using language that is devoid of culturally rooted values and stereotypes? For as soon as I begin this task, do people then not presume to have me figured out? I know my choice of words carries meaning, but is it what I want others to focus on?

I am complex; do others see that? Do they see beyond the implicit cultural meaning (and stereotypes) of my descriptors? Dare I feed stereotypes and say that I enjoy playing basketball, dancing, eating fried chicken and watermelon, drinking malt liquor, and dating white women? Yet, this is the reality of what it means to be me and my experiences; is that not enough? I never truly know what to do. When I tell people I am biracial, I am regularly responded to with a befuddled look. The sum of my being is much more (complex) than its parts; more than the multiracial union that brought me forth. While I am simply "me," this is a rather complex collection of two worlds, two realities. To present this to others is quite a challenge. I usually end up feeling misunderstood.

Societal Influences on Biracial Identity Development: Where Race and Language Meet

The general concept of identity development finds its roots in the search for the answer to a very basic question: "Who am I?" The search for self and identity is a critical facet of the human experience. It goes without saying that this is a lifelong endeavor, replete with twists, turns, and cumulative and cyclical features; and relies upon our interactions with others and society. Not only are we trying to "figure ourselves out," but we are trying to do so within a larger collective. Who I aspire to be, or who I see myself becoming, is inexorably related to the internalized notions of who I "may be" as communicated by family, peers, community, and society. Ultimately, the search for self represents "the negotiation between self-identity and world perception" (Hershel, 1995, p. 173). Identification and connection with others and a reference group are not only an integral component of identity formation, but a component within the hierarchy of human needs (Maslow, 1970). We seek to belong (to a group), as this provides some meaning to life as well as a psychological and behavior anchor. From our interactions with others in our family and community, we learn what it means to be "us." Moreover, we are (in the best of scenarios) able to learn these lessons in an atmosphere that provides us with a safe space and social support. Yet when belonging is not communicated, and individuals are not readily accepted into "the group," there is potential for problems. Without one's reference point, who does one then look to as a guide toward identity formation?

So begins the dilemma of biracial identity development. Its inception is located in the drive to simply develop into oneself within the harmonious family environment, where race and phenotype may be less of an issue. Many biracial individuals may readily embrace both racial heritages provided by their parents (Cooke, 1998). Intuitively, it seems that the result of this scenario would be a synthesis or the development of what Rockquemore and Brunsma (2002a) call a transcendent identity, and what Daniel (1996) calls a pluralistic identity. Both of these identity formations are characterized by the fact that they are relatively nonracial in their framework and represent a true multiracial existence. They are born from the blending and merging of multiple cultural traditions and are subsequently revealed in the embodiment of individual identity. However, as the broader influence of society comes to bear, with its implicit race-based categorization scheme, this specific developmental pathway is impacted, or interrupted (if you will), and it degrades into a framework that mirrors society's rigid rules. It is this socially rooted dichotomy of race that underlies the cultural umbrella under which biracial individuals find themselves: a system that requires them to be repressively categorized. There are discrete, mutually exclusive categories within which they are to place themselves: their identities and their being in the world.

The Awakening: Home as a Safe Place

My house was a safe place. I was just Matt. Not black, not white, not mixed—just me. I recall being identified more by roles and status (son, grandson, only child). Race was never a family issue, as my familial messages were clear: play with whomever you want, date whom you want, listen to whatever music you wish, to name a few. Ultimately the internalization of these messages was, "Be who you want to be; develop into you." Yet, existence eventually extends beyond the family boundaries and ultimately moves into the broader sociocultural context. The once-faded memories of my experience as a four-year-old would return as I expanded my horizons beyond the borders of my household. Within my family, I was never colored white or black with social crayons, but the world did not operate by the same rules that my house did. This would take some getting used to.

There is inadequate language and cultural reality to truly capture the biracial experience, as society constructs and relates a series of conflicting messages. As previously noted, both language and the American social structure take an "either-or" and rather rigid approach to racial categories, with a great deal of emphasis placed on excluding biracial individuals from the ranks of white society. Weisman (1996) notes that hypodescent assigns group membership to biracial individuals via appearance regardless of individual notions of identity and relationships to group(s); as society declares, "You look like them, so there you go." Thus the development of the pluralistic and transcendent identities is jeopardized and ultimately shattered, for they have no place in the current American cultural context. What results is a push/shove toward a singular identity (Rockquemore & Brunsma, 2002a), though more with the group of the minority parent. That places pressure upon individuals to accept a distinct identity that may contradict their notions of self, which initially comprised identification with both racial heritages. This forced monocultural identity is socially reinforced in time, as the demands and influences of society replace those found within the safe spaces of family. Regardless of the specific identity outcomes, given the phenotypic sight system, many biracial individuals may find themselves more likely to identify with the (day-to-day) *experiences* of the minority parent (Cooke, 1998).

Biracial individuals are more often than not defined as nonwhite using sociocultural definitions. Self-generated characterizations may also lead to this conclusion, especially given the fact that in many instances, minority communities are more likely to accept these individuals. However, this does not guarantee a successful identity or cultural "fit" for these individuals, for within these minority communities there may also exist the same "either-or" dichotomy leading to a less-than-steadfast acceptance of biracial individuals. Herein lies the contradiction; on the individual level, I may feel some connection to both reference groups and readily embrace my various racial heritages; yet at the societal level, both reference groups may be less than willing to view me as a full-fledged member. From an identity standpoint, individuals may develop a border identity (Anzaldua as cited in Rockquemore & Brunsma, 2002a), that is, an identity that stands apart from and is suspended between both reference groups. However, there is a danger inherent in this "middle" existence, for it may be accompanied by the psychological experience of marginalization, which is characterized by an exclusionary relationship with both reference groups (the dominant group [white] and other [nonwhite]) (Segall, Dasen, Berry, & Poortinga, 1999). Rockquemore and Brunsma (2002b) describe the negative treatment that many biracial individuals have felt from both reference groups, which opens the door to an identity purgatory of sorts.

The Awakening: Loneliness

The "middle margin" can be a lonely place. How do I as a biracial individual construct this notion of "me" and so reconcile seemingly contradictory aspects of my self that are communicated by the cultural nuances of the day? The imposed template does not fit with my reality. While the society imposes black or white, I look at my reality and feel both. I feel the pull from both sides; yet I feel strangely rejected, too. At times, I feel like a diplomat, brokering an uneasy truce between warring parties. However, at others, I get the impression that no one understands me and that I am destined to walk alone.

How is it that biracial individuals come to reconcile the identity dilemmas posited above? In the end, where does the push-pull of society and reference groups place us in relation to self? An existence "in between" reference groups may be fraught with isolation, and the option of pluralism is one that is frequently not available; although intuitively and futuristically, it is the one that makes the most sense and offers the most hope. Until that latter option is culturally legitimized, many biracial individuals find themselves developing a "migrant" notion of self, meaning they shuttle and move back and forth between both reference groups. This concept of an integrative identity (Daniel, 1996) or protean identity (Rockquemore & Brunsma, 2002a) has at its foundation situational and contextual variables that trigger reference group-specific attitudes, values, and behaviors. Great attention is paid to the details of self and others and the ensuing interpersonal interactions. While this is certainly not a feature unique to the biracial experience, as such analyses are undertaken within any interpersonal context; to many biracial individuals, this is a survival skill whose development and ultimate mastery are absolutely essential given the contrasting worlds they must traverse.

The Awakening: Anatomy of the Lunchroom . . . Where Do I Sit Today?

Ah, where to sit today? This is actually a more complex question than it appears to be. The joys of high school lunchroom politics. That was always the question as I walked down the steps around the noon hour. The options were rather numerous, each with its own set of rules, nuances, topics, and personalities. In retrospect, I have come to realize that each "neighborhood" represented a collection of stereotypes, some more accurate than others. There was the southeast corner of the cafeteria, or "Little Africa," as we proudly referred to it. Its refreshing atmosphere allowed for a linguistic break from the intellectual façade of standard English. There the language flowed colorfully and freely as we contemplated issues as diverse as the latest R&B and rap singles to which teachers and fellow students were the most racist. Another option was more centrally located, and while given no specific name, its relatively nondescript and white nature could be described courteously as mini-suburban. While in a distinctly different locale from Little Africa, it was many of these students with whom I shared classes. Replete with designer clothes and an air of *je ne sais quoi*, discussions of soon-to-be-purchased cars, SAT preparation, and college plans filled the air.

To see my cultural shifts was a thing of beauty. I was good. I could keep up with the best of them. Occasionally I would bring a friend from one group over to "the other side"; although this hardly ever ended well. The worlds were too different, too adversarial, too suspicious, and too foreign and strange to one another. At times I questioned whether these were even the same school. Inevitably I began such an endeavor with an introduction, as I was taught that a good host does such a thing. These were usually met with some token mumbles of acknowledgment, as everyone knew each other to some degree, yet interactions were rather rare. Then for the next hour I would initiate, translate, facilitate, and in the end, vacillate on the prudence of my decision to attempt merging my two worlds in the cafeteria, and ultimately hesitate to do it again.

TOWARD NEGOTIATING A "FIT"

Forcing the development of monoracial identity from multicultural ancestry serves as a constant reminder that someone does not "fit" with the current system that is in place (Daniel, 1992). A race-based cognitive dissonance results when personal identity (self-concept) does not coincide with group identity. This stems from the *denial of "fit"* with white society and the *reluctant "fit"* extended by the black community, both of which come laden with uncertainty and suspicion.

Kich (1992) presents a three-part process through which this negotiation of fit takes place: (1) awareness, (2) struggle for acceptance, and (3) acceptance. Awareness of difference begins early, as notions of self and "other" are readily apparent, both within the family and out, yet there may be varying degrees to which this notion of difference is emphasized. As the development of self-concept initiates, self-definition and those defined by "other" (parents, peers, society, etc.) begin to dominate the psychological landscape. Initially, it is parents who provide the language and foundations of this experience in a way that "conveys . . . a message of acceptance and positive valuation about being biracial" (Kich, 1992, p. 308). Yet as the spheres of influence widen beyond the safety of the family borders, the standard question posed to biracials ("What are you?") begins from peers and community. "Differentness" becomes more of a concern and issue as a place in the social hierarchy of childhood is established. Parents may be somewhat impotent to fully grasp the issues impacting their biracial children, as doing so represents an added layer of experience that they may not have gone through in their own development.

The Awakening: The Chameleon

Through family tradition and customs, I know that I represent a new type of person. At times I feel as if I have transcended race, but I do not feel free. By appearance and history I am black; but what about the "other" side of my being? Where does that come into the picture? No one ever seems to focus on that. I can deftly display a variety of aspects of self, from perspective-taking and ideological stances to speech patterns and dance moves. Who am I? I feel as if I do not own my racial heritage. It has been defined for me by the genes of my parents and by society's interpretation of my phenotype. Who am I? I am an actor in a play that just happens to be real life. As the performance begins, I am often compelled to ask, "Whom do you wish to know?" Tell me and I will produce him, like a magician pulls a rabbit out of a hat.

The resolution of this identity formation process is its final stage, self-acceptance (Kich, 1992). This represents the end result of the process whereby biracial individuals balance their self-perceptions (self-concepts) with the societal messages. While the positive psychological outcome of this process is a cohesive identity, how this may look will vary from person to person. There are varying degrees to which individuals internalize the potentially contradictory notions of race offered by socializing agents and the broader society. Other factors in this process that deserve consideration are physical appearance and individual and family responses to marginalization (Caluza, 2000). Of marginalization, a concept we have noted before, Tucker (as cited in Kich, 1996) states, "people . . . [are] ignored, trivialized, rendered invisible and unheard, perceived as inconsequential, de-authorized, [and as] 'other'" (pp. 270–271). Repeated exposure to marginalization may lead to the internalization of the societal love–hate relationship played out between reference groups (that is, black–white tensions) (Hershel, 1995; Kich, 1996). Being cast into the role of "other" by white society and "other among others" within the minority reference group presents a rather daunting place from which to develop a positive, self-accepting identity. Yet, the self-accepting biracial identity is "not dependent on the other person's recognition or confirmation and relies more on an integration [of a self] that includes a clearer and heightened awareness of [multiple] heritages" (Kich, 1992, p. 315).

The degree to which individuals develop an identity that allows them to "float" back and forth between reference groups can be related to components of the acculturation model offered by Segall et al. (1999). Irrespective of the previously noted quandary of reference group acceptance, the parallel process of adjusting to a culture provides a framework to refine our view of the variability of the integrative or protean identities and their related psychological and behavioral aspects. To begin with, there are varying degrees of how far an individual is willing or able to go in adhering to or shedding cultural characteristics. And while each of these reactions is not inherently positive or negative, keeping in mind that people frequently initiate a plan of action that they deem appropriate for their situation, there are potential rewards and pitfalls as individuals negotiate these waters. Each of these psychological responses within the framework of the integrative or protean identities does not represent static or fixed approaches, but rather represents fluctuating dimensions of self as biracial individuals actively attempt to garner a place for themselves in society, both psychologically and physically.

The process of assimilation results when an individual gravitates toward the dominant culture and attempts to shed aspects of his or her culture of origin (nondominant). Most noticeably, this may occur in language, style of dress, and other related observable elements, such as dating preferences. Within our context here, the more assimilated biracial individual will identify, even if unconsciously, with white America. In essence, this individual may feel a certain degree of comfort within white culture, especially if socialization experiences or scenarios, such as interracial adoption, provided minimal exposure to minority populations. Yet along with this assimilationist perspective has to come some understanding that acceptance will, at times, arrive minimally from the dominant culture, as the law of hypodescent ultimately assigns placement within the minority group. Individuals may actively reject this placement and characterization by responding to them with renewed efforts to be more like the dominant culture. These attempts to gain inclusion in white America may further alienate the biracial individual from the once moderately accepting minority reference group, as the group may begin to question the individual's group commitment and connection. The use of terms like *sellout* and *Oreo* (black on the outside and white on the inside) points to these concerns and questions generated by the minority group and further compounds the push-pull relationship that exists between biracial individuals and reference groups.

The Awakening: You on Our Team or What?

Why do you talk like that? What are you wearing? Why do you sit with them? What is that music you are listening to? Are you not one of us? The questions fly frequently and without mercy. Having to justify every facet of your existence is never easy or fun. In fact, it is just plain tiring. The questions, the looks, and other disapproving non-verbals seem to come more from blacks than whites, suggesting some degree of indifference to my partial membership in that latter group. I respond in word ("Yes, I'm down, I am a member") and in deed (I turn my R& B up for all to hear; I turn my "gangsta" rap up for all to hear). But part of me wavers, hesitates, and understands that it is not all that simple. Well, if I am honest, I really don't feel as though I completely belong; can I claim about 60 percent of "the black feeling"? Is that possible? Phenotypically, I stand out a bit; I've been followed in stores, pulled over by police, and viewed as a threat by mothers walking past with their children. But that hardly constitutes criteria for group membership, does it? There is still a feeling of being inauthentic if I leave it at those features alone—it just doesn't feel right. Maybe I am a sellout.

Another response that may reveal itself is what Segall et al. (1999) refer to as separation, which is an individual's maintenance of minority culture to the exclusion of the dominant one. Historically, this is a more difficult physical endeavor, as dominant culture features are everywhere, with the exception of ethnic enclaves like Chinatowns, but the concept ultimately refers more to psychological and ideological separation. As such, the biracial individual fiercely takes hold of all things ethnic and immerses herself in that world. While it may appear that this is a self-isolating stance, for some it surely provides comfort; but at the same time does it deny a component of self? This response of separation may not be rooted in the reality of the circumstances, for biracial individuals are inescapably linked to the dominant culture in some shape or form. To actively negate an aspect of self is destructive, regardless of its source. If others were to ascribe a singular identity to biracial individuals, we would label such an affront dehumanizing and look upon it unfavorably. However, when we self-select such an identity framework, it may certainly appear more palatable, but this may actually be more self-defeating to the broader development process, as it still removes us from potential social anchors and reference groups, namely dominant culture family members.

The Awakening: A View to a Crash—Bike Helmets, Roadside Ditches, and Poor Syntax

The words "Fuck you, mother nigger," stream from within the passing carload of white teenagers as it forces my bicycle (with me barely on it) off the road. I find some solace in the fact that my bicycle and I are not damaged, as I am still fifteen miles from home. I chalk it up as another incident for the teenage version of me to add to the list of things to tell my future children when they are old enough. As I resume my trek homeward, my shaken nerves are calmed by some of the amusement of what just took place. Oh, I certainly don't like getting run off the road, and the verbal and nonverbal messages were very clear; I think I will probably take a different route home the next time. But the hilarity of some fool's improper syntax strikes me as funny. I recall that public speaking can make some people a bit nervous and prone to such errors.

As I later relate the tale to some black friends, they offer that "white folks are such assholes!" I quickly agree, but later find myself a bit uncomfortable by having supported such a statement. Have my friends and I inadvertently included *my family* members in our philosophy? Do my friends know that I mean *those other white folks*, not my family? Come to think of it, whom do my friends really mean with that statement? Certainly not *my family*. Should I speak up to clarify for everyone? Despite the fact that I was the victimized one, I now feel guilty.

DEVELOPMENT OF A NEW VERNACULAR FOR BIRACIAL INDIVIDUALS

"What is a rebel? A man who says 'no' . . . whose no affirms the existence of a borderline. [A man who, in his act of rebellion], simultaneously experiences a feeling of revulsion at the infringement of his rights and a complete and spontaneous loyalty to certain aspects of himself . . . for with rebellion, awareness is born" (Camus, 1957, pp. 13–15). So begins *The Rebel*, written by the French existentialist Albert Camus, and while more of a political treatise, nonetheless it offers an apt starting point for our discussion on developing a new cultural and linguistic philosophy for biracial individuals. The words of Camus represent a call to psychological arms, as we endeavor to help biracial individuals produce a new set of meaning systems within the vernacular that more accurately affirm their uniqueness and provide the foundation for them to create a "safe space" psychologically. We strive to "rebel" against the current limiting and dehumanizing sociohistorical constructions of race and language and seek to expand the range of legitimacy afforded by the biracial experience.

To understand the phenomenological experience of biracial individuals, with the objective of creating sociocultural change, greater inclusion, and more self-defined identity development, it is essential to do so from a strong theoretical base. A variety of recent work has identified major spheres of influence upon biracial identity development, including family, accepting others, peers, school, and community, to name a few (Dovick, 2003; Gleason, 2000; Thompson, 1999; Tomishima, 2000; Wrathall, 2002). While focus on these features is indeed a useful endeavor, they must be explored and processed within the greater sociocultural context. To this end, the ecological systems model of Bronfenbrenner (1979) offers a starting point for deconstructing the broader environmental influences upon an individual's development. Furthermore, our premise throughout this work has been that the power of society exerts a narrow definition and unhealthy influence upon biracial identity development. A corrective goal would be to redistribute the descriptive power into the hands of biracial individuals themselves and allow them to reestablish their identity, through reframed definitions of self and a rejection of the narrow racial dictates of society. To this end, the empowerment model of feminist therapy (Worell & Remer, 1992) presents a means through which biracial individuals can validate their emerging views of self. This section will present both models, relate them to biracial identity development, and offer suggestions for present and future understandings of the biracial experience.

Ecological Systems Model

While the original model of Bronfenbrenner (1979) has gone through a variety of versions, it offers an excellent vehicle for viewing the interrelationship between society and individual development.

With the individual at its center, the model is organized into nested, or layered, systems of environmental influences, such as family, school, extended family, mass media, and culture—all of which impact the developmental process. Like concentric rings within a tree, each layer is impacted by another and eventually interacts with the individual. For our purposes the levels of note are first the innermost one, the microsystem, and the outermost one, the macrosystem. The microsystem comprises those entities and persons who represent immediate and daily (face-to-face) interactions for an individual (such as family, peers, and school). The macrosystem, which is the most complex system and is similar to a society's culture, comprises culturally based values, attitudes, and beliefs. Of note is the interaction that occurs between the micro- and macrosystems and the subsequent impact on development. At the microsystem level, families may recreate and "pass on" the societal messages that are rooted in the macrosystem. Another response could be that families alter or counter macrosystem influences, especially if there is the perception that they are potentially negative. However, there will eventually be some interaction between a developing person and macrosystem messages, and this will no doubt have some influence upon identity development. While family may create a specific type of environment for biracial individuals, as they venture out into society, they may be faced with a series of very different and potentially conflicting messages. All of this provides a framework to explore how the family of origin has created, communicated, and reacted to some of the broader culturally based messages about race.

Feminist Theory

As presented earlier, the historically dichotomous notions of race are embedded in the uppermost sphere of developmental influences: the macrosystem. Communicated through a variety of means within society, such as popular media, these impact the process of biracial identity development such that it is pressured to be framed as an either-or prospect. However, as we have seen, many biracial individuals utilize a more integrated approach, but the pressure of the dualistic distinction remains. The empowerment model of feminist therapy, with its inclusive themes of "both/and," offers applied tools to this dilemma (Worell & Remer, 1992). In a Bronfenbrennerian stance, the empowerment model recognizes the negative influence of society, via social and political factors that impact individual development. While the model was originally designed for use with women, its themes of recognizing, rejecting, and reframing society's narrow view of an individual and empowering one to validate oneself, parallels our biracial discussion. In direct opposition to the dualistic oppression perpetuated by society, the empowerment model strives to increase appreciation of multiple perspectives of self and allows them all to thrive simultaneously (Worell & Remer, 1992). This inclusive stance seems to mirror the natural developmental process of many biracial individuals who incorporate multiple traditions into their existence.

Aside from analysis of the broader, culturally based messages, some understanding of the individual perception of and reaction to sociohistorical construction of race are critical components to biracial identity. Identification of how these themes are internalized may well reveal them through linguistic expression. Language molds us, shapes our view of reality, and calls forth the appropriate social behaviors. However, there is no need to wait until language shifts at the macrocultural level to begin utilizing it to better relate to one's experiences. This adaptability of language provides a more inclusive approach to self-definition and behavioral expression, which ultimately liberates individuals from stifling cultural definitions and sociological conditioning (Daniel, 1996). Recognizing the subtlety with which we agree to social convention is called into question and challenged as the voices of the biracial collective proclaim, "[T]his has gone on for long enough; I will stand for no more. I chose my own terms and conditions for this [social] contract [of self-definition]" (Camus, 1957, p. 14).

FINAL THOUGHTS

We have charted how society has historically responded to the questions of race and racial identity with an either-or answer. For those of us who are multiracial, the result has often been a "forced fit" (physically, psychologically, and culturally) into one aspect of who we are as people. One way to alleviate this dilemma is presented in the framework that begins the biracial deconstruction of societally defined notions of self. From the ashes of this will arise a more self-generated concept of "who we are," and ultimately one that will give legitimacy to a new legacy of "unboxed identities" (Weisman, 1996). Derrida (1997) speaks to a similar process through which identity is internally differentiated, as he describes himself as a "European who does not feel European in every part" (p. 114). By this statement, he is deconstructing his identity and recognizing that it is a complex web impacted by features such as country of origin and immigration, which interact

Toolbox for Change

Maintenance of limiting images and perceptions of biracial people	For the biracial individual	For everyone else
Race and ethnicity are culturally seen as either-or concepts, whereby biracial individuals are frequently not "allowed" to simply be collective whole people.	In defining yourself, be aware of the society-level influences upon your identity development and how you may have internalized them; ask yourself whether you are developing into the person that *you* see or the person whom others have constructed.	Recognize the limiting characteristics of society's definitions of personhood and how these impact biracial people. Work to not recreate these limiting monikers of self.
The continued over-reliance on a flawed perceptual "sight" system that is used to determine initial conclusions about others.	Define yourself in a manner that fits your understanding of your reality and utilize an identity framework that fits *your* life.	Ask yourself, "*Why do I have to know*" what the racial/ethnic status of another person is to truly relate to them as an individual.
Sociocultural presentations (such as media) of biracial individuals rarely include the notion of a "both-and" philosophy, which limits our perception of their reality and ultimately our ability to relate to them.	Actively take hold of your identity and the language that displays it. Claim them as your own, regardless of where that "fit" places you in the eyes of others.	Strive to respond to others as individuals and not as representatives of a stereotype.
	Be true to yourself.	Delight in the diversity of the human constellation.

with family characteristics (like religion). As such, identity is both similar and different to itself. It represents a static and grounded entity, yet one that is constantly in a state of flux and rebirth.

It is through the deconstruction of a value-laden, culturally rooted identity that biracial identity will break free from its restrictive bonds. According to Camus, "Rebellion breaks the seal and allows the whole being to come into play" (1957, p. 17). As the population of multiracial individuals steadily increases in number, their collective voice in this new vernacular will be hard to ignore. As an ever-diversifying nation, we are compelled to initiate a cultural reevaluation and reconstruction of identities. What is necessary is accepting the autonomy to choose ambiguity. It is time for a new discourse to address the unshackling of multiracial identity from its oppressive and historically dichotomous bonds of marginalization. It is hoped that the day will come when multiracial people and their identities will no longer be forced to divide into unrelated, contradictory, and adversarial entities. That day is upon us now.

Awakened: Out of the Mouths of Babes

My response at four years of age to the elderly woman who called me a nigger was, "What? Speak up. I can't hear you!" As an adult processing this experience with my mother, we came to some conclusions of note. While my initial response was based upon the fact that I truly could not hear the woman clearly, another set of interpretations is offered: "Speak up" and let the world see your ignorance and lack of knowledge; and "I can't hear you" is more akin to I "do not" hear you, I choose not to, as your words do not penetrate my sense of who I am. There are no receptors here for that reality. It is not I.

I am my own person; my self is constructed by me, for me; it is mine alone to share with whom I choose, and how I choose to do it.

I am biracial, proud, and whole.

ACKNOWLEDGMENT

I would like to thank my mentor, colleague, and friend Dr. James Parker for his insightful critiques of this work.

NOTE

1. The terms *biracial, multiracial,* and *mixed race* will be used synonymously for ease of discussion. Additionally, unless noted, and given the author's background, the notion of "biracial" is rooted in white/nonwhite parentage, although it is acknowledged that a variety of equally beautiful familial scenarios could be considered biracial.

REFERENCES

Allen, T. W. (2001). The invention of the white race: Racial oppression and social control. In E. Cashmore & J. Jennings (Eds.), *Racism: Essential readings* (pp. 357–379). London: SAGE Publications, Ltd.

Bronfenbrenner, U. (1979). *Ecology of human development*. Cambridge, MA: Harvard University Press.

Caluza, K. T. (2000). A psychoeducational support group for multiracial adolescents: A twelve-session treatment manual (Doctoral dissertation, California School of Professional Psychology, 2000). *Dissertation Abstracts International, 61*(1), 561B.

Camus, A. (1957). *The rebel* (A. Bower, Trans.). New York: Alfred A. Knopf.

Cooke, T. I. (1998). Biracial identity development: Psychosocial contributions to self-esteem and racial identity (Doctoral dissertation, Arizona State University, 1998). *Dissertation Abstracts International, 58*(10), 5669B.

Daniel, G. R. (1992). Passers and pluralists: Subverting the racial divide. In M. P. P. Root (Ed.), *Racially mixed people in America* (pp. 91–107). Newbury Park, CA: SAGE Publications, Inc.

Daniel, G. R. (1996). Black and white identity in the new millennium: Unsevering the ties that bind. In M. P. P. Root (Ed.), *The multiracial experience: Racial border as the new frontier* (pp. 121–139). Newbury Park, CA: SAGE Publications, Inc.

De Saussure, F. (1959). *Course in general linguistics* (W. Baskin, Trans.). New York: Philosophical Library.

Derrida, J. (1997). *Deconstruction in a nutshell: A conversation with Jacques Derrida*. New York: Fordham University Press.

Dovick, S. M. (2003). Experiences of African American and Caucasian biracial/biethnic clients in psychotherapy (Doctoral dissertation, Pepperdine University, 2003). *Dissertation Abstracts International, 63*(7), 3469B.

Ferber, A. L. (1995). Exploring the social construction of race. In N. Zack (Ed.), *American mixed race* (pp. 155–167). Lanham, MD: Rowman & Littlefield Publishers.

Gleason, D. J. (2000). Racial identity development in biracial individuals: An analysis of therapists' accounts of psychosocial and psychological factors (Doctoral dissertation, California School of Professional Psychology, 2000). *Dissertation Abstracts International, 61*(1), 530B.

Hall, R. E. (2001). Identity development across the lifespan: A biracial model. *Social Science Journal, 38*, 119–123.

Hershel, H. J. (1995). Therapeutic perspectives on biracial identity formation and internalized oppression. In N. Zack (Ed.), *American mixed race* (pp. 169–181). Lanham, MD: Rowman & Littlefield Publishers.

Kich, G. K. (1992). The developmental process of asserting a biracial, bicultural identity. In M. P. P. Root (Ed.), *Racially mixed people in America* (pp. 304–317). Newbury Park, CA: SAGE Publications, Inc.

Kich, G. K. (1996). In the margins of sex and race: Difference, marginality, and flexibility. In M. P. P. Root (Ed.), *The multiracial experience: Racial border as the new frontier* (pp. 263–276). Newbury Park, CA: SAGE Publications, Inc.

Maslow, A. (1970). *Motivation and personality.* New York: Harper & Row.

Omi, M., & Winant, H. (1986). *Racial formations in the United States.* London: Routledge.

Rockquemore, K. A., & Brunsma, D. L. (2002a). *Beyond black: Biracial identity in America.* Thousand Oaks, CA: SAGE Publications, Inc.

Rockquemore, K. A., & Brunsma, D. L. (2002b). Socially embedded identities: Theories, typologies, and processes of racial identity among black/white biracials. *Sociological Quarterly, 43,* 335–356.

Root, M. P. P. (1992). Within, between and beyond race. In M. P. P. Root (Ed.), *Racially mixed people in America* (pp. 3–11). Newbury Park, CA: SAGE Publications, Inc.

Root, M. P. P. (1995). The multiracial contribution to the psychological browning of America. In N. Zack (Ed.), *American mixed race* (pp. 231–236). Lanham, MD: Rowman & Littlefield Publishers.

Segall, M. H., Dasen, P. R., Berry, J. W., & Poortinga, Y. H. (1999). *Human behavior in global perspective.* Boston: Allyn & Bacon.

Snyder, L. L. (2001). The idea of racialism: Its meaning and history. In E. Cashmore & J. Jennings (Eds.), *Racism: Essential readings* (pp. 91–97). London: SAGE Publications, Ltd.

Thompson, C. A. (1999). Identity resolution in biracial black/white individuals: The process of asserting a biracial identity (Doctoral dissertation, California School of Professional Psychology, 1999). *Dissertation Abstracts International, 59*(1), 6498B.

Tomishima, S. A. (2000). Factors and experiences in biracial and biethnic identity development (Doctoral dissertation, University of Utah, 2000). *Dissertation Abstracts International, 61*(2), 1114B.

U.S. Census Bureau. (2001). *The two or more races population: 2000.* Retrieved November 1, 2003, from www.census.gov/prod/2001pubs/c2kbr01-6.pdf

Vico, G. (1744). *The new science of Giambattista Vico* (T. G. Bergin & M. H. Fisch, Trans.). Ithaca, NY: Cornell University Press.

Weisman, J. R. (1996). The "other" way of life: The empowerment of alterity in the interracial individual. In M. P. P. Root (Ed.), *The multiracial experience: Racial border as the new frontier* (pp. 152–164). Newbury Park, CA: SAGE Publications, Inc.

Worell, J., & Remer, P. (1992). *Feminist perspective in therapy.* New York: John Wiley & Sons.

Wrathall, M. W. (2002). What about the children? The psychosocial well-being of multiracial individuals. (Doctoral dissertation, Azusa Pacific University, 2002). *Dissertation Abstracts International, 63*(1), 556B.

CHAPTER 5

Bias in Counseling Hmong Clients with Limited English Proficiency

Michael Goh
Timothy Dunnigan
Kathryn McGraw Schuchman

A hospital in a large midwestern city was trying to create a warmer welcome by displaying a sign in the hospital reception area that welcomed patients in the languages of its multilingual constituents. The new sign hung prominently as one entered the facilities, with the first line in English reading, "Welcome to our hospital. We're here to help you!" Just below it, the same phrase in Hmong read: "Welcome to our hospital. We're here to *hurt* you!" This story would be more humorous if not for the fact that it was true. It is a stark reminder of how even with the best of intentions, language, if not carefully treated, can have the most opposite and detrimental of consequences.

In Minnesota, Asians are the second largest racial group among all children of color. More than one third (38 percent) of Minnesota students who are English-language learners speak Hmong—the most common language among those 29,000 students. Over 45,000 Hmong were counted as residents of the Minneapolis–St. Paul (Twin Cities) metropolitan area in the 2000 census. They began arriving in Minnesota in the late 1970s as a traumatized refugee population. Significant immigration, both primary and secondary, continued through the early 1990s. The Hmong population in Minnesota is said to be the largest urban Hmong population in the world (The Minneapolis Foundation, 1999). Despite over two decades of immigration to the Twin Cities metropolitan area, mental health services for Hmong children and families are inadequate. While many community mental health centers provide quality care, mainstream institutions still lag in their ability to provide quality services that overcome cultural and language barriers.

Providing equal access to the health care system is the law. Title VI of the Civil Rights Act of 1964, which prohibits discrimination against any person on the basis of race, color, or national origin in any program receiving federal assistance, has frequently been understood to mean that qualified interpreters must be provided in health care settings.

Many Hmong families depended upon resettlement agencies and government programs for such basics as supplemental income, housing, and employment training. In recent years, Hmong have turned to other mainstream institutions to obtain forms of help that are relatively new to them, including mental health services. Mental health providers have had considerable difficulty understanding the viewpoints of Hmong clients, particularly those who are English-language learners and require interpreters. In recognizing the risk of poor communication, federal law mandates "linguistic accessibility to health care" under Title VI of the Civil Rights Act. In addition, Minnesota law also requires public health care institutions to provide services for English-language learners under the Bilingual Services Act of 1995 (MN Statutes 15.441, Subd. 1). However, Ohmans (1998) noted that Minnesota's English-language learners had a hard time accessing health care services because demand for interpreters far outstripped supply; and even when trained interpreters were hired, the system became overwhelmed.

An example was how one medical center's "46 interpreters made over 54,000 individual patient visits in 1997 . . . [and] the use of untrained, volunteer interpreters was rife with hazards . . . in one study of recorded ad hoc interpreter-assisted encounters, 25 percent to 50 percent of the words and phrases were incorrectly relayed" (p. 6). Ohmans (1998) reminds us that the common practice of using family members, friends, and children as interpreters not only undermines confidentiality and blurs family roles and boundaries but, more importantly, is considered a civil rights violation by the U.S. Office of Civil Rights. In mental health practice, when clients leave a clinician's office feeling misunderstood, misdiagnosed, and receiving less than adequate service because of language, this constitutes discrimination even if clinicians or the agency did not intend it. Ridley (1995) describes this as "unintentional racism."

Language discrimination in mental health practice is not something to be taken lightly. The surgeon general's report *Mental Health:*

Culture, Race, and Ethnicity (U.S. Department of Health and Human Services, 2001) concluded that culture matters in how ethnic minorities fail to access or confront barriers when trying to obtain help. In particular, the report noted, "a major barrier to effective mental health arises when provider and patient do not speak the same language" (p. 163).

In this chapter, we describe our process and work with the Hmong in Minnesota in overcoming language discrimination in mental health. While other cultures experience similar language discrimination, the complexities of Hmong language make this a unique challenge. By offering our process, our application of cultural semantics, and the guidelines for the use of interpreters we developed as a model for overcoming language discrimination in mental health, we hope that our efforts will help other culture groups that face similar challenges.

In the first section of this chapter, "Bridging Non-English–English Mental Health Concepts," we describe the development, process, and methods of a multidisciplinary investigative approach for bridging non-English and English-language mental health concepts. In the second section, "Cultural Semantics for Mental Health Providers," we illustrate the need for cultural semantics in mental health. Section three, "The Use of Interpreters in Mental Health Counseling," explores the issues of introducing interpreters into the provider–client relationship and suggests some guidelines for using interpreters in mental health counseling. In the summary section, we will review key implications for research and practice.

BRIDGING NON-ENGLISH–ENGLISH MENTAL HEALTH CONCEPTS: OUR PROCESS WITH THE HMONG

The challenge of crossing from American English into Hmong in a western mental health setting is a complex task with substantial barriers that can prevent clinical efficacy; it requires essential knowledge that is often difficult to ascertain. Because of the variation and complexity involved in bridging these cultures and languages, a group of clinicians and academicians in Minnesota, including the three authors of this chapter, began meeting and working on ways to remove language discrimination so that the Hmong could better access mental health services.

Differences in the ways Hmong and non-Hmong Americans conceptualize individual and family values, spirituality and religion, biological processes, and other natural phenomena can be extensive. Their respective views regarding health, illness, and healing are sometimes very difficult for westerners to reconcile. Under such circumstances, communication across the two cultures in mental health settings can be extremely challenging.

The process to bridge this language gap was led by an interdisciplinary group of professionals from such fields as social work, counseling psychology, medicine, cultural anthropology, linguistics, and linguistic anthropology. The team comprised both clinicians and academicians and included several Hmong members. The aim of the investigators from early on was to identify and compare key Hmong and English expressions for mental health conditions and treatments in order to increase mutual understanding between clinicians and clients. This group became the Hmong Mental Health Concepts Task Force, a working group of the Hmong Mental Health Providers' Network of Minnesota.

The Hmong Mental Health Providers' Network

The Hmong Mental Health Providers' Network of Minnesota was created in response to several tragic cases of violence within Hmong families. Representatives of Twin Cities Hmong mutual assistance associations, mental health clinics, hospitals, and other private and governmental agencies formed the Network in 1998. Its mission is to explore and establish ways in which service providers can better coordinate mental health and social services and share expertise, to expand and promote information and understanding of mental health and mental health services within the Hmong community, and to identify and provide guidance for research, policy, and legislative initiatives that promote positive mental health outcomes for the Hmong community.

Early discussions among mental health clinicians—social workers, psychologists, and bilingual staff who provided intervention and interpretation-identified problems with existing mental health services. One of the principal problems was inadequate language interpretation resulting in language discrimination. Practitioners emphasized as most problematic the scarcity of interpreters and delays in receiving interpretation assistance as much as the ineptitude of the interpretation.

Many mental health practitioners—both Hmong and non-Hmong—asserted that one solution to poor quality of services because of language barriers was to increase the number of bilingual clinicians trained in a variety of specialty areas within mental health services (psychologists, psychiatrists, etc.). However, most practitioners agreed that waiting for sufficient numbers of bilingual clinicians to be trained was not even within sight.

An overview of research and an examination of community practice standards revealed that there was a wide variation in the ways interpretation was provided in mental health settings. Also, little information was available about methods used in interpretation or guidelines for the translation of mental health concepts between Hmong and English.

Hmong Mental Health Concepts Task Force

Shortly after the establishment of this network, a subgroup of clinicians set out to investigate the problem of mental health interpretation, which led to the creation of a task force of researchers and practitioners. Initially called the Hmong Mental Health Concepts Task Force, members joined to study concepts of mental health and their application for services in the Hmong community. Details on the work of this task force are presented in the second section of this chapter.

Developing Key Collaborators and Identifying Important Contributors to Research

Finding professionals with the necessary expertise for this work was a uniquely challenging task, in part because the professionals who possess the needed expertise do not necessarily work in mental health or interpretation. For example, individuals who provided interpretation held a variety of positions in which interpreting was not their primary role. Often persons who interpret have no professional identification with the field of interpretation, so locating qualified persons required atypical searching.

It was also important that researchers have sufficient expertise in their professional fields as well as expertise in cross-cultural work. This was somewhat challenging but important for the cultural foci of our investigation. These professionals included psychologists with multicultural training and experience, a linguist with a foundation in anthropology, and a nurse with experience as an interpreter, among others.

What was perhaps most striking about our process was the diversity of disciplines represented. The members involved on regular and ad hoc bases came from backgrounds that included social workers, school counselors, licensed psychologists, anthropologists, linguists, academics, professional interpreters, community mental health practitioners, youth workers, religious workers, and medical practitioners, to name a few. It is symbolic that such an effort did not rest on the shoulders of any one particular provider, nor did it rest solely on representatives from one ethnic group. It further reflected the complexity of the task involved as well as the respect that such a task, if done well, required complex skills that no one discipline possessed. A natural consequence, however, has been the reality that teams take time to form and that the process of dialogue, debate, and discussion requires much time and patience.

Methods of Investigation

The initial task of this research was to produce a reference work to facilitate effective Hmong and English interpreting in mental health settings. Initially, members gathered to work on developing an encyclopedia to aid mental health clinicians and interpreters in their work with Hmong clients. There was consensus about the importance of the task force developing tools that would be tangible and applicable to clinical settings. The end result would need to make clinicians' interventions more facile and competent and make help more accessible and understandable for clients.

One of the first steps in the development of this reference work required practice and illustration of analyzing word meanings and how these efforts could be achieved in the process of interpretation. Actual case studies aided researchers in outlining key words and developing context and meaning. In this way, researchers used idiographic data to illustrate concepts—a method similar to creating an encyclopedia entry.

One important development through the research group has been a listserv: Hmong and English Mental Health Interpreting and Translating (HEMHIT). This listserv has provided an alternative way to facilitate discussion on these various research topics of Hmong mental health. Its overall goal is to aid in the improvement of communication between mental health professionals and their Hmong clients. Details about this listserv follow in the next section of this chapter.

As research directions were identified, the important function of the interpreter also became more illuminated. The literature and a community assessment of mental health interpreters revealed a multitude of ways in which mental health interpretation was provided in the clinical setting. The skills of the interpreter, the role of the interpreter, and the relationship between the interpreter and clinician vary widely among settings. Exploration into the role of the interpreter in mental health contexts is an area currently being studied (Goh, McGraw-Schuchman, & Yang, 2003), and is described in the third section of this chapter.

An important third component to this investigation was for the task force to be informed and educated about traditional and indigenous healing and helping systems within the culture. This provided a critical context for appreciating and understanding language use.

Parallel Projects

In the evolution of the Hmong Mental Health Concepts Task Force, it was discovered that the Minnesota Department of Human Services recently conducted a translation project. This process used expert reviewers along with other professionals to develop mental health education materials. The outcomes of the project included the development of a short glossary of mental health concepts translated into Hmong in print as well as audiotape media. Lessons learned from initial research cited the idiosyncratic nature of terminology as a barrier in translating. One problematic piece of feedback was that the publication was developed for western audiences and fell short of the explanations needed for English-language learners.

Prior to the start of the task force, we also learned that the Minnesota Department of Children, Families, and Learning had developed a dictionary for special education terms. Researchers were able to benefit from this unique project. The department had employed a team of professionals to brainstorm, analyze, and concur on definitions related to special education. The outcome was a lengthy document of terms that community providers have praised for its quality translation. One challenging entry on autism highlighted the complications that arise when there are no equivalents in the target language. The translated term resulted in a definition requiring half a page.

Other regional efforts were also uncovered, including the work of professionals in a Wisconsin community with a high Hmong population. In this area, Hmong social workers were developing a terminology list using consensus-building among bilingual mental health professionals to identify a standard of translation for a variety of mental health concepts. This group of providers is uniquely qualified to analyze mental health concepts in Hmong since, as bilingual professionals, they possess knowledge of both the Hmong language and mental health education and training. However, they faced challenges in mental health interpretation because of their limited understanding of linguistics and language analysis and the absence of research methods and protocols to aid consensus-building.

In recognizing the efforts of others in similar projects, our emphasis was to create a cooperative sharing network rather than any sense of competitiveness.

Evolution of Research Directions

Today the Hmong Mental Health Concepts Task Force—now called the Hmong Mental Health Research Group—studies mental health in the Hmong community by analyzing language, culture, indigenous healing methods, and western mental health practices. The task force studies them to increase knowledge and improve the effectiveness of mental health interventions within the Hmong community; to influence the development of western mental health concepts employed by Hmong to improve capacity; and to develop models of the best practices that can inform interpretation in other cross-cultural mental health contexts, including cross-cultural research and mental health outreach.

Members gather to dialogue, brainstorm, and collaborate on a variety of research topics on Hmong mental health. Their purpose is to demonstrate how we are attempting to compare key Hmong and English expressions for mental conditions, processes, disorders, and treatments in order to increase mutual understanding between clinicians and clients.

Throughout investigation, there has been consensus about the importance of keeping research and development grounded in the community. Inputs from community professionals, community members, and mutual assistance associations are frequently collected. The goal has been not only to identify terminology, but also to learn what is common and where there are conceptual differences. Participants discuss their experiences and challenges of this task and the challenge of translating and making understandable western concepts of mental health.

In the next two sections, we will illustrate two of the outcomes for overcoming language discrimination that resulted from the work of the Hmong Mental Health Research Group in Minnesota.

CULTURAL SEMANTICS FOR MENTAL HEALTH PROVIDERS

In this section, we present preliminary results of projects involving (a) the sharing of Hmong language data via an Internet listerv and

(b) the building of a Hmong–English dictionary at a publicly accessible web site. These results are presented in order to demonstrate the relevance of cultural semantics to the provision of mental health services in multilingual settings.

Cultural semantics is the study of culture-specific concepts by analyzing the use of key, everyday linguistic terms. In other words, cultural semanticists analyze how key linguistic terms are used in everyday discourse in order to understand and interpret culture-specific concepts. We recommend that mental health providers who serve linguistically diverse clienteles have a degree of formal exposure to the methodology of cultural semantics.

When mental health providers and their clients speak different languages, confusions arise that competent interpreting alone cannot dispel. Both sides tend to rely on culture-specific expressions, literal and figurative, that are very difficult for the other to comprehend. Responsibility for reaching cross-linguistic and cross-cultural accommodations falls mainly on clinicians. They must learn to employ language that is both adequately descriptive and amenable to interpretation. They also have to develop an ethnographer's ability to infer correct cultural meanings from the interpreted speech of their clients. Mental health clinicians who serve linguistically diverse clienteles unavoidably act somewhat like cultural semanticists. Although it is possible to perform these functions somewhat successfully at an intuitive level, we argue that the experience of consciously applying the principles and methods of cultural semantics helps one to discern the nature of, and to deal more effectively with, contrasting conceptual systems that are linguistically encoded.

In order to better understand the knowledge base that Hmong rely upon when dealing with mental health problems, the Hmong Mental Health Concepts Task Force was set up as described earlier in this chapter. The name of the task force proved infelicitous inasmuch as the name itself could not easily translate into Hmong. As one member observed, "The Hmong don't have a term for 'mental health,' and neither do we." For some Hmong, particularly those who had learned English as a second language, the term has an entirely pejorative meaning. An intelligent and well-educated Hmong individual once described the plight of a mutual acquaintance in the following way: "Things kept getting worse until pretty soon he was mental health." Being very aware of the negative connotations of the term *mental health*, Hmong sometimes substitute it for their own word *vws*, meaning "crazy" or "unable to control one's own actions."

Each meaning of "mental health," and of any other polysemous (having many meanings) English term, usually requires a separate Hmong definitional phrase. For instance, the Hmong expression for "well-being," *kev noj qab nyob zoo*, has been recruited to signify "mentally healthy state." The phrase *ntawm siab ntsws*, which literally means "pertaining to the liver (and) lungs," a standard metaphorical way of talking about feelings (or what English speakers call "emotions") is sometimes added after *kev noj qab nyob zoo* to make explicit the feeling dimension of well-being. When referring to various forms of emotional distress, Hmong describe the liver and/or lungs as being "difficult" (*nyuaj*) or "disturbed" (*ntxhov*). The phrase *kev nyuaj siab nyuaj ntsws* is now employed as the semantic near-equivalent of "emotional disturbance" in general and "depression" in particular.

The task force quickly appreciated how challenging it was to compare and contrast Hmong lexicalized concepts of thinking and feeling with those of English. We first had to adopt a more appropriate name, the Hmong Mental Health Research Group. Paraphrased as "The Group Who Studies Hmong Well-Being," our name could now be translated into Hmong. Several of us began reviewing English–Hmong word lists that had been compiled by bilinguals working for government health and social service agencies. The lists' purpose was to standardize word choices and ensure greater accuracy in interpreting and translating. English was usually the source language and Hmong the target language. The results ranged from poor to unusable. The following entry was taken from a preliminary list produced under the auspices of a Minnesota state agency.

> Mental health: *kev mob hlwb; kev ntxhov siab* (italics added)
> Way/sick/brain: way/disturbed/liver
> Brain disease: disordered feelings

Starting from a bare phrase, one often used as a euphemism for "mental illness," it is not surprising that the translator matched "mental health" with "brain disease" and "disordered feelings." The same gloss for "mental health" appears today on the Internet at the most frequently consulted English–Hmong dictionary website (ww2.saturn.stpaul.k12. mn.us/Hmong/sathmong.html).

The primary strategy has been to find a best fit between English and Hmong terms without taking into consideration the fact that meanings may vary widely over a range of possible contexts. Unfortunately, relatively little attention has been paid to the question that originally stimulated the interest of the Hmong Mental Health

Research Group. What can be learned about Hmong perceptions from how they talk about matters that we classify as mental health issues, and how might this knowledge be used to increase cross-cultural understanding?

Widening the Cultural Semantics Resource Base

Using a small grant provided by the University of Minnesota to encourage its faculty to become more engaged in projects that benefit the wider community, the second author (TD) organized the Hmong–English Mental Health Interpreting and Translating Internet Listserv (HEMHIT), and began promoting it as a public forum for comparing Hmong and English lexical resources for talking about *kev noj qab nyob zoo ntawm siab ntsws*, or "emotional/psychological well-being." Professional and lay language experts were invited to discuss their favorite Hmong and English terms for mental states and processes and to suggest ways of translating them in various contexts. The information derived from these discussions, it was explained, would be used to compile the web-accessible *Hmong–English Mental Health Dictionary* (fmdb.cla.umn.edu/hmong_dict/). English was chosen as the primary analytical language, or metalanguage, for the listerv so that persons with mental health expertise could participate even if they knew relatively little or nothing about the Hmong language. Despite the privileged status of English, we believe that data and critical perspectives contributed by bilinguals have prevented serious bias.

Building a Bilingual Mental Health Dictionary

With the help of a Hmong research assistant, we have begun composing entries for the *Hmong–English Mental Health Dictionary*. Basically, we extract crucial data from HEMHIT discussions and then ask listserv members to judge the results of our analyses. The main elements of an entry or dictionary page, which were carried over from another lexicography project, can be seen in the following example:

Emotion, feel negative emotion

Definition: *puas siab puas ntsws*.

Examples: 1. *Yog vim li cas nws ho puas siab puas ntsws?* Why is he/she feeling bad?

2. *Nws siab ntsws puas tag ntev lo lawm.* He/She has been emotional for a long time.

Notes: The English word *emotion* is most often used to refer to strong negative feelings. Hmong speakers use *puas siab puas ntsws*, which is literally "damaged liver damaged lungs," to talk about similar, but not conceptually identical, feelings. The phrase *nplooj siab nplooj ntsws*, "the liver the lungs," can denote good or bad feelings depending upon the context, but it's more likely to be the latter. The phrase can also be understood as referring to qualities of character and temperament, such as *Nws nplooj siab nplooj ntsws zoo li cas?* or "What is he/she like—What kind of a person is he/she?" Other metaphorical meanings are common, such as *Nws nplooj siab nplooj ntsws yog leej twg?* for "Who's his/her sweetheart?" English emotion has culture-specific meanings that cannot be readily interpreted or translated. Thus, using *emotion*, *emotional*, and *emotionally* to explain the meaning of any Hmong expression is a bit misleading. Regarding this point, see Wierzbicka's (1999) book *Emotions across Languages and Cultures: Diversity and Universals.*

    Related concepts: *siab, ntsws*

The entry word or phrase is classified according to its grammatical function. The idea of "experiencing emotion" is most often expressed in Hmong as a verb phrase that denotes a dysphoric state or condition. There any many Hmong terms for positive or good feelings. As is true of many other languages, Hmong has no general label for all the different kinds of affect, euphoric as well as dysphoric, that are technically categorized as emotions in psychological textbooks.

Immediately below the English entry in the dictionary is a short Hmong definition, actually a short gloss, which is back-translated into English. Next comes the example section with two typical sentences containing the Hmong expression *puas siab puas ntsws*. The notes provide additional information about the collocational (word combination) range of *siab ntsws* along with some observations about the nonequivalence of Hmong and English words for affective states. We are not sure whether the heading synonyms will prove useful enough to be retained, but do expect related concepts to come more into play as our understanding of Hmong conceptual organization increases.

Because "depressed" has a particular diagnostic significance in clinical settings, we decided to describe its most apparent and common symptoms in Hmong rather than provide a brief gloss like *nyauj siab*.

Depression
Definition: *Feem ntau Hmoob txhais lo lus Askiv depression ua kev nyuaj siab ntxhov siab.* Typically, Hmong translate the English word *depression* as "difficult, confused liver."

Examples: 1. *Nws muaj kev nyuaj siab ntxhov siab tas mus li*. He has depression all the time, He's depressed all the time.

2. *Ua neeg nyob muaj kev nyuaj siab ntxhov siab tas mus li*. To be human is to have some emotional turmoil all the time.

Notes: The Hmong expression *nyuaj siab ntxhov siab* can refer to feeling states that are negative but not as serious as depression.

related concepts: anxiety, *nyuaj siab*

In everyday Hmong conversation, the lexical label applied to a person's mental distress depends to some extent on its presumed causes. A number of Hmong figurative expressions of the form *modifier + liver/ lungs* have been used to interpret and translate "depressed," such as *nyuaj siab* (literally "difficult liver") and *ntxhov siab* ("confused liver") in the example sentences. These will eventually have their own entries and be distinguished on the basis of what Hmong regard as the usual causes and most typical manifestations of each condition.

The entry for *vwm* demonstrates how Hmong terms are defined, illustrated, and explained in the dictionary.

vwm

Definition: to be crazy, insane

Example: 1. *Tib neeg thwm hais tias ib tus neeg vwm thaum nws ua tsis raug kev raug cai vim nws khoo tsis tau nws tus kheej*. A person is said to be crazy when he violates normal standards of behavior because he can't control himself.

2. *Nws yog tus neeg vwm ua sim tua nws tus kwv*. He's the crazy person who tried to kill his younger brother.

3. *Nws muaj ntsis vwm rau qhov nws nyiam huv heev*. He's kind of crazy because he likes to be so clean.

4. *Nws vwm rau hluas nkauj*. He's crazy over a girl.

Notes: To be called *vwm* is very insulting. A person can become *vwm* from time to time without having an illness. The English term *mental health* is sometimes interpreted/translated as *vwm*. For instance, a mental health treatment facility may be characterized as a place for curing insanity, that is, *tsev kho mob vwm*.

Related concepts: mental health, mental illness

The definition is again back-translated, this time into Hmong, and the example sentences show how *vwm* matches fairly well in certain contexts with different meanings of "crazy."

The pejorative nature of *vwm* is explained in the notes. That Hmong may refer to mental health facilities with a phrase that back-translates as a "place for curing insanity" has obvious implications for promoting health care services in the Hmong community.

Even when an English term appears to have a Hmong equivalent, a comparison of their contextual uses often reveals important differences in meaning. Despite the fact that *quag dab peg* has been glossed in bilingual lexicons as "epilepsy" and as "an epileptic seizure," it more precisely denotes "convulsion" or "loss of physical control." Among the causes of such seizures are brain trauma, intoxication, and assault by a spirit. When talking about "epilepsy" to Hmong, care has to be taken to explain that the term denotes a persistent disease rather than an acute, temporary condition.

The final example taken from our nascent *Hmong–English Mental Health Dictionary* concerns the term *cultural competence*.

Cultural competence

Definition: *kev pab ib haiv neeg raws li lawv kev cai*. Helping a people in ways appropriate to their culture.

Example: *Nws qhia Miskas txog kev pab Hmoob raws li lawv kev cai*. He/She is teaching non-Hmong Americans to help Hmong in ways appropriate to their culture.

Notes: The U.S. Department of Health and Human Services (www.mentalhealth.org) has suggested that the Hmong phrase haum haiv neeg kev cai, ("fits a people's culture"), be used for cultural competence. HEMHIT members have also proposed: (1) haum ib haiv neeg twg kev coj noj coj ua, pertaining to how a particular group sustains itself, (2) kev txawj lis dej num rau lwm haiv neeg, knowing how to work with a people, and (3) paub kev cai dab qhuas, knowing the spiritual traditions.

Gloss 1 contains the phrase *coj noj coj ua*, which would be understood as referring primarily to the manner in which a people support themselves.

Gloss 3 may not be acceptable to some Christian Hmong inasmuch as *dab qhuas* refers specifically to non-Christian beliefs and practices.

Related concepts: culturally competent, *txawj*

The general idea of cultural competence is easily expressed in Hmong. Yet, as the notes indicate, it is unlikely that one Hmong phrase will ever become the conventional lexical symbol for all that "cultural competence" has come to mean and will come to mean. The same applies to other English terms that label semantically unstable conceptual categories within the domain of mental health, including the apex term itself.

Cultural Semantics as an Essential Aspect of Cultural Competence Training

Providers of mental health services must learn a great deal about the viewpoints, wants, and expectations of their clients in order to perform in a culturally competent manner. Acquiring such knowledge involves applying special skills and strategies. In reviewing two inter-linked projects involving the analysis of culture-specific terminologies related to mental states and processes, we have tried to demonstrate that the methodology of cultural semantics is an effective means to building a knowledge base for good communications between mental health providers and clients who are English-language learners. Cultural se-mantics also clarifies why cross-linguistic semantic equivalences aren't always achievable, and it better enables the clinician to work within present conceptual limitations while pushing against them. We are arguing that professionals who work with culturally diverse clienteles need to be formally exposed to this methodology. We are not sug-gesting that they be trained to function expertly as cultural semanticists, but only that they become acquainted with the advantages of compara-tive key term analysis, possibly during a single intensive workshop taken as one small part of their program of professional development.

THE USE OF INTERPRETERS IN MENTAL HEALTH COUNSELING

I had a very bad experience with an interpreter, which makes me very aware of how carefully you have to prepare before working together with a client. The hospital was attempting to provide counseling support to an unmarried Portuguese teen who had just delivered a baby. Since no one on the staff spoke Portuguese, a Portuguese-speaking priest was invited in to serve as an interpreter. I asked the priest to explain to the girl the services that were available to her in the community. The girl burst into tears. I asked the priest why the girl was crying and he said that he felt it was important to begin by reminding the girl that she had committed a mortal sin for which she must ask God's forgiveness. (Murphy & Dillon, 1998, p. 74)

In one widely cited incident, a seven-year old girl was asked to tell her mother what an ultrasound examination had revealed: that the woman's fetus was dead in utero. (Ohmans, 1998, p. 6)

A teenager incorrectly interpreted a Minneapolis physician's directive for x-rays, and told his mother that she was going to be microwaved. (Ohmans, 1998, p. 6)

Beyond understanding cultural semantics, clinicians need to know how to apply them in a clinical situation. Mental health counseling is complicated enough, given the dynamics between two people. Imagine adding a third person: in the cases of couples, family, or group counseling, the presence of additional persons can heighten already present feelings of suspicion and mistrust.

"Just translate word for word," a common instruction to interpreters, is laughable to many experienced users of interpreters who understand the fallacy of that logic, as we have illustrated in the previous section. There is no room here to list the hundreds of other anecdotes of misunderstandings and clinical mistakes that have occurred; some of the more poignant can be found in Fadiman's (1997) book *The Spirit Catches You and You Fall Down: A Hmong Child, Her American Doctors, and the Collision of Two Cultures.* As we have argued earlier in this chapter, the role of interpreters in mental health settings, therefore, clearly goes beyond literal translation of the spoken word. Quality interpretation is critical in assuring a meaningful therapeutic process and a successful outcome.

Clinical Issues in Mental Health Interpreting

Quality interpretation is central to overcoming the language discrimination experienced by refugee and immigrant populations when they try to seek help. Needless to say, in mental health counseling, communication is critical to the therapeutic process. In order for the provider to fully understand the information available about a patient or family, the skill of the interpreter is crucial. The interpreter is therefore essential not only to facilitate verbal communication but, more importantly, to understand what the information means. Practitioners sometimes struggle to convey important information to clients. This problem becomes even more challenging when providers and clients speak different languages and communicate through interpreters.

To date, the bulk of the literature on the use of interpreters in mental health settings focuses on psychiatric (medical) models. In these settings, interpretive challenges arise primarily in the accurate assessment and diagnosis of psychological illness. An interpreter, frequently a relative or child of the client, may lack the training needed to accurately translate medical jargon (Egli, 1987). Likewise, clinicians receive little training on how to effectively work with interpreters (Gong-Guy, Cravens, & Patterson, 1991). This unfortunate combination often results in interpretive distortions that compromise the clinician's ability to accurately assess the client's status. For example, an untrained interpreter may attempt to make sense of a client's incoherent utterances, and the clinician may miss a diagnosis of psychosis. Or, perhaps a clinician may not understand that cultural norms may cause a younger daughter to underreport or misreport her father's psychological symptoms. In either case, the messages conveyed may inaccurately depict the client's mental health status. All this runs contrary to Title VI of the Civil Rights Act of 1964 mentioned at the beginning of this chapter.

Social service organizations around the United States have begun to address these problems by training interpreters to work as paraprofessionals alongside clinicians. These interpreters not only bridge language gaps, but they also act as cultural brokers who explain cultural norms that may affect client–clinician interactions. In many cases, these paraprofessionals are trained to fulfill multiple roles such as counselor, community advocate, caseworker, and interpreter and translator (Egli, 1987). In 1987 and 1988, California sponsored federally funded training conferences for refugee mental health paraprofessionals. Most of the participants stated that it was their first organized training experience in refugee mental health (Gong-Guy et al., 1991).

The research on and successful use of paraprofessionals seems to have prompted the development of clear guidelines for interpreter training. For example, Downing (1992a, 1992b) recommends that interpreters learn the specialized vocabulary and concepts of the mental health field. He also recommends that interpreters' training include cultural "brokering" skills. That is, interpreters should be aware of the potential pitfalls that might arise in a clinic visit and alert the clinician when a cultural gap must be traversed. Pollard (1997) developed a video curriculum to assist interpreters and clinicians alike in learning how to work together to best serve the needs of their mental health clients. This video addresses some of the specific challenges for mental health interpreting. For example, an interpreter should recognize when an assessment tool is culturally inappropriate and communicate this to the clinician. These tools have good face validity but do not fully capture the complexities within the process of interpreting for mental health.

Mental Health Interpreting: What We Know and What We Need to Know

Recent reports and surveys indicate that the demand for paraprofessionals is likely to grow in the new millennium. A report from the Working Group of the Minnesota Interpreter Standards Advisory Committee (Ohmans, 1998) states that the demand for trained interpreters in Minnesota has vastly outgrown the supply. The report also outlines the human and monetary costs of misdiagnosing non-English-speaking clients when a trained interpreter is not present. A survey conducted by the Wilder Research Center in Minnesota (Mattessich & Parry, 2000) reports that nearly 20 percent of the 1,119 people surveyed indicated that they could not speak English at all. The report also asked participants to identify their greatest stressors. Language barriers were identified most often (26 percent of participants) as the greatest source of stress in these immigrants' daily lives.

The literature noted thus far speaks to the urgent need for trained professional interpreters in mental health settings, and many training programs have already been implemented, albeit mostly for medical settings. Researchers have also identified some of the specific psychological concerns that immigrants and refugees are bringing to mental health providers (Holtzman & Bornemann, 1990; Butcher, Egli, Shiota, & Ben-Porath, 1988). This information is critical for improving mental health services for immigrants, but it is not enough.

Research on interpretation in mental health practice is sparse. Aside from ethical standards, codes of conduct, or guidelines on interpretation procedures, there is little information available to guide mental health interpreting. This limitation has important implications for future study.

First, the professional role of the interpreter has been defined in the literature in broad aspects of interpretation, such as the importance of accurate interpretation and confidentiality practices. However, there is little guidance regarding the essential functions of an interpreter. Responsibilities of the interpreter that need further examination and development include, among others, the role of the interpreter in establishing trust, the responsibility of the interpreter to convey meaning about culture-based communications, and intervention methods for identifying miscommunication.

In addition, the necessary training and skills required for competent interpretation in the professional field of mental health have not been adequately addressed. There is no standard for competency in mental health interpretation and no training available that prepares interpreters to understand the complex arena of mental health and psychological practices. Moreover, there are few lists or dictionaries of mental health concepts available in Hmong (which is also true of many high-use languages), other than the works in progress mentioned earlier in this chapter, that could aid interpreters in translating western mental health concepts into the target language. Consequently, variability and inaccuracy are significant in the interpretation and translation of mental health terminology.

Last, the professional relationship between the interpreter and clinician and their joint relationship to their clients needs to be redefined and reinforced to adequately acknowledge the crucial role of the interpreter in mental health interventions and to establish guidelines for practice that are specialized and integrated into mental health treatment. Unfortunately, despite psychology's important contributions to the understanding of the therapeutic process, the field has yet to examine how the addition of an interpreter to the therapeutic setting influences processes and outcomes.

There is a clear lack of research on how interpreters actually affect the mental health counseling process. While much of the literature has addressed issues of interpreting in medical settings, less is said about the mental health counseling process. That is, how does the interpreter influence the client–clinician dynamic that is central to the therapeutic process? How does the presence of an interpreter impact the necessary ingredients of effective mental health counseling, such as building rapport, warmth, empathy, genuineness, positive regard, and other conditions? What if interpreters develop negative emotions or traumatic reactions to clients and clients' stories?

Initial Findings

At the time of writing this chapter, a grant-supported research project is being completed on the use of interpreters in mental health counseling (Goh et al., 2003). The goal of this research is to enhance the understanding of quality systems of care that involve quality interpretation and to influence improving health care practice to immigrant populations by providing a "best practices in mental health" interpretation to benefit interpreters, providers, and clients. We are trying to determine how to help our clients more effectively so that they feel understood, return for services, and benefit from the help provided. In the process, we believe that we are trying to communicate the mental health message in an effective way so as to increase mutual understanding between care providers and clients, thus overcoming language discrimination.

Utilizing a qualitative research methodology, thirty Hmong interpreters participated in ninety-minute structured in-depth interviews that covered such areas as (a) the models, process, and procedures that are used in their interpreting; (b) issues and dynamics in the client-provider-interpreter triad; and (c) issues of training and educating interpreters. Preliminary findings reflect a variety of interpreting models that range from little contact between interpreter and mental health provider to models where interpreters are as empowered as practitioners, participate in case consultations, and play a major role as cultural brokers for clinicians.

There is also great diversity in the amount of training; expectations of interpreters and clinicians about the roles and responsibilities of interpreters; and the need or lack of need for a strong, consistent working relationship with clinicians. Because of the lack of legislation in Minnesota on the need to provide interpreters in mental health counseling for clients who are English-language learners, there also appears to be a concomitant lack of education and training for those who claim proficiency as mental health interpreters.

A detailed presentation of our findings will be forthcoming. In the meantime, the following are recommended guidelines for using mental health interpreters, based on our preliminary findings, according to the various stages of mental health delivery.

Preparation for Clinical Sessions

Establish Goals and Procedures
Establish goals and procedures for the session.
Explain confidentiality/limits, if necessary.
Provide the interpreter with a brief summary of the client.

Establish Roles and Understand Relationships
Consider the interpreter a member of the health care team.
Discuss the client and interpreter's background to learn about the impact of gender, age, social or ethnic issues, and dialects.
Determine how the interpreter's position in or relation to the community may impact interpreter/client relations.

Review Terms and Topics
Explain the purpose of the session.
Discuss technical terms that may be used.
Discuss sensitive topics to be discussed.
Discuss whether the interpreter is likely to feel uncomfortable.
Discuss interpreter "censorship/editing."
Learn some basic words and phrases in the client's language.

Beginning the Session

Discuss Confidentiality
Explain how provider and interpreter keep confidentiality, and explain the limits of confidentiality.

Explain to the client that the interpreter and provider will discuss everything the client says.

Explain that interpreter and provider may take notes to help achieve accuracy; it helps to prepare the interpreter to paraphrase and summarize and allows the provider to understand and clarify.

Establish Speaking Time

Remember to allow extra time, since everything has to be said twice and explanations will generally take longer.

Explain that the interpreter may interrupt dialog talking to allow for accurate interpretation.

Explain that questions may need to be asked.

Remember there may be times when it is important for the client to speak to the interpreter without stopping.

During the Session

Practice Good Communication

Face the client and/or family members and speak directly to him/her/them.

Speak slowly and clearly in a regular tone of voice.

Use simple language and straightforward sentences; avoid metaphors, slang, and jargon.

Use nouns rather than pronouns whenever possible; this way the referent will be clear.

Practice good English communication; some clients may still understand English.

Allow Time for Questions and Clarification

Allow time for the interpreter to talk with the client; this may be necessary if the client needs further clarification to understand what has been said, or if the client does not understand certain western practices or technical terms.

Discuss with the interpreter concerns about client's understanding or interpreter's separate conversation with the client.

Allow time for the interpreter to talk with the provider; this is important for the interpreter to gain clarification about practices and technical terms.

Allow time for the interpreter to explain the culture to the provider when simply interpreting the words is not enough.

Allow Time to Summarize

Ask clients to summarize or repeat information to help determine whether concepts have been properly translated and understood.

Providers and interpreters can summarize issues discussed.

Use the Time during Interpretation

Observe body language and use the interpreter to help you understand nonverbal messages.

Use the time to plan the next response.

Use the time to evaluate what has happened in the session.

After the Session

Allow time with the interpreter after the session to obtain information about nonverbal cues, speech pattern and tone, and cultural information that may be useful to understanding the client/context.

Discuss the interpreter's impression of the client's problems or misunderstandings, and other issues that could not be discussed.

Seek feedback from the interpreter.

SUMMARY OF KEY IMPLICATIONS FOR RESEARCH AND PRACTICE

To overcome language discrimination experienced by mental health clients who are English-language learners, our knowledge of how to cross cultures through language needs to expand. At the present time, we believe that the theory, research, and training around language issues in mental health counseling are insufficient to adequately prepare clinicians for multicultural work requiring second-language competencies. To ignore issues surrounding language barriers to mental health would be considered unethical (Sue, 1998), racist (Ridley, 1995), and "cultural malpractice" (Hall, 1997).

Currently, theories of practice that examine and illustrate methods of practice for clinicians and interpreters are not readily available. Codes of conduct, ethical standards, and styles of communication are some of the guidelines available to clinicians and interpreters that direct behavior and practice. However, these principles and procedures are remote from the theory needed to inform practice and guide clinical intervention. Theories are needed that hypothesize and promote not just access to language but key dimensions important to the quality of access.

For example, the theories needed to advance the role of the mental health interpreter should be related to skills, methods, approaches, and constructs relevant to communication and relationship development within the interpreter–clinician–client triad. These theories need to explore and define the use of interpreters in mental health counseling and postulate various mental health interpreter models—highlighting their processes, strengths and weaknesses, and recommending the best applications.

It has also been suggested here that guidelines about the professional roles and functions of the multicultural clinician and mental health interpreter need to be further investigated to establish criteria for competence and practice. For example, further analysis may continue to establish that one function of the cross-cultural clinician may be that of linguistic analysis that will require the training of specific competencies (such as an introduction to cultural semantics) and other professional development issues (such as learning to work collaboratively with an interpreter in the therapeutic relationship). Furthermore, from our own experience, we see the task of the cross-cultural interpreter to also be that of linguistic innovation, where new uses of words are developed in both English and the target language, and oftentimes require split-second spontaneity and ingenuity. More study into the processes of mental health interpreting will help advance cross-cultural understanding of the processes that ethnic minorities and new immigrants, specifically English-language learners, experience in mental health.

Among the most vulnerable areas of clinical application is that of psychological assessment using standardized assessment instruments to determine cognitive, mental, or affective states. There are inventories in use that have been translated or are used with verbal interpretation. While these instruments may be some of the tools available for assessment conducted cross-culturally, many that have been translated have not been validated through research for use in cross-cultural psychological interpretation. The Beck Depression Inventory is one such instrument that has been used but largely unstudied in its application to diverse ethnic populations. The Beck Depression Inventory (BDI) has been used with the Hmong population, but lack of validating research raises serious questions about its utility. First, the translation of the inventory is still in debate among bilingual mental health professionals, which is in itself problematic. The question of face validity is certainly relevant, since clinically it could be demonstrated that alternative symptoms of depression may be more relevant to measure within the Hmong

Toolbox for Change

For	Images/perceptions	Strategies for change
Individuals	That English language learners are somehow incompetent.	Try learning to speak a second language. Language acquisition, especially for adults, requires tremendous skill and commitment. Individuals who cross cultures not only have to overcome language barriers but also adjust socially, culturally, physically, politically, and psychologically. When operating in their native tongues, these individuals are highly competent.
Community	That individuals and families who do not speak English should learn to speak English. That English language learners are not entitled to share in community resources.	No one chooses to experience language discrimination. It is often a consequence of circumstance. The priority of learning to speak English competes with other demands of finding shelter, social support, familial ties, and financial security. It is exactly community resources and support that they need to help them take the steps needed to overcome language discrimination.
Practitioners/educators	That clients need to speak English in order for proper mental health services to be rendered.	To discriminate against and withhold services for anyone based on any personal characteristic, in this case language, is clearly unethical and against the law. In many states it is required by federal law that interpretive services be provided for clients who are English-language learners.

That the responsibility for overcoming language discrimination is the sole responsibility of the client.

That the responsibility for overcoming language discrimination is the responsibility of the interpreter.

That all interpreters can be mental health interpreters.

That the delivery of mental health services to clients who are English language learners is the job of bilingual therapists.

Clinicians are in the best position, because of their understanding of the therapeutic relationship, to effect positive action in overcoming language discrimination. Clinicians need to obtain some understanding of cultural semantics, the use of mental health interpreters, and health/mental health practices of the target culture. While interpreters can play a critical role in eliminating language discrimination, it is the clinician's job to brief interpreters about expectations, roles, and responsibilities during the session. If you are committed to working with this population for the long term, it would be helpful to learn some key phrases in your client's language. The training interpreters receive is not consistent across disciplines and around the country. Mental health interpreting requires specific skills that pay attention to linguistic, cultural, as well as process cues. Bilingual therapists are not necessarily trained to be interpreters and may consider their strength to be in their clinical skills rather than their language skills. Until educational programs around the country see a surge in the recruitment and training of bilingual therapists, such a goal continues to be far from reality.

population (such as somatic expressions). In addition, of course, the empirical evidence available for the BDI has been established largely with English-speaking white individuals. For instruments like the BDI to be confidently used with other ethnic populations, the best translation or even a new development of inventory items needs to be established.

Further research also needs to be conducted to increase our understanding and integration of alternative healing concepts and practices. Through an increased understanding of traditional approaches to healing, mental health clinicians gain important insight into help-seeking behaviors, problem identification, treatment expectations, and methods of care important for working with other ethnic populations. This knowledge may help identify correlates to care that can be useful to augmenting western mental health care. It can also help identify important distinctions that will help clinicians to bridge care. Through exploration, practice methods that promote collaboration between traditional and western healers can also be defined. Alliances with indigenous healers and helpers can be established. In this way, helpers can work cooperatively to complement care provided to Hmong families, identify problems more effectively, and determine the need for referral to other healers more efficiently.

In addition to theory and research, components of practice need to be established. First, education and training for clinicians and interpreters are essential. The field of interpretation will need to continue to establish its authority in a variety of disciplines and professional positions that involve interpretation. Interpreters and educators will need to appreciate that interpretation of mental health concepts is a challenging task, and that bridging concepts in mental health is an additional layer of complexity in translation that requires additional knowledge and training. Clinicians will need to acquire complementary skills that facilitate the interpretation of mental health concepts. Clinicians will also need to study, learn, and practice the special set of skills required to establish effective working partnerships with interpreters and to apply the necessary interventions at all stages of treatment as in any other treatment modalities (family therapy, group therapy, therapy with children, etc.).

The guidelines and qualifications of multicultural clinicians and mental health interpreters with regard to overcoming language discrimination in mental health will need to be established for the field to advance and for quality of care to continue improving. Interpreters and clinicians, together and through their independent professions, need to establish standards of practice to benefit their clients. They will need to join forces to address the challenges of this work in order to establish relevant terminology, develop interview protocols, and enforce preferred models of interpretation, among other guidelines.

Part of the task of developing appropriate standards of care will likely require advocating the development of policy that will benefit our clients. Sorting out meaning across cultures is laborious and costly, as it increases the amount of time a clinician spends developing accuracy in communication. New systems will need to be determined and implemented in order to adequately compensate all professionals involved in client care and for the same scope of care provided to English-speaking clients. Systems and providers will need to be held accountable for overcoming language discrimination. In turn, clinicians will need to contribute to the resolution of these and similar problems.

There are many challenges that confront the clinician when treating clients who are English-language learners and have little experience with American culture. How effectively professional mental health expertise is integrated with a target language and culture is the important task of this clinical encounter. Success creates the understanding and empathy so important for human relationships and good clinical work. Quality care and competent care standards for English language learners will need to contain some criteria that address the importance of language that leads to effective communication. Standards will also need to assert the value of the alliance between clinician and interpreter in achieving this end. These standards for language access will be the only way new Americans will be able to overcome language discrimination. In this way, new Americans will have an equal opportunity to experience the same levels and quality of mental health care as everyone else.

REFERENCES

Butcher, J. N., Egli, E. A., Shiota, N. K., & Ben-Porath, Y. S. (1988). *Psychological interventions with refugees.* Minneapolis, MN: University of Minnesota.

Downing, B. T. (1992a). *Professional interpretation: Insuring access for refugee and immigrant patients.* Minneapolis, MN: University of Minnesota.

Downing, B. T. (1992b). The use of bilingual/bicultural workers as providers and interpreters. *International Migration, 30.*

Egli, E. A. (1987). *The role of bilingual workers without professional mental health training in mental health services for refugees.* Minneapolis, MN: University of Minnesota.

Fadiman, A. (1997). *The spirit catches you and you fall down: A Hmong child, her American doctors, and the collision of two cultures.* New York: Noonday Press.

Goh, M., McGraw-Schuchman, K., & Yang, P. (2003, January). *The use of interpreters in mental health counseling: Issues and guidelines for best practice.* Paper presented at the American Psychological Association National Multicultural Conference and Summit, Hollywood, CA.

Gong-Guy, E., Cravens, R. B., & Patterson, T. E. (1991). Clinical issues in mental health service delivery to refugees. *American Psychologist,* 46(6), 642–648.

Hall, C. C. I. (1997). Cultural malpractice: The growing obsolescence of psychology. *American Psychologist, 52*(6), 642–651.

Holtzman, W. H., & Bornemann, T. H. (Eds.). (1990). *Mental health of immigrants and refugees.* Proceedings of a conference sponsored by Hogg Foundation for Mental Health and World Federation for Mental Health. Austin, TX: University of Texas.

Mattessich, P., & Parry, K. (2000). *Speaking for themselves: A survey of Hispanic, Hmong, Russian, and Somali immigrants in Minneapolis-St. Paul.* St. Paul, MN: Wilder Research Center.

The Minneapolis Foundation. (1999, Fall). *Minnesota, nice or not?* Minneapolis, MN: Author.

Murphy, B.C., & Dillon, C. (1998). *Interviewing in action: Process and practice.* Pacific Grove, CA: Brooks/Cole.

Ohmans, P. (Ed.). (1998). *Bridging the gap: How to meet the need for interpreters in Minnesota.* St. Paul, MN: Working Group of the Minnesota Interpreter Standards Advisory Committee.

Pollard, R. Q. (1997). *Mental health interpreting: A mentored curriculum* [Videotape]. Rochester, NY: University of Rochester.

Ridley, C. R. (1995). *Overcoming unintentional racism in counseling and therapy: A practitioner's guide to intentional intervention.* Thousand Oaks, CA: SAGE Publications, Inc.

Sue, S. (1998). In search of cultural competence in psychotherapy and counseling. *American Psychologist, 53*(4), 440–448.

U.S. Department of Health and Human Services. (2001). *Mental health: Culture, race, and ethnicity—A supplement to mental health: A report of the surgeon general.* Rockville, MD: U.S. Department of Health and Human Services.

Wierzbicka, A. (1999). *Emotions across languages and cultures: Diversity and universals.* Cambridge, MA: Cambridge University Press.

CHAPTER 6

A Quest for Identity: Racism and Acculturation among Immigrant Families

Sandra Mattar

"Mom . . . what am I?" This simple question from my twelve-year-old daughter was enough to raise my anxiety as a parent. She had asked me this question before, but this time the question was delivered with a punch, a cry for self-definition, very much consistent with her entrance into the adolescent world. Her question came with a distressed tone—an indication of an active struggle to attain psychological adjustment and a mental and physical well-being.

I immediately knew that she was asking me about race. She wanted a category. She explained that she needed an answer for her friends at school: "They keep asking me, and I don't know what to tell them." I thought that being the only nonwhite in her class at a private school, a straight-A student with a Spanish name, both her South American parents holding graduate degrees, and with an upper-middle-class background, she did not fit the mainstream stereotype of a "Latina." Therefore she confused her friends who wanted an answer. I thought, *Welcome to the world of stereotypes, of prejudice and discrimination.*

"Well," I answered calmly, trying not to dwell on my feelings as "the other," a feeling I had faced since becoming an immigrant in the United States, "I don't have an easy answer. Let's see: Your maternal grandparents are from Lebanon, and your paternal grandparents are from Portugal. Your dad and I were born in South America (Venezuela), and you were born in Boston, Massachusetts." My answer must have been too complicated because she said, "I'll tell them I am from Boston." Yes, probably this is less complicated, as is the fact that her classmates have changed her name from Maria to "Mia" because, I suspect, it sounds "less ethnic." This answer is not only less "complicated," but is an example of a decontextualization that is typical in countries where the "self-made" individual represents an image to strive for. In this sense, there are seldom references of "place" and of the influence of the intergenerational transmission of culture, context, and history (P. Hull, personal communication, 2003).

AMERICA: WHITE OR BROWN?

At a time when the "browning" (Rodriguez, 2002) of America from an increasing Latino and Asian immigration seems an imminent possibility, questions such as "What am I?" are gaining salience among mental health workers across the nation. According to Schmidley (2001), in the year 2000 the number of immigrants and first-generation children in this country reached an unprecedented 56 million, or one-fifth of the entire U.S. population. The U.S. Bureau of the Census in 2000 revealed important demographic changes: "The Asian American/ Pacific Islander population increased by almost 50 percent, the Latino/ Hispanic population by over 58 percent, African Americans by 16 percent, and American Indians/Alaska Natives by 15.5 percent, in marked contrast to the 7.3 percent increase of whites" (U.S. Bureau of the Census 2000, in Sue & Sue, 2003).

Trimble (2003) speaks of the need to pay attention to the personality changes produced by social change and acculturation in a century where acculturation due to global mobility is so pervasive. Sue and Sue (2003) also talk about living with a "clash of worldviews, values and lifestyles" and the potential conflictive implications. Cuellar (2000) also warns of the importance of better understanding the mental health consequences of the acculturation process.

Reaction of some form is not an uncommon response to culture contact. On some extreme positions, people become violent and attempt to extinguish or exterminate cultural symptoms or beliefs of others, including the people who support those systems. These reactions occur when people are threatened by some cultural feature of others. As the United States become increasingly more multicultural or culturally diverse, does this increase risk for psychological conflicts due to acculturation processes and forces (p. 48)?

TENSION BETWEEN CLINGING TO THE PAST AND BELONGING

The question "Who am I?" is not uncommon among adolescents, especially children of immigrants. This question was a dreaded one for me growing up, and one that still echoes in my mind. As a daughter of Lebanese immigrant parents in Venezuela, who I was remained elusive to me. At school, I could not fully identify with my peers, nor see myself portrayed in Venezuelan history lessons. At home, the use of the Arabic language, which sounded impossibly guttural to me, made talking in Spanish a preferable option. Maybe a need to belong among my peers also made it more attractive to me.

My daughter's question brought back to me, in the words of Falicov (1998), "the issue of belongingness, the agony of whether I should return to my roots or stay close to the new life created in my adoptive country." Returning to one's roots is an automatic reaction that works as a defense mechanism in times of anxiety. Immigrant parents tend to cling to their old ways in times of uncertainty. In fact, raising children in a country different from one's native country thrusts one into an unknown world where there are no solid personality anchors. In other words, a lasting sense of security and confidence may be difficult to maintain when there is little understanding of social outcomes that are expected. Many of the things that parents from the mainstream U.S. culture were able to take for granted, I had to learn and relearn. During this process, my children were forced to pay for my cultural inexperience.

ACCULTURATIVE STRESS AND CULTURE SHOCK

> Thou shalt leave everything beloved most dearly; and this is the shaft which the bow of Exile first lets fly. Thou shalt prove how salt the taste is of another's bread, and how hard a path it is to go down and up another's stair. (Dante, *Paradiso, The Divine Comedy*)

My experiences of distress have been referred to in the mental health literature as "acculturative stress" (Berry & Kim, 1988), which involves "a personal crisis . . . (where) the old social order and cultural norms often disappear, and individuals may be lost in the change . . . hostility, uncertainty, identity confusion and depression may set in" (p. 246). The term *culture shock* has also been coined to describe the consequences of an uprooting experience, or "the uprooting of established ways of thinking and doing, and the massive, abrupt exposure to a new language and new way of life (which) precipitates psychological distress" (Falicov, 1998, p. 55).

There are several factors that moderate the relationship between acculturation and stress. Among these are the nature of the larger society (the ethnic diversity, cultural pluralism and social/cultural supports, exclusion practices, among others), the type of acculturating group (third world versus first world immigrant), modes of acculturation (marginalization, separation, or integration from/to the host society), demographics and social characteristics of the individual, and the psychological characteristics of the individual (Berry, 1990).

EXPERIENCES OF DISCRIMINATION AND ETHNIC IDENTITY

My daughter's question also brought up my first encounter with racism in this country, an experience I had never confronted before in Venezuela. In Venezuela, racial discrimination is much more subtle than in the United States, where "race is an elusive, perplexing, troubling and enduring aspect of life" (Carter, 1995). Indeed, unlike in Venezuela, in the United States there is a history of slavery that still permeates every aspect of American life; as well as tremendous human diversity, perhaps unlike any other country in the world. The way the history of relations between minorities and mainstream culture plays out in the United States is also very different. The prevalent notion in the United States is that diversity equals race, not that diversity equals culture. Culture and race are considered one and the same.

SOCIETAL PRESSURES AND THE NEGOTIATION OF NEW IDENTITIES

My first experiences with discrimination were very painful. I was caught off guard in a world of social nuances based on race and hate. I lacked the intellectual and emotional arsenal that would have helped to cope with the humiliation. I learned that some of these skills were taught to children belonging to certain groups in the United States even before they started walking. As an upper-middle-class woman growing up in Venezuela, where the development of an ethnic identity was a nonissue (it was taken for granted), I did not have to negotiate my identity. I belonged to the group in power, and therefore there was no need to articulate who I was. Just like in the United States, "ethnic" conversations are only for "the other."

It was not until coming to the United States that I was consciously impacted by the issue of ethnic identity. I struggled to find a category that would include my Venezuelan and Lebanese heritages. It was my Spanish accent that finally determined who I was, as my physical traits were confusing to many. People could not place me into one racial category. Many times I passed as white as long as I did not open my mouth. Root (1992, 1996, in Sue & Sue, 2003) indicates that this dilemma is typical of multiracial children who are constantly confronted with ambiguous reactions from people who cannot place them inside a clear racial category. The pressure to choose a race can result in "invalidation, conflicting feeling of loyalties to the racial/ethnic identities of parents, internal trauma, and confused identity development" (Sue & Sue, 2003, p. 368).

In my case, society eventually categorized me as a Latina, not a Venezuelan-Lebanese. The label *Latina* was an ethnic category imposed from the outside. It was not a category that I built on my own. I resented this imposition because it discounted the totality of who I was. My background had been reduced to an accent, and it came with numerous stereotypes. Eventually, I adopted this identity because doing so was easier than not doing so. I did not have to explain myself anymore. In a way, I thought, "If people want a category, I will give them just that." I also fell prey to group pressure. Coming from Venezuela made me an official "Latina," no doubt. The process of representing myself as a Latina is the result of a reaction against an imposed ethnic identity, a representation created by social pressures to conform to prescribed labels, and one that is closely connected to a process of stereotyping and discrimination. It is also equally connected to my previous privileged history in Venezuela, where people like me were not part of "the other" group.

CHOOSING BETWEEN "NATIONALITY" AND "ETHNIC IDENTITY"

The process of "choosing" or embracing ethnic labels, I learned later, is common among immigrants who come from countries where nationality, rather than race, is emphasized as a major identity descriptor. Upon arrival in the United States, immigrants become "the other," which is the first blow to their identity. From being "one like the rest," the immigrant becomes "one unlike us." This is, no doubt, a narcissistic injury of major proportions. However, this process is less shocking when immigrants move into neighborhoods in the new country that are microcosms of their countries of origin. For these immigrants, being among countrypeople buffers them from the reality of being different and the treatment that comes with it. For those of us who may not fit the mainstream culture's somewhat simplistic definition of ethnic identity, our identity seems to be more imposed from without than willfully adopted from within. This is the dilemma of the multi-ethnic immigrant such as myself, and of many Latin Americans who, upon becoming immigrants in the United States, learn that they are not white but rather "people of color." Eventually, they also learn the disparaging societal treatment that comes with that label.

SOURCES OF CONFLICT AND AMBIGUITY

For the immigrant, defining ethnic/racial identity is part of a developmental process that is closely tied to acculturation (Phinney, 2003). The process of defining ethnic identity becomes an active negotiation with the environment, and as Berry (1990) indicated, it is mediated by many forces. As I try to define myself in a new world, there are several questions that I struggle to answer in my varied roles as a cross-cultural psychologist, teacher, immigrant parent, and woman:

> How do immigrant children who do not fit a clear-cut stereotype of their immigrant group fare in life?
>
> Who defines self-identity, race, and culture, thereby silencing other discourses and narratives?
>
> What might be the price children pay for growing up in a world of rigid and stereotyped racial/ethnic categories?
>
> How might children of immigrant parents establish a coherent sense of self while often living out their lives between two distinct worlds, and what additional developmental tasks might children of immigrant parents need to navigate?
>
> How might immigrant parents negotiate their own personal identities while facing the challenges of raising children in a country different from their own?
>
> How might immigrant parents support the development of their children's ethnic and cultural identities?
>
> How might the parents avoid alienating their children's desire to belong to the country in which they live, whether it is rightfully theirs by birth, or by adoption?

How can parents promote their children's attachment to their new country?

What might be the price in mental health that both immigrant parents and their children are forced to pay in order to flourish in the new country?

Would a healthy outcome be the same between immigrant parents on the one hand, and their children on the other?

Additionally, related questions emerge about the acculturating process of white-appearing immigrant children compared to immigrant children who do not "pass" as white. Do they "acculturate" faster because they look white? In other words, how do race and social class affect the course of children's ethnic identity development, and their successful adaptation to mainstream society?

DEVELOPMENTAL TASKS FACING IMMIGRANT CHILDREN

> Cultural identities are not solely determined in response to racial ideologies, but racism increases the need for a positive self-defined identity in order to survive psychologically. (Tatum, 1997)

This chapter focuses on immigrant individuals as well as individuals who are in intercultural relationships. However, the literature on black racial/ethnic identity (Helms, 1990) development proves very helpful in illuminating the struggles faced by both immigrant children and their parents. After all, black children have to grow up in a country that still, in the twenty-first century, remains segregated in many more ways than one, thereby creating two separate cultures.

Also, like many Native American children, immigrant children often have to deal with issues of competing national loyalties, expressed both in language and country allegiances, racism and discrimination, and a redefinition of skin color and social class, among others.

Studies on biracial children help us understand the developmental tasks faced by immigrant children. Like the latter, the former group faces mixed and ambivalent reactions from mainstream populations, not much different from my daughter's classmate's question "What are you?" Biracial/bicultural children also struggle with "imposed" identities or "the pressure to choose sides," which are a product of the American history of racial categorization (Tatum, 1997). The 2000 U.S. Census provided more choices around racial categories. However, it stills falls short in capturing the multidimensionality of several immigrant groups in the United States, such as Latinos and Asians.

IMMIGRANT ADOLESCENTS AND THE MULTICULTUAL EXPERIENCE: WHAT DOES IT MEAN TO BE AMERICAN?

Through their development, children of immigrants face issues similar to those faced by the aforementioned groups. These issues become more salient during adolescence, when they are already struggling with an ever more confusing world, as they try to sort out their bicultural or even tricultural experience. Adolescence also gives them the cognitive tools to understand the nuances of racist treatment and discrimination, and the notions of injustice and unfairness. Many immigrant children learn, for the first time, that there are different rules for them simply because of their foreign backgrounds. They also struggle to integrate different lifestyles into their lives, and their understanding of who they are.

Unlike the majority of her white peers, my daughter is going through adolescence with an extra developmental task. Managing this task can deeply affect her self-esteem and her need to belong to a community that she can trust. This is the task of understanding that she is not like the rest of the group, and that her parents are different, as well. She needs to negotiate how "American" she is. She also needs to learn to deal with the culture shock she experiences in her travels between school and home, which, in essence, sometimes becomes an international trip. My daughter constantly reminds me that "we are in America, not in Venezuela," a statement that reflects her need to define herself in "American" terms, as well as to test my limits of what is acceptable! As far as she is concerned, I can toss out every learned rule on childrearing because "the rules are different here." Alluding to a similar experience, Suarez-Orozco and Suarez-Orozco (1995) state that immigrant children "typically do not share their parent's dual frame of reference. They cannot frame their current experiences in terms of the old country ideals, standards and expectations" (p. 326).

DEVELOPMENTAL PSYCHOLOGICAL THEORIES AND IMMIGRANT CHILDREN

According to Hardy and Laszloffy's (2000) review of major psychological developmental theories, the majority of the theories fail to address the experiences of children and families of color. From Freud to Erikson, Piaget, and Kohlberg, to name a few, they have all failed to address issues of race and ethnicity. In this sense, Hardy and Laszloffy (2000) indicate, "Because of the specific challenges created by living in (such) oppressive contexts, children and families of color must negotiate several unique tasks in addition to those that are specified in traditional developmental theories" (p. 109). Among these unique tasks are the following:

- **Living with racism and the development of coping mechanisms**: Hardy and Laszloffy indicate that children have to "negotiat(e) the dilemmas of silence and of speaking" in the face of racism and injustices. Here, I am reminded of the time when I was completing one of the requirements for my doctoral clinical training at an all-white, upper-middle-class elementary school in the Boston suburbs. In this place, I was the target of the most humiliating and disparaging treatment I had ever received. My supervisor, a black woman, encouraged me to take a stand against this treatment. When I told her I did not know how to deal with such racism, I learned something interesting, and maybe matter of fact for people used to living with discrimination. I learned from her that black mothers typically taught their children how to manage racism as soon as they learned how to talk. This coping mechanism is a way of surviving growing up in an oppressive environment (J. Turner, personal communication, 2003). As an immigrant who was not used to discrimination, the notion of using my own voice when I had been silenced was new and uncharted territory for me. It was also a territory that caused me severe distress.

- **Living with rage**: The second task that children of color need to master, according to Hardy and Laszloffy (2000), is "negotiating the dilemma of rage," or how to express the suppressed negative emotions that result from society's constant mistreatment of such children.

- **Internalized oppression**: A third task is "negotiating the dilemma of self-hate," which refers to the phenomena of internalized oppression, and adopting the language and behaviors of the oppressor.

FURTHER DEVELOPMENTAL TASKS

What Language Should I Speak?

Just like black children, immigrant children of color also seem to struggle with the aforementioned tasks. However, as Zavala (in Tatum, 1997) indicates, the choice of what language to speak also forms an integral part of these children's identity formation and constitutes an extra developmental task to negotiate. It is no surprise to me that along with my daughter's quest for discovering "who" she might be, she expressed a desire for reinforcing her Spanish language skills. There are several possible explanations why she expressed this desire. One can speculate that she likes to "show off" her Spanish language skills because being bilingual is fashionable in some middle-class circles. Another possibility is that she wants to reaffirm her connection with her parents' native country in order to understand who she really is. A third possibility might have to do with her newly developed awareness of discrimination. She might be, according to Phinney (1989), in the period of exploration, "where young people typically learn the history of their group and become more aware of discrimination, a process that may lead to a deeper commitment to their ethnicity" (p. 77).

The choice of language has tremendous implications for personality development. In this sense, Espin (1997) indicates,

> Language and speech do not occur in a vacuum. In the United States, the dominant society ascribes inferior social status to Black English and to bilingualism. The differential valuing of languages and accents has a profound impact on the development of self-concept and identity. When bilingual skills are devalued, also devalued are those parts of the self that have developed in the context of another language. (p. 76)

Language Use and Acculturation Level

Espin further suggests that ethnic language use is another indicator of acculturation level and is related to ethnic identity. However, she does not view it as a necessary predictor of the latter. According to Marsella and Yamada (2000), the notion of ethnocultural identity is a good indicator of the variation that exists within ethnic groups. Ethnocultural identity is the "extent to which an individual endorses and manifests the cultural traditions and practices of a particular group . . . the extent to which (he/she) is identified with and practice(s) the lifestyle of that group" (p. 13). I believe that this concept is more accurate than the concept of acculturation to describe the extent to which an individual subscribes to a particular culture.

Stereotypes and Self-Identity, Self-Esteem, and Internalized Racism

Another task closely connected to the immigrant children's well-being and quality of life is how to deal with a world that stereotypes immigrants as "less than" and supports myths that portray particular groups very negatively. My daughter has already asked me questions such as, "Why are all Latinos poor?" I can hardly control myself when I hear questions like this, but I am also aware that she is being raised in an upper-middle-class, mainly white community. The way she has internalized society's negative messages about Latinos is appalling and frightening. Also, she appears at times not to be connected with the group identified as Latinos. In the meantime, she struggles at school because, while she loves to "show off" her Spanish-language skills, she does so in an environment that tells her "you are not like them." There is no doubt that she is internalizing the latter message. But I cannot forget that both my husband and I are parts of the equation in this racial/ethnic internalization game. How can you teach your children to be proud of their ethnicity when the message in the community around you is "you either assimilate or else you don't belong." There is no possibility of embracing one's culture unless mainstream society confronts its own fears around difference and is willing to embrace "the other" as he/she is. Phinney (2003) states that, "Perhaps the most fundamental aspect of ethnic identity is its strength and valence, or how positively individuals feel about their group membership." In this sense, immigrants have a better chance at mental health when they feel proud of who they are as a group. However, the degree of pride that any immigrant group may be able to achieve is, in many ways, limited by the amount of pride allowed by the new culture. Speaking of this positive self-identification among immigrant groups, Falicov (2002) indicates,

> Striving for the dream of stability in a new land is riddled with pressures to subscribe to the dominant culture's story, which negatively judges dark-skinned, poor immigrants. . . . The social climate of structural exclusion and psychological violence suffered by immigrants and their children is not only detrimental to their participation in the opportunity structure but it also affects the immigrant children's sense of self, through a process of what Carola Suarez-Orozco (2000) aptly calls "social mirroring." (p. 281)

Falicov's statement makes me think of the host culture's reaction to personal identity's threats. What is the mainstream reaction when immigrant groups try to assert themselves and show pride in who they are? As with the black experience, social reactions by the dominant culture tend to be toward silencing those voices.

ACCULTURATION AND RACISM

Marginalization and the Search for Ethnic Identity

Experiences of discrimination determine, at some level, the immigrant's motivation to undertake further exploration of his/her ethnic identity. Rumbaut (1994, in Phinney, 2003) found an inverse connection between the adolescent's experiences of discrimination and his/her self-identification as American. In other words, the more you are the target of discrimination in the United States, the less American you will feel. This process represents an irony in that the dominant group's reaction against the immigrant's self-definition results in a strengthening of these groups' ethnic identities.

Cultural Allegiance

Along with the task of choosing what language to speak, which is a task faced by both immigrant parents and children, there is also the "cultural allegiance" dilemma, or the "identity as a member of the larger society" (Phinney, 2003). This task refers to a child's sense of cultural identification with a country, a flag, history, and cultural traditions: it is also known as patriotism. For an immigrant parent, this is a very challenging and heated issue. The family's dilemma of "choice of country," or which country they adopt, is not an isolated choice. There are numerous factors that determine this choice, such as the family's racial and socioeconomic background, degrees of technological development similarities between one's former and adoptive country, the degree of segregation in the community lived in, level of education, work and visa-status issues, and the ways in which parents encourage a particular identification, among others.

Acculturation Conflicts

Along the same lines, Sue and Sue (2003) indicate that many minority ethnic groups are confronted with a society that has a very different set of values. The resolution of this conflict takes several routes: some individuals maintain their native cultures, while others assimilate and exchange their values for those of the host culture. A third group of people become bicultural and "fare much better because of an ability to accept and negotiate aspects of both cultures" (p. 352).

Situational Acculturation

Trimble (2003) describes a phenomenon called "situational accul-turation," whereby the outcomes of an individual's acculturation process are a unique combination and interaction of variables.

The situation and the corresponding demands of the *dominant or contributing* culture may contribute considerably more to people's choice of behavioral repertoires than the general acculturating expectations that they have learned (Trimble, 2003, p. 10).

Racism and discrimination "have profound effects on individuals' level of acculturation, their concurrent acculturative stress, and the level of personal identification with the culture of origin and the dominating or contributing culture" (p. 9).

The most recent trends around ethnic identity models suggest that the development of ethnic identity is context-sensitive. Kim-Ju and Liem (2003) found correlations between ethnic self-awareness and ethnic group status, group composition, and ethnic identity orientation. In other words, the social context influences ethnic self-awareness. For example, factors of social class and occupation can interact with the individual's age and gender, as well as with the given social setting (racial makeup) in which that person is immersed.

Overall, there is an assumption in the literature on acculturation that becoming "acculturated" is a goal, rather than a process that is very much determined by the particular combination of individual and contextual variables.

The Interaction between Acculturation and Ethnic Identity

Phinney (2003) emphasizes a multidimensional understanding of ethnic identity in relation to acculturation, stressing the inadequacy of linear models to understand how, for example, immigrants and their children develop an ethnic identity vis-à-vis the majority. Phinney stresses that ethnic identity varies along several dimensions: over time or across generations, in different contexts, and with age or development. The notion of "true assimilation" may be an anathema (Trimble, 2003). Along similar lines, Suarez-Orozco and Suarez-Orozco (1995) stress that

> [m]igration is an open-ended process that differentially affects the experiences of various generations, the U.S.-born second generation, the third generation, etc. Hence, we are critical of theories of immigrant assimilation and acculturation that tend to offer premature closure (e.g.,

"by the second generation group X was fully assimilated") to what is, in our estimation, an intergenerational dynamic process. (p. 324)

MUTUALITY VERSUS POWER: IMPLICATIONS FOR ETHNIC IDENTITY

While Phinney (2003) acknowledges a close connection between ethnic identity and the experience of discrimination, she does not address how mainstream America's willingness to engage in conversations of ethnic identity, race, and discrimination could affect how people of color define themselves. In my personal experience, these conversations almost never happen. This should be a bilateral process: that which is defined cannot escape the influence of who the definer is. In other words, the dominant group's urge to define "the other" needs to include a discussion of who the dominant group is. In this sense, object and subject are intrinsically connected. Benjamin (1988) has spoken of the mutuality that needs to exist between self and other:

> A condition of our own independent existence is recognizing the other. True independence means sustaining the essential tension of these contradictory impulses; that is, both asserting the self and recognizing the other. Domination is the consequence of refusing this condition. (p. 53)

Indeed, asserting the self and recognizing the other is the only way to a harmonious coexistence in our society. However, as Benjamin suggests, this process cannot take place in an environment where domination of self over the other exists. This is part of the cycle of oppression that keeps people from developing a healthy sense of self.

Promoting a Positive Racial/Ethnic Identity

One of the major challenges that I have confronted as an immigrant parent of three children is how to teach them to keep a dignified sense of themselves as minorities in this country without "contaminating" them with my own negative encounters with racism. But nothing in my life prepared me for the painful experiences of witnessing the disparaging treatment of my own children.

Upon having my first child, I decided, like many parents do, that she had to know that she had the exact rights every child in America had. This was the way I grew up—no doubt a privileged view of the world. I wanted her to experience how being in the majority felt. I was, in Parham's model of racial identity, in the pre-encounter phase, which is characterized by a lack of racial awareness. It was when my daughter reached preschool that I realized that my efforts at ignoring my children's ethnicity were senseless. She came home at four years old and told me that she was "brown and different." This was not an insight that she had come upon on her own. Her teacher had used her and two others in the classroom as examples of how people are different. I suspect that this was the result of the additive teaching and training model of the 1990s, still practiced today, where people "celebrate the differences" in skin color, giving a lip service to diversity. My daughter seemed genuinely concerned that she was unlike the majority of her peers. She had not noticed that her skin was brown until that moment. Probably none of the other children had noticed, for that matter.

Is it Validation or Invalidation?

What was presumably intended as a celebration of human diversity by the preschool teacher became an experience of domination. The assumption behind the teacher's comment was that "this is how the other" looks. I was infuriated with the teacher for making my daughter stand out in the group and making her feel different. Of course, this was very naive on my part, a result of not having those experiences growing up. As I became more acculturated, and through my children's experiences, I realized that even in the first years of elementary school, children start to sort themselves out on their own, culminating in a clear segregation once they reach high school and start dating (Tatum, 1997). Interestingly enough, this phenomenon occurs in many Latin American countries, but around class. It is not surprising then that in Latin American countries there are so many upheavals around economic inequality, which is a clear form of discrimination.

Had I brought up the incident of the skin color with the school, it would have fallen on deaf ears. This was a mainly white school, and we were clearly in the minority. Both my husband and I spent several sleepless nights pondering the dilemma of what to do with our children's education. We decided to live in our current neighborhood because of the quality of the public schools. Unfortunately, living in a very diverse city would mean significantly lowering the education level of our children. In a way, we were pioneers in our city. My children were just a handful of nondominant children in their schools.

"Don't Be So Sensitive"

How much one chooses to share, and the support one gets, are mediated by contextual variables. I could not share with my white friends, for fear of being misunderstood. They would also have had a hard time relating to my story. My relatives in South America were not a support either because they have never experienced what it means to be a "minority." The only support I found was at work, where I interacted with colleagues who were not only people of color, but also had the same interest in diversity I had.

It is clear that the way we dealt with racism and discrimination with our children very much paralleled our own racial identity development and acculturation process as immigrants.

PSYCHOLOGICAL ADAPTATION AMONG IMMIGRANT PARENTS AND THEIR CHILDREN: SOME SUGGESTIONS

As I start writing this section, I am aware of the inherent biases that I bring as an immigrant with a mixed ethnic background, and with my particular demographics. I will try to stay away from universal claims. What I present next reflects not only my clinical observations and readings on the subject of protective factors that help individuals cope with race and discrimination, but also my own experience as an immigrant woman.

Tatum (1997) indicates that some of the factors associated with a positive psychological adjustment in multiracial families are variables such as "higher socioeconomic level, attending integrated schools, living in multiracial neighborhoods, having a multicultural social life, enjoying open, warm relationships with parents . . . it also helps to have positive race-consciousness that includes a willingness to talk to children openly about issues related to identity" (p. 175).

There are strategies prevalent among black families that may be useful to immigrant parents in their efforts to cope with the hardships of acculturation and racism/discrimination:

> [T]o maintain a positive self-image, have connections to the community, maintain an accurate connection of what is happening in the environment, cope with stressors and adapt to the environment, have emotional intimacy with others, maintain a sense of competence, and work productively. (Ramseur, 1991, as cited by Illovsky, 2003)

Furthermore, Ramseur suggests that immigrant parents have kinship and extended family networks; work toward harmony, cooperation and interdependence; accept differences; foster internal development, work, and achievement orientation; adhere to tradition; have strong male and female bonds; have adaptable and flexible roles; develop support to deal with stressors (for example, obtain emotional support from others and appreciate one's roots); respect and utilize the skills and wisdom of senior family members; and emphasize children.

In the Toolbox for Change, I offer a series of suggestions for immigrant parents, educators, and practitioners.

SUMMARY AND CONCLUSION

> Although categorical self-labels are important indicators of identification . . . they do not encompass the full range of the psychological meaning of ethnic identity. (Phinney, 2003, p. 68)

Immigrant children and their first-generation parents face numerous developmental tasks that are disregarded by major psychological developmental theories. They face a daunting task of trying to sort out who they are in the midst of very contradictory messages and situations. They try to maintain cultural allegiances for their parents' sake, while at the same time they are being pushed by their mainstream peers to accept mainstream discourses and deny their backgrounds. Part of this is a result of an acculturation force that teaches people to embrace a country and its traditions. However, there are other factors that permeate everyday interactions. The notion of acculturation, while useful in understanding immigrants' mental health, is archaic in its linear conceptualization. Issues of ethnic identity development are as important in the immigrant's mental health as are the notions of racism and discrimination.

I believe that in studying the development of ethnic identity and acculturation, it is imperative to address not only the individual variables, such as age, gender, and class, but also the mainstream's social status given to a particular race (for example, Asian versus black, where it is clear that whites tend to marry more Asians than blacks, or the stereotype that Asians are smarter than Latinos and blacks). Also, it is important to address the pressure to conform imposed by the majority group, and its implications for a person's livelihood.

A serious redefinition of what it means to "have" an ethnicity in the United States is imperative. Reviewing the notions of "majority" and "minority" is necessary when notions of pure racial groups are

Toolbox for Change

For	Strategies for change
Immigrant parents and their children	• Expose your children to role models along different cultural lines. Mirroring is a powerful tool for developing a child's behavioral repertoire. When a child cannot see herself portrayed in the mainstream social channels, both her self-esteem and her potential for growth are limited. Having a multicultural repertoire of role models results in multiple possibilities for that child, as well as teaching her about human potential regardless of personal characteristics. • Be surrounded by a diverse group of friends. Heterogeneous groups are more creative and more validating of our multiplicity of experiences as human beings. A diverse group also avoids the parochial experiences that make racism and discrimination so prevalent. Diverse groups carry the message that "one size does not fit all," thereby freeing the individual of rigid behavioral expectations and feelings of entrapment. • Always remember that this is a country of immigrants. Because you arrived later, it does not mean that you are entitled to fewer rights than the rest of the population. No one can tell you that. Know what your legal rights are. • Raise U.S. citizens, but also raise them as citizens of the world. In this era of globalization and continuous cross-cultural encounters, such practice might help your children experience less stress, as well as help them to become more adaptive. Teaching such concepts also sends immigrant children the message that "they do not have to live between two worlds" (Gopaul-McNicol & Armour-Thomas, 2002, p. 178). It is also important to keep in mind that the acculturation process is different for immigrant parents and their children. Strong cultural allegiances and identities do subside over time for both immigrant parents and their children (Gopaul-McNicol & Armour-Thomas, 2002). • Teach your children about racism and the injustices that result from it. Give them examples of both blatant and hidden racism. Most importantly, teach them about institutionalized racism and the negative impact it has on people's lives.

For	Strategies for change
	• Parental involvement in the schools is crucial to educating teachers around their own cultural traditions and ethnic notions. Raising the level of awareness around the different needs different populations have might increase tension between parents and teachers, because the prevalent assumption is that "you don't have a right to question the status quo . . . this is how we have done it for years . . . you are not going to change it . . . go back to your country." These are actual covert and overt reactions I have personally both received and witnessed when I or others have demanded change. It is important to keep in mind that tensions will always arise when individuals come with a new paradigm. The key issue here is how to engage the whole system in supporting your claims. Civil rights laws have made it possible to demand the changes necessary for everyone's welfare.
	• Demand representation of your own ethnic and cultural group. Educate mainstream citizens about people like you in order to challenge prevalent stereotypes. Also remember the relevance of a two-way communication channel. You break barriers when you reach out. However, remember that this is not your sole responsibility. Groups in power need to engage in this dialogue, too.
	• Be proud of who you are. By choosing to live and work in the United States, you are contributing to the diversity of thinking that makes this country so powerful. Remember that homogeneous thinking leads to stagnation, which in turn results in self-destruction.
	• Allow your children to share traits of both your country of origin and the United States. Isolating children from mainstream influences just for the sake of cultural preservation is selfish and maladaptive. As Gopaul-McNicol and Armour-Thomas state (2002), "parents must understand that the strong cultural identity may dissipate over time, as each new generation becomes more Americanized" (p. 148).

continued

Toolbox for Change (continued)

For	Strategies for change
Practitioners/ educators	• Continue to work around self-awareness of your own biases and prejudices toward people different from you. Learning to feel comfortable with "difference" is an invaluable asset in your professional life. Along with self-awareness, it is imperative to learn the professional skills necessary to deal with particular groups such as immigrants in the United States. Good intentions are not enough. • Clarify personal notions of "acculturation." What does an acculturated person look like? Keep in check your urges to indoctrinate people with your own life values. • Clarify your personal notions about what it means to be American and/or patriotic. In an era of globalization and with exposure to an increasingly diverse population in the United States, groups in power might experience a nostalgia to return to a "safer" time, when there were fewer heterogeneous forces in power to threaten the makeup of the "American fabric" (mainly, a white view of the world). Working with immigrants can be refreshing and disturbing at the same time. It can become a threat to an individual's sense of identity, because it challenges his/her ethnocentrism and universal assumptions. Immigrants also represent a threat to people's livelihood because accepting them means having to share economic resources that can seem limited at times. • Be constantly aware of mainstream society's pervasive and insidious negative messages about minority groups. While this might seem a daunting and unnecessary task, it is crucial to keep in check how groups in power promote institutionalized racism. • Encourage conversations about difference, power, and oppression. Whether because of guilt or an inability to relinquish power, these conversations are not happening in our society, thereby promulgating the cycle of oppression. • Empower immigrant families by providing them with the available system resources. Parents cannot advocate for their children when they are not clear on how the system works and what their rights are.

Toolbox for Change

For	Strategies for change
	• Promote the creation of broader definitions of race to include the multiple realities that are part of a growing number of children in this country. The increasing immigration rate in the United States, as well as factors such as geographic mobility and multiracial unions, among others, make the notion of race seem rigid and static. We need to teach our children to think of race not in terms of skin color, but rather in terms of multiple identities. Also, engage in a serious conversation about who defines those categories and for what purpose. The notion of race only serves one purpose: to oppress those who do not look like "us."

becoming outdated in such a multicultural country as the United States. This reviewing should include issues of power. More recent generations of white Americans are wondering whether they have an ethnicity. It is no surprise then to see hordes of white teenagers adopting black mannerisms and lifestyles. There is also a recent interest in finding relatives (no matter how distant) who may provide one with a minority status for job seeking or college applications. This phenomenon was very clear in Venezuela once the European Union was formed. Those who made fun of the country's numerous Spanish and Portuguese immigrants made a sudden reconnection to their Spanish and Portuguese roots in order to obtain EU passports.

Economic issues are also closely connected to acculturation and ethnic identity. In my experience as a third-generation immigrant across three continents, I have observed a close connection between economic prosperity and a more adaptive acculturation process. In this sense, who retains the economic power is key to understanding how immigrant groups adapt to a new country.

The way we talk about ethnic identity of immigrants in the United States also needs to change because ethnic/racial labels impose social constructions that, in many cases, are not shared by immigrants themselves. It is important to examine the immigrants' ecological context, or what Falicov (2002) calls the "ecological niche," including economic and social/political pressures in their adoption of racial/ethnic categories. A very well-to-do immigrant I once met told me that home was where you found economic prosperity. But, in my view, "home" is also a place where you feel you belong, where you do not have to worry about some law changing and robbing you of your immigrant status; or where you know your child is going to be treated fairly, no matter his/her ethnic/racial background. I will feel at home when I am no longer forced to be the "other," or what the rest of the group wants me to be in order to diminish its own anxieties. Home means peace, and peace means exactly what the Pledge of Allegiance prescribes: "liberty and justice for all."

As I look back at my experiences as an immigrant parent, it is clear that my initial response to my daughter's question "What am I?" was rather naive. Maybe it was just the beginning of a developmental process for *me*, a process that was activated by her quest for identity. My answers to her will vary through the years as I try to unravel and articulate the mysteries of who I am.

REFERENCES

Benjamin, J. (1988). *The bonds of love*. New York: Pantheon Books.

Berry, J. (1990). Psychology of acculturation: Understanding individuals moving between cultures. In R. W. Brislin (Ed.), *Applied cross-cultural psychology* (pp. 232–253). London: SAGE Publications, Ltd.

Berry, J., & Kim, U. (1988). Acculturation and mental health. In P. Dasen, J. Berry, & N. Sartorius (Eds.), *Health and cross-cultural psychology* (pp. 207–236). Newbury Park, CA: SAGE Publications, Inc.

Carter, R. (1995). *The influence of race and racial identity in psychotherapy*. New York: John Wiley & Sons.

Cuellar, I. (2000). Acculturation and mental health. In I. Cuellar & F. Paniagua, (Eds.), *Handbook of multicultural mental health*. San Diego, CA: Academic Press.

Espin, O. M. (1997). Psychological impact of migration on Latinas: Implications for psychotherapeutic practice. In O. M. Espin (Ed.), *Latina realities: Essays on healing, migration, and sexuality*. Boulder, CO: Westview Press.

Falicov, C. J. (1998). *Latino families in therapy: A guide to multicultural practice*. New York: Guilford Press.

Falicov, C. J. (2002). Ambiguous loss: Risk and resilience in Latino immigrant families. In M. Suarez-Orozco & M. Paez (Eds.), *Latinos: Remaking America*. David Rockefeller Center for Latin American Studies and the University of California Press.

Gopaul-McNicol, S., & Armour-Thomas, E. (2002). *Assessment and culture: Psychological tests with minority populations*. San Diego: Academic Press.

Hardy, K., & Laszloffy, T. (2000). The development of children and families of color: A supplemental framework. In W. Nichols & M. Pace-Nichols (Eds.), *Handbook of family development and intervention* (pp. 109–128). New York: John Wiley & Sons.

Helms, J. (Ed.). (1990). *Black and white racial identity: Theory, research and practice.* Westport, CT: Greenwood.

Illovsky, M. (2003). *Mental health professionals, minorities and the poor.* New York: Brunner-Routledge.

Kim-Ju, G., & Liem, R. (2003). Ethnic self-awareness as a function of ethnic group status, group composition, and ethnic identity orientation. *Cultural Diversity and Ethnic Minority Psychology, 9*(3), 289–302.

Marsella, A., & Yamada, A. M. (2000). Culture and mental health: An introduction and overview of foundations, concepts and issues. In I. Cuellar & F. Paniagua (Eds.), *Handbook of multicultural mental health: Assessment and treatment of diverse populations.* San Diego, CA: Academic Press.

Phinney, J. (1989). Stages of ethnic identity development in minority group adolescents. *Journal of Early Adolescence, 9,* 34–49. In K. Chun, P. B. Organista, & G. Marin (Eds.), *Acculturation: Advances in theory, measurement, and applied research* (p. 77).

Phinney, J. (2003). Ethnic identity and acculturation. In K. Chun, P. B. Organista, & G. Marin (Eds.), *Acculturation: Advances in theory, measurement, and applied research* (pp. 63–81). Washington, DC: American Psychological Association.

Rodriguez, R. (2002). *Brown: The last discovery of America.* New York: Penguin Putman.

Schmidley, D. (2001). *Profile of the foreign-born population in the United States: 2000* (Current Population Reports, Series P23-206). U.S. Census Bureau, Government Printing Office. Retrieved June, 17, 2003, from www.census.gov/prod/2002pubs/p23-206.pdf

Suarez-Orozco, C., & Suarez-Orozco, M. (1995). Migration: Generational discontinuities and the making of Latino identities. In Lola Romanucci-Ross & George De Vos (Eds.), *Ethnic identity: Creation, conflict and accommodation* (3rd ed.). Walnut Creek, CA : AltaMira Press.

Sue, D. W., & Sue, D. (2003). *Counseling the culturally diverse: Theory and practice.* New York: John Wiley & Sons.

Tatum, B. (1997). *Why are all the black kids sitting together in the cafeteria?* New York: Basic Books.

Trimble, J. E. (2003). Introduction: Social change and acculturation. In K. Chun, P.B. Organista, & G. Marin (Eds.), *Acculturation: Advances in theory, measurement, and applied research* (p. 10). Washington, DC: American Psychological Association.

CHAPTER 7

Coping with Immigration: New Challenges for the Mental Health Profession

Linna Wang
Darryl Freeland

Immigration and immigrants have for decades received attention in cross-cultural mental health studies. However, following U.S. Census 2000 data and the tragic events of September 11, 2001, the immigrant who has been spotlighted by these most current, disturbing events confronts as never before the mental health profession. This new encounter between immigrants and mental health professionals highlights the need for a new knowledge of care and service delivery, which can add another enriching dimension to multicultural studies and practice.

This chapter utilizes a cross-disciplinary approach to the issue in two parts. First, it briefly surveys studies on, and issues of, immigration and immigrants from both national and international perspectives, including the immigrant's unique experience in this society, which presents both similarities to and differences from both domestic and racial minorities. The second part proposes that to integrate the newcomers into this society, public policies that promote multiculturalism and integration must be established and activated from government levels.

This chapter identifies three major factors that contribute to the failure of the mental health system in serving immigrants' needs. The "silo state" (described later) of the current mental health system is oppressive to the newcomers, more so than to the general consumers of mental health services. The Eurocentric values of the American mental health professions conflict with the cultural values of many immigrants, and the *etic* (culturally universal) approach to mental health by professionals on the individual level constitutes the major force that keeps mental health services out of the reach of immigrants. To work with immigrants, to improve their general wellness and mental health, the mental health systems and their constituent professionals must make a paradigm shift in their views and in their orientations—a shift from an inward convergence to integration that reflects the characteristics of an international and global society. This shift will require systemic, structural changes that necessitate cross-disciplinary, preventive means of meeting the mental health needs of immigrants.

NATIONAL AND INTERNATIONAL PERSPECTIVES OF IMMIGRATION

According to the U.S. Census Bureau, the foreign-born population in the United States has been increasing steadily since the 1970s. By March 2003, the foreign-born population exceeded 32 million and accounted for 11.5 percent of the U.S. population (U.S. Census Bureau, 2003)—up from 4.7 percent in 1970, the lowest point in U.S. history. The rapidity of this increase was prominent in the last few decades of the twentieth century (from 6.2 percent in 1980 to 7.9 percent in 1990 and 10.4 percent in 2000). The population change, however, has not been limited to the increased numbers only. The feeding countries have also changed. As a percentage of the total, immigration from European countries decreased from about 62 percent in the 1970s to 15.3 percent in 2000, while immigration from Latin American countries increased from about 19 percent in the 1970s to 51 percent in 2000, and immigration from Asian countries increased from about 9 percent in 1970 to 25.5 percent in 2000. While the United States is experiencing the second great wave of immigrants in its history, the newcomers of this wave are very different from those in the last wave. This difference has profound and multidimensional implications, from national immigration policy to management of daily interaction with the new immigrants.

Put into a global, ecosystemic perspective, however, the drastic change in the U.S. population is but an integral part of the interdependent global web of economic, political, social, technical, and environmental events, forces, and changes. The rapid increase in the foreign-born U.S. population reflects a high level of international migration during the past generation. In the last few decades of the twentieth century, almost every continent in the world experienced similar population change. About one million legal and 500,000 illegal immigrants enter into European countries annually, and about one third of jobs were filled by foreign laborers in some Asian countries. Australia has the highest portion (about 24 percent) of the foreign-borns in its population. While economists cheer global immigration as the fastest way to boost globalization (*The Economist*, 2002a), that immigration also poses international political challenges. Immigration tests the host country's sense of "self," challenging policymakers to find management methods for the influx, including integration of the newcomers. Additionally, and of crucial import, how immigration and immigrants are managed and *integrated* directly affect world peace.

Immigration can be identified as a human experience, which has occurred almost as long as human history has. However, immigration is more than an individual decision: governments leave their fingerprints on this human experience. Historically, colonial countries have imported laborers from their colonies or have exported them from one country to another—for example, France imported people from its North African colonies. From the Indian subcontinent, Great Britain imported Indians as well as exported them to Africa. Currently, the U.S. government imports skilled workers via H-1 working visas from Asian countries to staff its fast-growing high-tech industries, while excluding workers from other selected countries, rendering those immigrants "illegals." Refugee immigration is the result of government actions, whether these actions are in the form of violence (civil war, international war, etc.) or persecution (political or religious). Still significant, government-sanctioned slave trades produced "forced immigration" onto Africans.

Factors that contribute to individual decisions to immigrate include economic gain, family reunification, and asylum from persecution. Economic gain itself sometimes is not a strong-enough incentive for an individual to embark on such a hard journey. Economic incentive is often driven by or coupled with conditions in a failing state, a context that can produce hopelessness in the minds and hearts of potential immigrants. The transition from such a state can include a foreign destination occupied by family and friends who have settled down in the country, and relationships that can decrease the barrier and the cost of the immigration, thus making the trek and the transition easier for others to follow. That phenomenon can explain the frequently observed clustering of immigrants from the same regions of the sending countries. Indeed, a primary condition of destination is frequently not economic gain but kinship.

People who immigrate for economic reasons and family reunification tend to be voluntary immigrants. They start the psychological preparation for the new country long before the journey begins. By contrast, people who seek asylum as refugees from political oppression, religious persecution, or war are more likely to be involuntary immigrants. They have to abandon all of their possessions, leave their homeland at short notice, and escape to foreign environs with deficits of language and psychological preparation. They may perceive immigration as being imposed on them. The imposed immigration may create more helplessness and less willingness to interact with the hosting culture.

International immigration surveys also indicate that internal immigration (migration within the home country) and external immigration (migration out of the home country) are often intertwined, while large-scale immigration usually occurs at the onset of industrialization (*The Economist*, 2002b). This variant process can partially explain the global phenomenon of immigration in the last two decades of the twentieth century: economic globalization jump-started industrialization in many Latin American and Asian countries. In that context, a farmer's wife may start to work in a sweatshop in a nearby city (internal immigration) to accumulate the needed funds for her husband's later migration to another country (external immigration). After he settles down in the other country, she and the children will follow, as will then the extended families and friends (family reunification) follow the initial familial group.

ACCULTURATION: ASSIMILATION VERSUS INTEGRATION

Acculturation, a process that individuals undergo in response to a changing cultural context (Berry, Poortinga, Segall, & Dason, 1992), is inevitable in the immigration experience. The course of acculturation, however, is a two-way, interactional process between the newcomers and the hosting society. The course of acculturation is decided by the immigrant on an individual, pragmatic, and psychological level, as well as by the hosting country at the population level. That acculturation complex contains changes in social structure, economic base, and political organization (Graves, 1967). How immigrants are treated and what is expected of them are closely associated with the political structure and public policies of the hosting country. Such treatment depends on the orientation of the hosting country—whether it is a multicultural society or monoculture society. A monoculture society privileges a singular presentation: one language, one religious practice, and one ethnic group. As the Australian minister for immigration in the late 1960s claimed, a monoculture society is *one*, "everyone living in the same way, understanding each other, and sharing the same aspirations" (Bullivant, 1985, p. 12). In a monoculture society, the immigrant's acculturation is socially constructed (and therefore expected) as a linear, convergent *assimilation* process: in that mode of acculturation, individuals acquire the second culture while letting go of their original culture. But such linear singularity contains a prejudicial discrepancy that can doom human dignity, cultural integration, and sociopolitical engagement. Deceptively, "on the one hand it seems like a simple enough proposition: an outcome of adaptation of new environments, a process of 'learning the ropes' and 'fitting in' through which 'they' become like 'we,' a convergence hypothesis, a sort of regression to the mean. . . . But on the other hand, it is an explosive term, value laden with arrogant presumptions of ethnic superiority and inferiority and fraught with the bitter baggage of the past—and the politics of the present, to be sure" (Rumbaut, 1997, p. 483). Monoculture society and its assimilation orientation are the fertile ground for anti-immigrant public policies and sentiment.

In contrast to a monoculture society, in a *multicultural* society, pluralism is valued by its population and by its government policy. A central issue of concern to the multicultural society is how to manage that part of its cultural diversity that is associated with immigration. Instead of the focus on assimilation typical of a monoculture society, a multicultural society promotes *integration* for its newcomers, a process wherein individuals can develop healthy identities and mutually positive intergroup attitudes in a multicultural, sociopolitical context. In such societies, public policies are positively linked to pluralism (Berry et al., 1992). No ethnicity is "superior" to any other, and intergroup relationships are characterized by mutually respectful partnerships. Canada is an example of a multicultural society. In its dual-language system, no one language takes precedence over the other, nor does any ethnic group over any other. Similarly, after realizing that assimilation never worked, the Australian government in 1978 formally endorsed a multicultural policy, proudly announcing itself as one of the most cosmopolitan societies on earth (Bullivant, 1985), thus setting Australia on the course of actualizing multiculturalism. In Sweden, an explicit multiculturalism policy was adopted in 1975, with three goals: equality, freedom of choice, and partnership. These goals in Sweden aim to give immigrants the same living standard, to assure ethnic and linguistic minorities a genuine choice between retaining and developing their cultural identity, and to create an environment wherein immigrants, minority groups, and native populations all benefit from working together (Lundstrom, 1986).

Like the majority of the state-nations in the world, the United States, although multiracial, is a monoculture society. Even though as a whole the benefits of immigration to the U.S. economy outweigh its costs, federal assistance to immigrants has been declining. For example, the end of the State Legalization Impact Assistance Grants (SLIAG) in 1994 diminished federally funded, targeted-education, health, and social services programs for immigrants. The passage of the Personal Responsibility and Work Opportunity Act of 1996 banned most forms of public assistance and services for legal immigrants who remained noncitizens. The lack of multicultural policies at the federal level has created a void that leaves room for anti-immigrant policies/propositions to be put onto states' ballots. A notorious example is California Proposition 187, passed in 1994, which attempted to prohibit virtually all health care for 1.6 million immigrants residing in California, and to force over 300,000 of their children out of the school system. Although a U.S. district court judged the prohibition unconstitutional, the initial passage of the proposition gave a boost of confidence to the anti-immigrant forces nationwide, provided legal sanction to the harassment and discrimination against immigrants, and set precedent for other anti-immigrant propositions to be put onto the ballot, such as California Proposition 227.

As a monoculture society, the United States tends to favor an *assimilationist* orientation to its newcomers. America's schools and other institutions consciously turn immigrants into Americans. The cry for the need of assimilation and the lament of its inadequacy were recorded as early as 1880: "There is a limit to our powers of assimilation and when it is exceeded the country suffers from something very like indigestion. We know how stubbornly conservative of his dirt and his ignorance is the average immigrant who settles in New York, particularly if he is of a clannish race like the Italians. Born in squalor, raised in filth and misery and kept at work almost from infancy, these wretched beings change their abode, but not their habits in coming to New York" (quoted in Chavez, 1996, p. 251). Assimilation is seen as a linear process for immigrants to merge into the "core society." That assimilation process begins early, when the newcomers set their feet on the soil of the new country, with a final product of "identificational assimilation," a self-image of the unhyphenated American (Gordon, 1964). This process is usually accomplished within two to three generations. As a nation, the United States demonstrated an exceptional capacity for assimilation, absorbing tens of millions of people from every corner of the world. At the same time, the process of "becoming American" has been a process far from linear, neither straightforward nor uniform (Rumbaut, 1997). As noted, the process of acculturation or Americanization can begin years before the immigration actually occurs, as potential immigrants psychologically prepare themselves for the longest journey of their lives. For example, nearly half of the new immigrants in the United States can speak English well or very well (Rumbaut, 1994), and many people have visited America before they immigrate (Massey & Espinosa, 1997). This linguistic knowledge and cultural familiarity are a reflection of globalization and widespread contact with American culture and lifestyle (Rumbaut, 1997), acquired through family connections (Massey & Espinosa, 1997) and worldwide adoption of English education.

ASSIMILATION PARADOX

Assimilation is reported to be positively associated with the advancement of the immigrant's life quality when its criterion is income. For example, evidence from Britain shows that, when assimilation level is measured by language acquisition, which is considered the key to assimilation, fluent English boosts an immigrant's earnings by around 17 percent an hour (*The Economist*, 2002c). When assimilation is measured by the length of stay in the host country, Mexican Americans enjoy wage growth of 30 percent or more between the first and second generations (Reyes, 2001). However, a survey of public health literature has disclosed the existence of an "assimilation paradox," a negative correlation among assimilation, physical health, and mental health. Some "high risk" groups of immigrants who are "less assimilated" to the U.S. culture, particularly low-income immigrants from Mexico and Southeast Asia, show unexpectedly favorable outcomes when health and mental health are concerned. Markides and Coreil (1986) refer to this phenomenon as an "epidemiological paradox" of assimilation. Several pregnancy outcome studies have indicated that less-assimilated immigrant women (new immigrants) actually have had better pregnancy outcomes than have more assimilated (second generation) women, as the outcomes are measured by birth weight and infant mortality rates—despite the fact that these women are of the poorest group, and they tend to utilize prenatal care much later than do other groups (Williams, Binkin, & Clingman, 1986; Scribner & Dwyer, 1989; Weeks & Rumbaut, 1991; Yu, 1982). Contrary to conventional wisdom, the relationship between social economic status and health (poor people tend to have poor health, a condition also apparent in the general American population) usually does not repeat itself among the new and therefore less-assimilated immigrants and their children (Beiser, Hou, Hyman, & Tousignant, 2002.) Indeed, public health data indicate another pattern: increased assimilation is often associated with increased health risk behaviors (Marks, Garcia, & Solis, 1990), such as smoking (Haynes, Harvey, Montes, Nicken, & Cohen, 1990), drug use (Amaro, Whitaker, Coffman, & Heeren, 1990), and alcohol use (Gilbert, 1989).

In terms of mental health, different sources yield different results. Clinical studies on immigrants and refugees tend to focus on depression and anxiety, indicating that a large number of refugees experience severe clinical depression, anxiety symptoms, and/or posttraumatic stress syndrome—disorders that are attributable to preimmigration conditions, such as multiple traumatic experiences before emigration (Allodi, 1991; Chung & Kagawa-Singer, 1993; Mollica & Lavelle, 1986; Nguyen, 1989). Community-based studies (using nonclinical samples) tend to indicate that new (thus less-assimilated) immigrants are less likely to suffer lifelong depression than are more-assimilated immigrants, and their anxiety and depression are more likely to be situational, affiliated with postimmigration factors such as discrimination, unemployment, and daily hassles (Beiser et al., 2002; Pernice & Brook, 1996a). Studies on refugees indicate that diagnoses of schizophrenic disorders occur with greater frequency among refugees than among non-refugee immigrants (Krupinski, Stoller, & Wallace, 1973), although the prevalence is rather low (Gong-Guy, Cravens, & Patterson, 1991). Within refugee groups, diagnoses of brief reactive psychoses, particularly those characterized by paranoid reactions and hysterical psychosis, occur with far greater frequency than do diagnoses of schizophrenic disorder (Lin, 1986).

Those data seem to confirm once again that immigration *per se* may not necessarily compromise immigrants' health or mental health (Aronowitz, 1992; Munroe-Blum, Boyle, Offord, & Kate, 1989). Rather, assimilation may be a process highly stressful for immigrants. This process of "they" becoming "we" gives legitimacy to the superiority of the "core society," a process that endorses discrimination, which has been identified as the major acculturative strain clearly associated with psychological symptoms among immigrants (Carter-Pokras & Woo, 1999; Dion, Dion, & Pak, 1992; Pernice & Brook, 1996a; Sanchez & Fernandez, 1993; Sandhu & Asrabadi, 1994; Ying, 1996). In this converging process of regressing to the mean, "they" have to let go of whatever differences they do have before "they" can become "we," even though these differences may be vital to the physical and mental well-being of the immigrants. This process is especially stressful at the beginning stage of relocation, when the newcomer is over-whelmed with daily hassles (Abouguendia & Noels, 2001), poverty (National Council of Welfare, 1998), and discrimination (Jasinskaja-Lahti & Liebkind, 2001). It remains controversial whether new immigrants actually go through a euphoric phase before they are hit by the stressful reality of relocation, as proposed by some researchers (Leherher, 1993; Brink & Saunders, 1976; Rumbaut, 1985). Most of the studies indicate that mental health risk occurs soon after resettlement (Tyhurst, 1982; Sluzki, 1986). Ritsner and Ponizovsky's (1999) cross-sectional and in part longitudinal study with a large community sample indicates a two-phase temporal pattern of development of psychological stress, consisting of escalation and reduction phases. The psychological distress escalates right after the immigrant's arrival, and peaks at twenty-seven months. The distress then starts to decline. The reduction phase continues to the end of the fifth year. This study, consistent with Beiser's (1988) and Pernice and Brook's (1996b) data, did not support the existence of any distress-free period during the first 2.5 years after immigration. In fact, refugees may remain at heightened risk of paranoid disorders that occur many years following resettlement because of social and linguistic isolation (Hitch & Rack, 1980).

IMMIGRANTS AND INDIGENOUS RACIAL MINORITIES: SIMILARITIES AND DIFFERENCES

Research findings indicate that there are similarities and differences between the new immigrants and the U.S. indigenous racial minorities. Given their short history in this country, most of the immigrants have not had the same history of racial discrimination and oppression that blacks have had. The second wave of immigration started in the early 1980s, and most of the newcomers in this wave did not experience the civil rights movement (including the women's movement) of the 1960s, and they may have limited knowledge of that history

and significance. However, the discrimination that immigrants experience is still race-based. As Pernice and Brook's (1996a) data showed,
while all other immigrant groups in New Zealand reported experiences
of discrimination, British immigrants in their sample not only did not
report such experiences, they did enjoy increased status in their new
country. New immigrants, however, do experience prejudice and discrimination different from that of the indigenous minority groups—
black men are stereotyped as violent, Asian immigrants are perceived
to be taking jobs from the natives, and Latino immigrants are portrayed as draining national resources. The experience of assimilation
and its impact are different among immigrants: they differ according
to the reasons for immigration and the immigrant's social class in the
home country. For instance, Asian Indians with highly transferable
human capital, such as computer and science technology skills, tend
to immigrate to the United States for further career development.
They tend to be from middle or higher social classes, have studied in
an English language education system before immigration, are more
likely to be professionals in the United States, and are generally of a
much higher socioeconomic group (Mehta, 1998). Their experience
of discrimination (or sometimes their lack of such experience) is not
only drastically different from that of, say, black Americans, but their
experience of prejudice can also be very different from that of other Asian
immigrants, such as the Vietnamese, who as a group may have had
limited English or transferable skills. Most of the immigrants are from
relatively more homogeneous populations. They tend to be from the
majority population group (some from the privileged group) in their
home countries. The new status of "minority" and the discrimination
that comes with it can be shocking to them, leading to their disillu-
sionment about the pursuit of the American dream. Compared to
domestic racial groups that have a long history of racial oppression,
immigrants without such history of victimization can be less prepared
psychologically and less strategically skillful in the grueling task of
handling discrimination and prejudice, subtle or blatant; an innocence
that in turn exacerbates the immigration stress. Tension, animosity,
and disrespect among ethnocultural groups are often observed, as well.
In the process of assimilation, immigrants often get the same message—
"get with the program"—from both the dominant Caucasian and
indigenous minority groups. Thus ironically, if not tragically, the
achievement of certain immigrant groups is often used as evidence to
enhance the racial discrimination against indigenous minority groups
and other immigrant groups.

FAILURE OF THE MENTAL HEALTH SYSTEMS
FOR THE NEWCOMERS

The American mental health system, as an integral subsystem of the monoculture society, favors an assimilationist orientation as well, and much research has been cast in a similar, inwardly bound mold—that is, how to help immigrants fit into the core U.S. culture. The majority of clinical literature on helping immigrants has focused on how to moderate the existing theories and models to work with immigrants, stressing the importance of acculturation in clinical considerations. Research has indicated that, indeed, the more-acculturated immigrants have consumed more mental health services than have less-acculturated ones (Kung, 2003; Vega, Kolody, Aguilar-Gaxiola, & Catalano, 1999). It has been known for decades, since the groundbreaking research by Sue and McKinney (1975), and confirmed time and again by others (Nguyen, 1985) that immigrants and ethnic minorities tend to under-utilize mental health services. The underutilization, however, has been attributed to immigrants' lack of knowledge or appreciation of psychological treatment. Perceived as the immigrant's failure to utilize a modern method of psychological care, that nonparticipation or under-utilization is not taken as a hint to the possible incompatibility between the newcomers and an American mental health system rooted in an American culture. Although some researchers have tried to identify the gap between the American mental health system and immigrants' characteristics and needs, in its attempts to provide service to the newcomers, the mainstream mental health field remains unchanged, perpetuating a system that is clinic-oriented, individual-oriented, and provider-oriented. In that system, good-willed but otherwise naive professionals may have joined forces with the general societal values, perhaps unintentionally but nevertheless disparagingly engaging in the practice of prejudice and discrimination against immigrants by imposing culturally incompatible values, norms, practices, and service delivery formats onto immigrants. The mental health professionals have demonstrated admirable compassion in rendering help to the immigrant community. Help, however, must be a statement of outcome rather than a passionate declaration of intent (Gist, 2002). This outcome should be judged by the well-being of the new members—the immigrants themselves—on their own terms, not by the service providers' demonstration of compassion alone.

The finding that consumption of mental health services only rises with immigrants' acculturation level (Wells, Hough, Golding, Burnam,

& Karno, 1987; Wells, Golding, Hough, Burnam, & Karno, 1989) must not be taken as a permission to wait for the immigrants to achieve a certain level of acculturation first, before mental health professionals provide services to them. Assimilation did work for the immigrants of European heritage coming in the first wave of immigration in the history of this country. But that assimilation took about 100 years. The majority of the first wave of immigrants were Caucasians. European cultures, although different both among themselves and from the American culture, tended to cluster with or be close to American culture (Hofstede, 1991). The immigrants coming in the second wave are visibly different in appearance; they are from cultures that are categorically different from American culture, and they have a much shorter history in this country (the median length of residence in the United States is only 14.4 years for the total foreign-born population, according to the U.S. Census Bureau, 2001). Their acculturation tasks involve much more than changing lifestyle and getting rid of accents. There is no guarantee even then that they would be accepted as unhyphenated Americans, even if they accomplished these tasks, as many third- and fourth-generation visibly different groups, such as Asian Americans, could testify. Most of the European immigrants coming in the first wave bought one-way tickets to the new continent, and they could never look back. With the advanced technology of modern communication and transportation, the new immigrants can have much stronger ties with their home country roots. The mental health system simply cannot afford to wait passively for immigrants to acculturate before the systems deliver quality services to them. The mandate to mental health professionals to engage in social responsibility and social advocacy requires that mental health professionals serve the less-acculturated immigrants and their families.

BARRIERS OF THE NEW IMMIGRANTS TO THE ACCESS OF MENTAL HEALTH SERVICES

The American mental health system has not been merely unsuccessful in meeting the mental health needs of Americans in general—as stated in the Commissioner's Report on the mental health system (President's New Freedom Commission on Mental Health, 2003)—the mental health system has failed miserably to serve the immigrants. Critical factors that contribute to such failure are identified here as the "silo" structure of the mental health system on the system level, the pathology orientation of mental health disciplines on the content of service level, and the *etic* view of cultures held by many mental health professionals on the individual level.

The System Level

The current mental health system is inwardly fragmented and separated from other disciplines, such as the public health and physical health systems. Within the mental health system, there are clear divisions among disciplines, not limited only to psychiatry, psychology, social work, marriage and family therapy, public sector and private practice, and so on and so forth. There exists an often-unspoken yet very apparent pecking order, with psychiatry at the top, social work at the bottom, and testing and psychotherapy in between. Medication is superior (at least in terms of payment) to talk therapy, while "clinical work" is superior to "non-clinical social support." Interdisciplinary integration and cooperation are preliminary (Meyerson, Chu, & Mills, 2003). Turf war among the disciplines commonly protects a status quo in the name of enhancing professional identity. Such division is further perpetuated by licensing laws, funding systems, and codes of ethics of each discipline that are punitive to any attempt to cross a disciplinary line or to negotiate cross-disciplinary integration. For example, the code of ethics of the American Psychology Association, the American Counseling Association, and the American Association of Marriage and Family Therapy all state that their members should practice only within the boundaries of their competence, based on their education, training, supervised experience, consultation, study, or professional experience—a requirement that on the face is designed to ensure that the mental health professional does no harm by wandering into an area where s/he lacks sufficient training but, again, "ethical guidelines" too often serve as barely veiled turf claims whose bottom line is commodification of the discipline for financial gain or, at the very least, a posture of superiority of orientation. How to coordinate with professionals from other disciplines is not a required training component of any of the disciplines. If a professional attempts to step out of the office and coordinate with others, s/he may risk behaving unethically, at the risk of a lawsuit. The ever-increasing complexity and bureaucracy of such a self-serving system leaves millions of Americans lost in a maze, in the process of being "referred" to different subsystems. Such complexity is even beyond the coping skills of some mental health providers who opt to take cash for their services, leaving consumers to deal with a maze of common, conflict-ridden systems such as those involving insurance claims—if they (much less immigrants) even have insurance coverage! If the coordination of care falls squarely on the backs of consumers, such a system is virtually inaccessible to immigrants who are from different social and health care systems. The structure alone of such a health care system reflects the traditional assimilation orientation toward the newcomers, as that orientation requires newcomers to acquire a highly sophisticated knowledge of the mental health system before they could even begin to navigate the maze of the system.

The Content of Service Level

On the content level, a number of researchers (many of them minorities or immigrants themselves) have made substantial contributions to the understanding of the barriers that hinder immigrants' access to the mental health services. A number of barriers have been identified, such as the high rate of uninsured (Ku & Matani, 2001), lack of language skills to understand the mental health system (Fan, 1999), lack of bilingual staff, lack of knowledge about mental health systems and western psychology concepts (Marwaha & Livingston, 2002), absence of targeted programs (Gong-Guy et al., 1991), and so on. These barriers are both explicit and intuitively identifiable. The implicit barriers, however, lie in the conflict between immigrants' cultural values and the hidden values inherent in the American mental health system. While less recognizable, these surreptitious values probably constitute the major force that keeps mental health services from the reach of the newcomers in U.S. society. For example, while even native-born Americans find mental health interventions stigmatizing, this stigma has, however, a different connotation for many immigrants. With high family and group orientation, immigrants are reluctant to seek counseling because psychotherapy can stigmatize not only the person who needs help but also that person's entire family system. The obligation to protect the family name and sometimes the reputation of the whole group (for example, the "model minority" reputation) is an added dimension of social stigma for immigrants. Some researchers and practitioners have recognized and then written about the conflict between these culturally rooted antipathies (Das & Kemp, 1997; Meadows, 2003; Phan & Silove, 1999). Notably, Sue and Sue (2003) have done a fine job conceptualizing and summarizing such discrepancies.

According to Sue and Sue (2003), western psychology and psychotherapy prize the values of individual focus, expressiveness (verbal, emotional, and behavioral), insight searching, self-disclosure, scientific empiricism, and distinctions between mental and physical functioning and ambiguity. Each of these values potentially conflicts with immigrants' cultural values; therefore, these western psychology values become a barrier to immigrants' access to mental health services. For example, verbal, emotional, and behavioral expressions are highly valued by American psychology and are capacities often taken as indicators of progress. Some therapy models emphasize the importance of the ability to recognize, acknowledge, describe, and verbally communicate emotions. On the contrary, high-context cultures (cultures where communication is highly contextual and where a lot of information is delivered nonverbally and/or assumed in the context) tend to view such open expression of emotions as lack of maturity and self-control. What is more valued is what is assumed and unspoken yet well understood by the people from the same high-context culture. While psychology jargon has become part of mundane language in psychology-minded American culture, in many other cultures people are more likely to explain the causes of their emotions rather than to label their emotions (Cervantes, 2002). Among certain immigrant peoples, emotions are often communicated through subtle nonverbal cues, gestures, and behavioral interactions that may be missed by the verbal communication-oriented U.S. professionals. Great discomfort and feelings of inadequacy may arise when immigrants are confronted with the unfamiliar task of labeling and verbally communicating their emotions—in a word, communicating in a fashion that is considered inferior. Asian immigrants value harmony, which dictates that people should anticipate the emotional needs of others, should not express strong feelings at the expense of interpersonal harmony, and, in an effort to maintain harmony in a disagreement, should overlook the differences (Kim, Li, & Liang, 2002). Noh and Kaspar's (2003) study on Korean immigrants also found that active, problem-focused coping styles were more effective in reducing the impacts of perceived discrimination on depression, while frequent use of passive, emotion-focused coping had debilitating mental health effects.

Most cultures in the world do not differentiate mental health and physical health as clearly as does the U.S. culture. In the home countries of many Latino and Asian immigrants, somatization is well accepted as a way of expressing emotions (Lee, Lei, & Sue, 2001; Isaac & Janca, 1996), while the definition of problems can be drastically different from that of western psychology. For example, it is well accepted in Chinese culture that anger increases the probability of liver problems, that fear hurts the kidneys, that sadness injures the spleen, and that even happiness—if it is extreme—can be harmful to the heart. Somatization and social stigma of emotional disturbance naturally land immigrants in physicians' offices more than in mental health facilities. If those persons are referred to the mental health providers, and if they can then find their way there at all, their definition of the problems (spirit possession, heartache, weak nerves, loss of soul substance, etc.) (Azhar & Varma, 2000) may be considered mysterious at best, misunderstood, and thus discredited. What is clearly defined as pathological by western psychology—such as delusion and hallucination—can be considered desirable by some immigrants (McDaniel, 1989). The unfamiliar definition of a "problem" marks only the beginning of difficult and frustrating experiences for both the mental health provider and the consumer.

While the content of American psychotherapy contains values that conflict with many immigrant traditions, an additional but less noted values conflict occurs in the office-based, talk-cure format. That format can account for immigrants' underutilization rate of mental health facilities. Talk therapy has its roots in white, middle-class values of meaning-searching and insight-seeking. An assumption in those values is that the problem resides either inside the person or inside the family system of the person; therefore, transformation is to occur through the intrapersonal mechanism of cognitive or emotional change or interpersonal interaction change. The bottom line is "they have a problem and it is our job to find it out." The linear, scientifically oriented psychotherapy designed to treat both individuals and family systems starts by defining the problem and then helping the individual or family to take responsibility for owning and solving the problem. In other words, problems are within either the person or the family, and so are the solutions. This individualized pathology orientation determines the format of service delivery as one that is office-bound. This format—confining the person, couple, or family to a formal setting, disclosing intimate information to a stranger on a limited fifty-minute time frame in an arbitrarily fixed weekly schedule, and negotiating payment for solving the problem that is defined in strange terms—is anything but familiar to the new immigrants.

Again, immigrants are likely to experience transitional depression and anxiety related to postimmigration factors, such as discrimination, language barriers, and lack of housing, employment, and medical assistance. These are problems that cannot easily, if at all, be talked away, regardless of how much new meaning can be reframed into the immigrants' experiences. The talk therapy format simply does not make much sense to them. It is frustrating to the clinician whose skills are confined in insight and personal skills-seeking, as well as to the immigrants who would like to know how to deal with "real life" problems. The immigrant's constant talk about the problems encountered in the new country can be perceived and interpreted by the clinician as a deficit of external locus of control that borders on pathological "resistance," "non-compliance," or merely an unwillingness to take personal responsibility—conditions familiar to the mental health worker that can be interpreted as real problems that are worth treating.

The format of talk therapy is not only unfamiliar to the new immigrants: if it is imposed on them, it can do them harm. The new immigrants tend to be from community-oriented cultures, and they tend to pool community means to deal with hardship or problems in life. As Sun and Steward (2000) found, Hong Kong Chinese people, regardless of gender and education level, use social support as a means of coping, and their social interactions increase when stressors become more threatening. New immigrants rely on the family and community, and they often opt for familiar traditional healing practices (Nguyen, 1984). When office-based talk therapy is adopted as a means of solving problems, immigrants are taken from their social contexts, and they are required to focus on an internal resolution, an action that can cut them off from their natural sources of coping and strength. They may be trapped in a paradoxical box: the more progress they make in learning skills that are valued by the U.S. culture, such as assertiveness and "emotional independence," the more distant they can become from their source of strength and familiarity. The more they are required to become independent individuals, the farther they get from their primary value of community. The negotiation of those two poles can be a complex and stress-producing task that, when imposed, can be more harmful than helpful.

The Individual Level

On the individual provider's level, the good-willed and passionate mental health professional, when not in touch with and not knowledgeable of the biases and Eurocentric nature of her or his own values, assumptions, and beliefs as well as those of the profession, may unknowingly provide a low quality of service to new immigrants. Such racial superiority and Eurocentrism can take forms from blatant to subtle, ranging from a barely veiled prejudicial recommendation, making insensitive or even insulting suggestions (such as "Have you thought about naturalization or religious conversion?" offered to a Middle Eastern Muslim woman immigrant who has been experiencing intense discrimination since 9/11), to providing immigrants with the same treatments that have "proved effective" for white Americans, regardless of the fact that most of the psychology research was done on the white U.S. population (Graham, 1992). Well trained in the Eurocentric systems, many providers take the *etic* (culturally universal) position in working with the new immigrants. That *etic* position can involve the process of "naming," a process involving an assumption that there is only one and "correct" way of defining normality and abnormality—a belief that there exists for an individual or family an ideal status of being, and that there is an objective standard for functional human behavior. While professionals with an *etic* position may not deny the importance of culture to a certain extent, they may also view culture as merely one of the many independent variables that are an optional consideration, rather than understanding culture as the background of human behaviors—indeed, as the backdrop of authentic human drama, often comprising rich and heroic proportions. These good-willed professionals are too often willing to perform the minimum modification in diagnosis, treatment, and interaction with immigrant clients. With the sanction of the dominant societal force, the professional structure and the professionals' own *etic* position, many mental health providers continue to propose white solutions, regardless of the identity of the immigrants with whom they are working (Atkinson, Morten, & Sue, 1989, 1998). When cultural contextual variables are ignored, dominant culture prevails. The cultural imposition of dominant group values can lead minorities to internalize negative self-images (Espiritu, 1997). Immigrants can adopt a sense of inferiority and a desire to conform to those values and expectations that are glorified as normal in the mainstream society (Pyke, 2000).

Ethnocentric monoculturalism is a powerful social force that is dysfunctional in the U.S. pluralistic society. The U.S. mental health system, with its goals and service delivery process that are informed, influenced, and determined by this powerful force of monoculturalism, inevitably has been ill-equipped to address the needs of immigrants in the pluralistic society and has therefore failed to serve the needs of the diverse members of that society. The problems at the system, professional, and individual levels overlap and intertwine, with each supporting and maintaining the status quo of the others. The system has become self-perpetuating, "stuck in a status quo approach to care that accepts tradition and mediocrity rather than demanding innovation and excellence" (Kelly, 2002, p. 1). The world, however, is not stuck in the status quo. The accelerating process of globalization draws people from different geographic and cultural origins into close contact and relationships. As Marsella (1998) notes, the world has become a global community in which lives have become increasingly interdependent, where most global events and forces increasingly become local events and forces. Since the abuse, suffering, and victimization of any person or people has implications for all, the health and well being of all human beings must be assigned a new priority in all our lives. Mental health professions must respond to this interdependence with determination and rigor.

NEW CHALLENGES TO THE U.S. MENTAL HEALTH SYSTEM

To demonstrate with integrity its essential value to the national economy and the overall health of the nation's population and to keep abreast of the needs of a society that is rapidly changing to be more international and global, the mental health system has no other choice but to face decisively the challenges in this new era. There must be a paradigm shift from the inwardly converging orientation that requires assimilation before treatment to the outwardly embracing orientation that seeks to integrate and accommodate all cultural variations and perspectives. The goal, however, should not be to provide "equal treatment" to immigrants but "equal access" (Sue & Sue, 2003) to create an opportunity for the new members of the society to have equal access to the services that are available to the rest of the population. To achieve this goal, changes must occur at all three levels—system, professional, and individual. The outcomes for those goals should be those that are considered desirable and valuable by the immigrants. Similarly, those outcomes should be measured by the criteria of the immigrants' general functioning in U.S. society, the immigrants' economic gain, and the value that their position merits in the society. However, such outcomes can be achieved only through matching services to the pressing needs of immigrants—namely, the needs to overcome language barriers, to obtain assistance in employment training and opportunities, to acquire housing, to access medical care, and to gain knowledge and skills in dealing with daily hassles and hardships. By their very nature, these needs require services that are prevention- and education-oriented rather than clinical treatment-oriented. The delivery format of such services, therefore, will most commonly also be community-based rather than office-based.

Challenges on the System Level

No change on the system level can materialize without a change in funding systems. Since the federal government is the single biggest payer for the nation's health care, federal funding has to reflect the value of prevention and cross-system coordination. It needs to prioritize allocation to such programs as housing assistance, employment training and assistance, and care coordination. Cross-system coordination should include the interface between mental health and physical health and between mental health and federal and local governmental policymakers and agencies. Instead of functioning as an ambulance parked at the bottom of a cliff, waiting for people to fall, the mental health system must become an active player in prevention, in bettering the society and the life of its citizens, proactively providing society with its expertise in the knowledge of human behavior, providing such information to society and policymakers. The mental health system should take a systemic approach, orchestrating with all the systems involved to develop working relationships and partnerships with other systems to establish different levels of "wraparound" programs. The expertise and strength of the mental health professions should be used constantly to survey the playing field in a timely manner, to identify the underserved population, and to provide pertinent information to decision-makers who can change policies and reallocate resources to the most-needed areas.

U.S. foreign policy by and large influences which group of people are the next coming into the country. Therefore, especially in the case of refugees, the mental health system should have a close, interactive working relationship with government foreign policymakers, should be informed by those policymakers of who will be the next group of newcomers, and should reciprocally inform policymakers of the availability of social resources. That reciprocal information should include whether the society at large is ready to provide humanitarian support to the potential newcomers, thus collaborating with policymakers on resource allocation that respects the needs of immigrants and the society that can integrate them. With its knowledge and expertise, mental health professionals can rather accurately predict the needs and behavioral patterns of different groups of immigrants and refugees; therefore, the mental health system should take a leadership role, offering its expertise to anticipate the needs of the next wave of new-comers, and to develop assistance programs according to the specific needs of the newcomers even before they set their feet onto U.S. soil. For example, if it were known that one group of newcomers possessed limited skills but were from countries/regions where the education system was English-based (as in some African countries that had been British colonies) and the other group were people with more transferable skills (although there, the education system might be local language-based), then assistance programs for the first group would be more employment capacity-enhancing, and assistance programs for the second group intuitively would focus more on language training. Such programs can be developed in anticipation of the next wave of immigrants and refugees, to embrace them and integrate them as soon as they arrive. As advocates for immigrants' general well-being, mental health professionals must work with the local government to create tax incentives for businesses to create employment opportunities, as is often done for the American disabled population.

The wall between mental health and physical health care systems has to be knocked down. No discipline, no single approach, and no solitary action or intervention can reliably provide the comprehensive and overarching support for this most marginalized population. As a partner, not as a competitor, the mental health profession should stand side by side with primary care services, to coordinate the care that is of immigrants' choice. Service must be delivered within the immigrants' contextual environment, such as in their homes, community centers, schools, religious institutions, regional associations (immigrants from the same region often organize their own association as a social sup-port), social/festive events gatherings, etc. The mental health system has to go to those places where the problems and needs are, to tackle the problems on the spot, preventing them from further festering to a degree that requires costly and stigmatizing psychological treatment. Many existing wraparound programs that offer services to the youth (Chenven & Brady, 2003) can be borrowed as models for such services to the immigrants.

Challenges at the Professional Content Level

The content of mental health service to immigrants should steer away from the traditional *DSM* (*Diagnostic and Statistical Manual*)-based diagnoses and internally focused interventions. Instead, the ser-vice should be heavily educational (Kagan & Shafer, 2001), providing information that is crucial to survival in this country—for example, the norm of childrearing practice; information and direction to social resources; the general social rules and norms, regulations, and policies in U.S. society; the differences between the political, financial, educational, and medical systems in the United States and those of their home countries; immigration regulations and policies, etc. Help-seeking immigrants should be regarded as people who *encounter* problems in their lives, not as people who *have* problems (Sue & Sue, 2003). Problems should be externalized, and the first move should be strengths-searching and resource-identifying, not pathology-hunting. Community resources and "alternative" measures should be utilized in problem-solving. Alternative measures, much to the discomfort of many western practitioners trained primarily in the reductionism tenets of the natural sciences, often include religion and spirituality. While mental health professionals have to make room for and learn to coexist with other healers and healing mechanisms, such as religious priests or monks, spiritual healers or counselors, shamans, herbal treatment, yoga, massage therapy, prayer, ceremonial rituals, and so on, most non-western cultures do not have clear separations among religion, spirituality, and healing. These healers and healing mechanisms can have equal, if not more, healing power to the immigrants who share the same belief systems. These healers and healing mechanisms should be treated as valid allies that are, for many immigrants in belief and in practice, on a par with other professionals.

While it is vital to fight against the social stigma of mental illness, there should be the same rigor in fighting the social stigma of being "foreign." This action is vital for immigrants if they are to develop healthy cultural identities that, in the process of acculturation, have been identified as strong predictors of mental health. As long as stigmas are attached to "foreign" accents, "foreign" looks, or "foreign" beliefs, immigrants will always get the same message—that being "foreign" is less than red, white, and blue—that being "foreign" disqualifies and discredits them by default, and that they are not welcome unless they become nonhyphenated Americans.

No discipline or profession can function without basic theory guidance and tenets. Especially in mental health work with immigrants, there must be a well-articulated theoretical perspective. While most of the psychological theories and concepts are severely limited in their compatibility to the values and world views of the immigrants, it is believed that to engage in professional mental health work with immigrants, social constructivism and systems theory are theories of choice (Marsella, 1998), for these theories share the holistic views held by most non-western cultures. These theories broke with earlier scientific linear causality, moving toward a psychology and anthropology compatible with and similar to that of eastern philosophy. They share the philosophy that emphasizes the embeddedness of different levels of life contexts and activities within ever-ascending dimensions and interrelatedness of every social group. They recognize the interdependent and interconnected nature of the world, and they strive for the balance of forces and powers—especially the hidden forces and powers. They recognize the validity of and give legitimacy to indigenous psychologies and healing practices, and they strive to give a voice to those who are easily overridden by the majority. These theories provide understanding and use of conceptual and theoretical perspectives that link global forces to microsocial, psychosocial, and biopsychosocial levels of human behavior.

Challenges at the Individual Level

With the challenges and required changes on the systems and professional content levels, individual mental health professionals also have to face the challenge of acquiring another skills set that includes a knowledge base that is culturally competent to work with immigrants. These mental health professionals must have higher tolerance for ambiguity and uncertainty, because whenever they walk into any one group of immigrants' lives, those lives are a new unknown. They must embrace a capacity to lean into their discomfort, to recognize and to challenge the Eurocentric nature of the assumptions, values, and concepts held both by themselves and by their professions. They must be flexible, willing to switch roles when such shifting is necessary and helpful. They should be able to switch frequently from clinician to consultant, to Internet technician, to social advocate, to community activist, and so on. Mental health professionals should be able to apply their research skills to assess quickly the immigrants' needs, deficits, and strengths and to design programs that meet culture-specific or group-specific needs by utilizing the immigrants' strengths and available means. They have to acquire knowledge of the immigration process, which includes the differential treatment that the U.S. government issues to immigrants of different status. They need to be informed of national and international issues and events and educated on U.S. foreign policy and geopolitics. Clinicians must learn how U.S. foreign policy is carried out in different countries or regions and how that policy affects international immigration.

As an example, without knowing the historical background, current events, and U.S. role in the Middle East, a mental health professional can never fully understand and therefore work effectively with Palestinian immigrants. Without the knowledge of the historical, political, and financial relationships between Japan and Korea and the geopolitics in Asia, mental health professionals may easily misinterpret as prejudice the comments of mistrust that Korean immigrants express toward Japan, and the mental health worker may take a wrong turn from there.

Challenges to Academic Training

When culture competency is being discussed, one cannot *not* talk about training. Mental health education, as an integral component of the nation's health care system, is shaped and defined not only by the dominant societal views and values but also by the profession's values and assumptions. The *status quo* of mental health training is consistent with that of the mental health system. With its curriculum content dominated by western theories and treatment modalities, it caters to the white middle-class audience, as evidenced in most psychology programs' predominance of Caucasian faculty and student bodies. The education system has to change with the rest of the mental health system to produce professionals well prepared to serve the changed population. The curriculum changes should inquire about such topics as economics, politics, and climate—conditions that vastly affect life and human beliefs and behaviors.

Currently, the public health perspective has little attention in mental health education, as the private practice or specialty clinic model dominates the U.S. free market health care system. As an unprecedented number of immigrants are coming into this country, with most of them coming from places where socialized primary care medicine or indigenous and spiritual healing practices are more prevalent, the enormity of mental health needs and tasks will inevitably require more economically feasible alternatives to current office-based specialty clinic interventions. A greater attention to environmental factors and social policies and practices that contribute to depression, anxiety, aggression, and the like can help produce more culturally consonant and economically cost-effective solutions to mental health problems. In contrast to the present training models and curriculum, this concentration would require a training regimen of broader scope that focused on larger organizations that involved mental health services.

Toolbox for Change

For	Images/perceptions	Strategies for change
Individuals	*They* versus *we*. "Foreign" equals "less." Foreigners fleece the American people. They take jobs away and drive wages down. If you don't love this country the same way that we Americans do, go back to your own country. Get with the program.	Public campaign to fight the social stigma of being foreign. Promote integration rather than assimilation. Promote social awareness of immigrants' contributions to the nation. Educate self in foreign affaires and U.S. foreign policy. Broaden view by learning from the foreigners in the U.S. and other countries.
Practitioners	We treat you just like any other human being. I can't help you if you don't understand my culture or the way we do business here. Please teach me about your culture. It is beyond my training to help you, so let me make a referral.	Awareness of Eurocentric nature of the mental health profession. Acquire new knowledge and skills. Take preventive and public health approaches. Get out of office and go to where the problems are. Do not wait for the problems to come to you.
Community/ society	No orchestrated assistance system designed for immigrants. Immigrants are left alone to swim or sink. Anti-immigrant legislature.	System changes at all levels. Special funding for culture/group-specified programs. Interface of all systems. Get politically involved in monitoring and opposing anti-immigrant legislature.

CONCLUSION

The trend of immigration is going to continue in the United States and globally. With one of the best economies and a large number of the best-trained mental health professionals in the world, the United States is in an advanced position to respond to increased global interdependency and its consequences. How immigrants are treated in this society has far-reaching impacts on world peace. If the United States is to play a leadership role in the international arena of peace and the advances of civilized humankind, there is no other choice but to face the challenge to improve the welfare of the new members of the American society. Mental health professionals, as social advocates and agents of change, have a significant role in this endeavor.

To summarize the images of oppression and the suggested strategies to combat such oppression at different levels refer to the toolbox for change.

REFERENCES

Abouguendia, M., & Noels, K. (2001). General and acculturation-related daily hassles and psychological adjustment in first- and second-generation South Asian immigrants to Canada. *International Journal of Psychology, 36*(3), 163–173.

Allodi, F. A. (1991). Assessment and treatment of torture victims: A critical review. *The Journal of Nervous and Mental Disease, 179*, 4–11.

Amaro, H., Whitaker, R., Coffman, J., & Heeren, T. (1990). Acculturation and marijuana and cocaine use: Findings from HHANES, 1982–1984. *American Journal of Public Health, 80*, 54–60.

Aronowitz, M. (1992). Adjustment of immigrant children as a function of parental attitudes to change. *International Migration Review, 26*, 89–110.

Atkinson, D. R., Morten, G., & Sue, D. W. (Eds.) (1989). A minority identity development model. In *Counseling American Minorities: A cross cultural perspective* (3rd ed.) (pp. 35–52). Dubuque, IA: W. C. Brown.

Atkinson, D. R., Morten, G., & Sue, D. W. (1998). *Counseling American minorities* (5th ed.). Boston: McGraw-Hill.

Azhar, M. Z., & Varma, S. L. (2000). Mental illness and its treatment in Malaysia. In I. al-Issa (Ed.), *Al-Junun: Mental illness in the Islamic world* (pp. 163–186). Madison, CT: International Universities Press.

Beiser, M. (1988). Influences of time, ethnicity and attachment on depression in Southeast Asian refugees. *American Journal of Psychiatry, 145*, 46–51.

Beiser, M., Hou, F., Hyman, I., & Tousignant, M. (2002). Poverty, family process, and the mental health of immigrant children in Canada. *American Journal of Public Health, 92*(2), 220–228.

Berry, J. W., Poortinga, Y. H., Segall, M. H., & Dasen, P. R. (1992). *Cross-cultural psychology: Research and application*. New York: Cambridge University Press.

Brink, P. J., & Saunders, J. M. (1976). *Transcultural nursing: A book of reading*. Englewood Cliffs, NJ: Prentice-Hall.

Bullivant, B. (1985). Educating the pluralist person: Images of society and educational responses in Australia. In M. Poole, P. de Lacey, & B. Randhawa (Eds.), *Australia in transition: Culture and life possibilities*. Sydney, Australia: Harcourt Brace Jovanovich.

Carter-Pokras, O., & Woo, V. (1999). Health profile of racial and ethnic minorities in the United States. *Ethnicity and Health, 4*(3), 117–120.

Cervantes, C. A. (2002). Explanatory emotion talk in Mexican immigrant and Mexican American families. *Hispanic Journal of Behavioral Science, 24*(2), 138–164.

Chavez, L. R. (1996). Borders and bridges: Undocumented immigrants from Mexico and Central America. In S. Pedraza & R. Rumbaut (Eds.), *Origins and destinies: Immigration, race and ethnicity in America*. Belmont, CA: Wadsworth.

Chenven, M., & Brady, B. (2003). Collaboration across disciplines and among agencies within systems of care. In A. J. Pumariega & N. C. Winters (Eds.), *Handbook of child and adolescent systems of care: The new community psychiatry* (pp. 66–81). San Francisco: Jossey-Bass.

Chung, R. C. Y., & Kagawa-Singer, M. (1993). Predictors of psychological distress among Southeast Asian refugees. *Social Science and Medicine, 36*, 631–639.

Das, A. K., & Kemp, S. F. (1997). Between two worlds: Counseling South Asian Americans. *Journal of Multicultural Counseling and Development, 25*(1).

Dion, K. L., Dion, K. K., & Pak, A. W. (1992). Personality-based hardiness as a buffer for discrimination-related stress in members of Toronto's Chinese community. *Canadian Journal of Behavioural Science, 24*, 517–536.

The Economist (2002a). The best of reasons: Who gets in. Nov. (2).

The Economist (2002b). Irresistible attraction: Who moves, and why. Nov. (2)

The Economist (2002c). Feeling at home: Why some immigrants settle in faster than others. Nov. (2).

Espiritu, Y. L. (1997). *Asian American women and men*. Thousand Oaks, CA: SAGE, Publications, Inc.

Fan, C. (1999). A comparison of attitudes towards mental illness and knowledge of mental health services between Asian immigrants and Anglo-Australians. *Community Mental Health Journal, 35*(1), 47–57.

Gilbert, M. (1989). Alcohol consumption patterns in immigrant and later generation Mexican American women. *Hispanic Journal of Behavioral Sciences, 9*, 299–313.

Gist, R. (2002). What have they done to my song? Social science, social movements, and the debriefing debates. *Cognitive and Behavioral Practice, 9*(2), 273–279.

Gong-Guy, E., Cravens, R. G., & Patterson, T. E. (1991). Clinical issues in mental health service delivery to refugees. *American Psychologist, 46*(6), 642–648.

Gordon, M. M. (1964). *Assimilation in American life: The role of race, religion, and national origins.* New York: Oxford University Press.

Graham, S. (1992). "Most of the subjects were white and middle class": Trends in published research on African Americans in selected APA journals, 1970–1989. *American Psychologist, 47*(5), 629–639.

Graves, T. D. (1967). Psychological acculturation in a tri-ethnic community. *Southwestern Journal of Anthropology, 23*, 337–350.

Haynes, S. G., Harvey, G., Montes, H., Nicken, H., & Cohen, B. H. (1990). Patterns of cigarette smoking among Hispanics in the United States: Results from the HHANES, 1982–1984. *American Journal of Public Health, 80*, 47–53.

Hitch, P. J., & Rack, H. (1980). Mental illness among Polish and Russian refugees in Bradford. *British Journal of Psychiatry, 137*, 206–211.

Hofstede, G. (1991). *Cultures and organizations: Software of the mind.* London: McGraw-Hill.

Isaac, M., & Janca, A. (1996). Somatization—a culture-bound or universal syndrome? *Journal of Mental Health, 5*(3), 219–222.

Jasinskaja-Lahti, I., & Liebkind, K. (2001). Perceived discrimination and psychological adjustment among Russian-speaking immigrant adolescents in Finland. *International Journal of Psychology, 36*(3), 174–185.

Kagan, H., & Shafer, K. C. (2001). Russian-speaking substance abusers in transition: New country, old problems. In S. L. A. Straussner (Ed.), *Ethnocultural factors in substance abuse treatment* (pp. 250–271). New York: Guilford Press.

Kelly, T. A. (2002). Dealing with fragmentation in the service delivery system. Retrieved on Aug. 25, 2003, from www.mentalhealthcommission. gov/presentations/kelly.doc

Kim, B. S. K, Li, L. C., & Liang, C. T. H. (2002). Effects of Asian American client adherence to Asian cultural values, session goal, and counselor emphasis of client expression on career counseling process. *Journal of Counseling Psychology, 49*(3).

Krupinski, J., Stoller, A., & Wallace, L. (1973). Psychiatric disorders in East European refugees now in Australia. *Social Science and Medicine, 7*, 31–49.

Ku, L., & Matani, S. (2001). Left out: Immigrants' access to health care and insurance. *Health Affairs, 20*(1), 247–257.

Kung, W. W. (2003). Chinese Americans' help seeking for emotional distress. *Social Service Review, 77*(1), 110–135.

Lee, J., Lei, A., & Sue, S. (2001). The current state of mental health research on Asian Americans. *Journal of Human Behavior in the Social Environment, 3*(3–4), 159–178.

Leherher, Z. (1993). *The psychology of immigration: A literature review.* Jerusalem: Israeli Defence Forces & JDC-Brookdale Institute of Gerontology and Human Development.

Lin, K.-M. (1986). Psychopathology and social disruption in refugees. In C. L. Williams & J. Westermeyer (Eds.), *Refugee mental health in resettlement countries* (pp. 61–73). Washington, DC: Hemisphere.

Lundstrom, S. (1986). Opening address to IACCP conference. In L. Ekstrand (Ed.), *Ethnic minorities and immigrants in a cross-cultural perspective* (pp. 9–13). Amsterdam: Swets & Zeitlinger.

Markides, K. S., & Coreil, J. (1986). The health of Hispanics in the southwestern United States: An epidemiological paradox. *Public Health Reports 101*, 253–265.

Marks, G., Garcia, M., & Solis, J. (1990). Health risk behaviors in Hispanics in the United States: Findings from HHANES, 1982–1984. *American Journal of Public Health, 80*, 20–26.

Marsella, A. J. (1998). Toward a "global-community psychology": Meeting the needs of a changing world. *American Psychologist, 53*(12), 1282–1291.

Marwaha, S., & Livingston, G. (2002). Stigma, racism or choice: Why do depressed ethnic elders avoid psychiatrists? *Journal of Affective Disorders 72*(3), 257–266.

Massey, D. S., & Espinosa, K. W. (1997). What's driving Mexico-U.S. migration? A theoretical, empirical, and policy analysis. *American Journal of Sociology, 102*(4), 939–999.

McDaniel, J. (1989). *The madness of the saints: Ecstatic religion in Bengal.* Chicago: University of Chicago Press.

Meadows, G. (2003) Buddhism and psychiatry: Confluence and conflict. *Australasian Psychiatry, 11*(1), 16–21.

Mehta, S. (1998). Relationship between acculturation and mental health for Asian Indian immigrants in the United States. *Genetic, Social & General Psychology Monographs, 124*(1).

Meyerson, B., Chu, B., & Mills, M. V. (2003). State agency policy and program coordination in response to the co-occurrence of HIV, chemical dependency, and mental illness. *Public Health Reports, 118*(5), 408–415.

Mollica, R. F., & Lavelle, J. P. (1986). *The trauma of mass violence and torture: An overview of the psychiatric care of the Southeast Asian refugee* [Report]. Boston: Indochinese Psychiatry Clinic, St. Elizabeth's Hospital.

Munroe-Blum, H., Boyle, M. H., Offord, R., & Kates, N. (1989). Immigrant children: Psychiatric disorder, school performance, and service utilization. *American Journal of Orthopsychiatry, 59*, 510–519.

National Council of Welfare. (1998). Poverty profile 1996. Catalogue H67-1/ 4-1996-E. Ottawa: Minister of Public Works and Government Services Canada.

Nguyen, S. D. (1984). Mental health services for refugees and immigrants. *Psychiatric Journal of the University of Ottawa, 9*(2), 85–91.

Nguyen, S. D. (1985). Mental health services for refugees and immigrants in Canada. In T. C. Owan (Ed.), *Southeast Asian mental health: Treatment, prevention, services, training, and research* (DHHS Publication No. ADM 85–1399, 261–281). Washington, DC: U.S. Government Printing Office.

Nguyen, S. D. (1989). Towards a successful resettlement of refugees. In M. Abbott (Ed.), *Refugee resettlement and well-being* (pp. 71–86). Auckland, New Zealand: Mental Health Foundation.

Noh, S., & Kaspar, V. (2003). Perceived discrimination and depression: Moderating effects of coping, acculturation, and ethnic support. *American Journal of Public Health, 93*(2), 232–239.

Pernice, R., & Brook, J. (1996a). Refugees' and immigrants' mental health: Association of demographic and post-immigration factors. *International Journal of Social Psychology, 136*(4).

Pernice, R., & Brook, J. (1996b). The mental health pattern of migrations: Is there a euphoric period followed by a mental health crisis? *International Journal of Social Psychiatry, 42*, 18–27.

Phan, T., & Silove, D. (1999) An overview of indigenous descriptions of mental phenomena and the range of traditional healing practices amongst the Vietnamese. *Transcultural Psychiatry, 36*(1), 79–95.

President's New Freedom Commission on Mental Health. (2003). *Achieving the promise: Transforming mental health care in America*. Retrieved July 29, 2003, from www.mentalhealthcommission.gov/reports/ FinalReport/CoverLetter.htm

Pyke, K. (2000). "The normal American family" as an interpretive structure of family life among grown children of Korean and Vietnamese immigrants. *Journal of Marriage & the Family, 62*(1), 240–256.

Reyes, B. I. (2001). *A portrait of race and ethnicity in California: An assessment of social and economic well-being*. San Francisco: Public Policy Institute of California.

Ritsner, M., & Ponizovsky, A. (1999). Psychological distress through immigration: The two-phase temporal pattern? *International Journal of Social Psychiatry, 45*(2).

Rumbaut, R. G. (1985). *Mental health and the refugee experience: A comparative study of Southeast Asian mental health: Treatment, prevention, services, training and research*. Rockville, MD: National Institute of Mental Health.

Rumbaut, R. G. (1994). Origins and destinies: Immigration to the United States since World War II. *Sociological Forum, 9*(4), 583–621.

Rumbaut, R. G. (1997). Paradoxes (and orthodoxies) of assimilation. *Sociological Perspectives, 40*(3), 483–511.

Sanchez, J. I., & Fernandez, D. M. (1993). Acculturative stress among Hispanics: A bidimensional model of ethnic identification. *Journal of Applied Social Psychology, 23*, 654–668.

Sandhu, D. A., & Asrabadi, B. R. (1994). Development of an acculturative stress scale for international students: Preliminary findings. *Psychological Review, 75*, 435–448.

Scribner, R., & Dwyer, J. (1989). Acculturation and low birthweight among Latinos in the Hispanic HANES. *American Journal of Public Health, 79*, 1263–1267.

Sluzki, C. E. (1986). Migration and family conflict. In H. Mooz (Ed.), *Coping with life crises*. New York: Plenum.

Sue, S., & McKinney, H. (1975). Asian Americans in the community mental health care system. *American Journal of Orthopsychiatry, 45*, 111–118.

Sue, D. W., & Sue, D. (2003). *Counseling the culturally diverse: Theory and practice* (4th ed.). New York: John Wiley & Sons.

Sun, L. N. N., & Steward, S. M. (2000). Psychological adjustment to cancer in a collective culture. *International Journal of Psychology, 35*(5), 177–185.

Tyhurst, L. (1982). Coping with refugees. A Canadian experience: 1948–1981. *International Journal of Social Psychiatry, 28*, 105–109.

U.S. Census Bureau. (2001). *Profile of the foreign-born population in the United States: 2000*. Retrieved Aug 25, 2003, from www.census.gov/prod/2002pubs/p23-206.pdf

U.S. Census Bureau. (2003). *Foreign-born population surpasses 32 million, Census Bureau estimates*. Retrieved Aug 25, 2003, from www.census.gov/Press-Release/www/2003/cb03-42.html

Vega, W., Kolody, B., Aguilar-Gaxiola, S., & Catalano, R. (1999). Gaps in service utilization by Mexican Americans with mental health problems. *American Journal of Psychiatry, 156*, 928–934.

Weeks, J. R., & Rumbaut, R. G. (1991). Infant mortality among ethnic immigrant groups. *Social Science and Medicine, 33*(3), 327–334.

Wells, K., Golding, J., Hough, R., Burnam, M., & Karno, M. (1989). Acculturation and the probability of use of health services by Mexican Americans. *Health Services Research, 24*, 237–257.

Wells, K., Hough, R., Golding, J., Burnam, M., & Karno, M. (1987). Which Mexican-Americans underutilize health services? *American Journal of Psychiatry, 144*, 918–922.

Williams, R. L., Binkin, N. J., & Clingman, E. J. (1986). Pregnancy outcomes among Spanish-surname women in California. *American Journal of Public Health, 76*, 387–391.

Ying, Y. W. (1996). Immigration satisfaction of Chinese Americans: An empirical examination. *Journal of Community Psychology, 24*(1), 3–16.

Yu, E. (1982). The low mortality rates of Chinese infants: Some plausible explanations. *Social Science and Medicine, 16*, 253–265.

CHAPTER 8

Multiple Minority Individuals: Multiplying the Risk of Workplace Harassment and Discrimination

Nicole L. Nelson
Tahira M. Probst

The dawn of the new millennium brings with it a revolutionary change in the way we view the workforce. For the first time ever in the United States, women and minorities are entering the workforce in greater numbers than white men (Offermann & Gowing, 1990). In fact, as of the year 2000, women and minorities will make up 85 percent of the entering workforce, and by the year 2021, at least 25 percent of the workforce will be age 55 or older (Blank & Slipp, 1994). Latinos already comprise the largest minority group, and it is estimated that by 2050 one out of every two Americans will be a minority. In addition, by 2050, immigration will have increased the total U.S. population by 80 million people, and two thirds of immigrants arriving annually will be of working age (Toossi, 2002). This will cause a shift in the composition of the workforce in which, eventually, young white males will become the minority population.

BENEFITS AND CHALLENGES OF WORKPLACE DIVERSITY

Although there are many benefits of organizational diversity (for example, enhanced recruiting from a tight labor pool, increased creativity, and organizational flexibility), research suggests that minority status is associated with a number of negative outcomes. For example, absenteeism and turnover rates are generally higher among women and minorities than they are among white men. According to Meisenheimer (1990), women in the U.S. workforce have an absenteeism rate that is 58 percent higher than that of men. Another study of American employees revealed that the turnover rate for women and blacks was more than double that of white males (Hymowitz, 1989). Cox (1994) cites lack of career advancement and lack of fit with the organizational culture as reasons for these higher rates of turnover and absenteeism. In addition, women and minorities often feel they have limited access to informal networking and mentoring opportunities, which can be critical for career success (Ibarra, 1993).

NEW THOUGHTS ON REAPING THE BENEFITS AND OVERCOMING THE CHALLENGES OF DIVERSITY

There is relatively little research to explain why diverse groups of employees often experience negative workplace events (Cox & Nkomo, 1990). In addition, most studies of discrimination and harassment tend to limit their focus to one minority group at a time (blacks, Asian Americans, Latinos, etc.) and do not consider multiple forms of diversity—reflecting, for example, racioethnicity, gender, disability, age, and sexual orientation. To rectify this oversight, we introduce in this chapter the concept of "multiple minority status" and propose that belonging to more than one minority group simultaneously—in other words, having multiple minority identities—will have a significant impact on the work experiences of minorities. As of yet, there has been little research done in this area. However, based on research suggesting that minority group members experience a host of negative physical, psychological, and job-related outcomes, we expect that being a multiple minority will further increase the likelihood of experiencing these negative outcomes.

In this chapter, we also consider the critical role that the *organizational diversity climate* can play in the workplace experiences of employees. Because of the challenges brought about by today's rapidly changing workforce, organizations need to focus on monitoring their climates for diversity, in addition to the typical focus on modifying individual employee behavior via diversity-training initiatives. Unfortunately, while many companies are concerned with fostering a positive diversity climate within their organizations, there are few tools available to

Figure 8.1 Antecedents and consequences of workplace discrimination and harassment

organizations to quickly and effectively diagnose their diversity climates. Thus, a second goal of this chapter is to present such a tool, which can provide a comprehensive assessment of organizational diversity climate that takes into account gender, age, race/ethnicity, disability, and sexual orientation.

A BRIEF OVERVIEW OF THE PROPOSED MODEL

To frame our investigations into the antecedents and consequences of workplace harassment and discrimination, an integrated model of the workplace experiences of minorities was developed (see Figure 8.1). This model theorizes three major factors that influence the level of harassment and discrimination experienced in the workplace: (1) the organizational diversity climate, (2) the employee's multiple minority status, and (3) the employee's identity importance. In turn, harassment and discrimination have repeatedly been shown to lead to lower levels of employee job satisfaction, increases in absenteeism and turnover, decreases in corporate loyalty, and increased levels of psychological distress and physical health complaints.

What Is Organizational Diversity Climate?

An organization's climate can be defined as a set of shared perceptions regarding contingencies between individual behavior within organizations and organizational consequences resulting from that behavior (Naylor, Pritchard, & Ilgen, 1980). As a result of these shared perceptions, individual behaviors that lead to negative outcomes for an employee will be avoided, whereas individual behaviors that lead to positive outcomes will be reinforced. In a similar fashion, an *organization's diversity climate* reflects shared employee perceptions regarding the predicted consequences of various forms of workplace harassment and discrimination. In other words, a positive organizational diversity climate will be intolerant of workplace harassment and discrimination, whereas a negative diversity climate will convey to employees that harassment and discrimination are tolerated by the organization.

Because of today's shifting demographics, organizations are becoming increasingly concerned with ensuring that they foster a positive climate for diversity within their workplace. A recent survey by the Society for Human Resource Management (2001) found that 66 percent of Fortune 1000 companies have initiated diversity training, education, and awareness efforts to foster better working relationships. Yet, despite these efforts, nearly a quarter of respondents also reported that these training programs were ineffective in reaching their goals. More disturbing, the number of workplace discrimination and harassment complaints filed with the Equal Employment Opportunity Commission (2002) has remained virtually unchanged over the past decade, with complaints totaling 80,840 and settlements nearing a quarter of a billion dollars.

These data reinforce the notion that diversity training is not the sole solution to addressing the challenges brought about by today's rapidly changing workforce. Rather, organizations also need to focus on monitoring their climates for diversity, in addition to the typical focus on modifying individual employee behavior through diversity training efforts.

While there are few studies documenting the impact of organizational diversity climate on workplace discrimination and harassment, there has been substantial research on sexual harassment. Specifically, Hulin, Fitzgerald, and Drasgow (1996) developed a measure of organizational climate related to sexual harassment called the Organizational Tolerance for Sexual Harassment Inventory (OTSHI). This measure assessed employee perceptions regarding organizational contingencies between sexually harassing behaviors and subsequent consequences. Subsequent research conducted by them and colleagues (Fitzgerald, Drasgow, Hulin, Gelfand, & Magley, 1997) found that the organizational tolerance of sexual harassment was the largest predictor of sexual harassment in the workplace, accounting for nearly five times the variability in sexual harassment episodes over other common predictors such as job gender context (that is, the proportion of men to women in the organization). This research was groundbreaking because it provided a framework for diagnosing organizational tolerance for workplace discrimination and harassment—a framework that was expanded upon by Probst and Nelson (2003) to develop a broader measure of organizational diversity climate that can be used to assess organizational tolerance for multiple forms of workplace discrimination and harassment.

Based on the theory and research described above, the first proposition set forth in this chapter is offered.

Proposition 1

Organizational diversity climate will be the largest predictor of employee experiences of workplace discrimination and harassment.

Defining Multiple Minority Status

Before one can study outcomes of minority status, there must be an agreed-upon definition of what constitutes a "minority" classification. According to Cox (1994), diversity may be defined as "otherness." Characteristics that make people diverse may be categorized as either primary or secondary dimensions. Primary dimensions include relatively unchangeable aspects of a person, such as race, age, gender, ethnicity, sexual orientation, physical ability, and cognitive ability. The majority of these primary dimensions are covered by equal employment opportunity legislation, due in part to the general permanence and often visually identifiable nature of these characteristics. Secondary characteristics, in contrast, are generally more malleable traits, such as socioeconomic status, political views, marital status, parental experience, and work experience. Because secondary characteristics are less outwardly obvious and (most argue) can be changed, many are not currently protected under law. Since primary dimensions of diversity are generally more salient and form the basis of the major civil rights legislation in the United States, these were the characteristics used to define minority status in our study.

Under Title VII of the Civil Rights Act of 1964, individuals must not be discriminated against due to their race, color, religion, sex, or national origin. Therefore, in this study, *racioethnic minority status* was defined as any nationality/ethnicity other than white (non-Latino) European. According to Smith (1984), data from the nationwide General Social Survey show that 64 percent of Americans are Protestant, 25 percent are Roman Catholic, 2 percent are Jewish, and 7 percent have no religious preference. Accordingly, *religious minority status* was defined as any affiliation with a religion other than Protestant.

The 2000 U.S. Census reports that females actually make up a numerical majority of America's population (51 percent). However, they were accorded *gender minority status* in this study due to their historic underrepresentation in the workplace, particularly in positions of power. The Age Discrimination in Employment Act of 1978 protects workers over the age of forty from discriminatory practices; therefore, *age minority status* was accorded to workers over the age of forty. *Disabled minority status* was defined, according to the Americans with Disabilities Act of 1990, as having an impairment that substantially limited one or more major life activities. Currently, there are no federal laws to protect people from employment discrimination due to their sexual orientation, despite multiple introductions of the Employment Non-Discrimination Act of 1997 (ENDA). At this point, only ten states and the District of Columbia have passed legislation making it illegal to discriminate based on sexual orientation or gender identity. Nonetheless, *sexual minority status* was defined as any sexual orientation other than heterosexual. Finally, because of employment discrimination faced upon returning from the war, Vietnam veterans were accorded equal opportunity employment protection under the Vietnam Veteran's Readjustment Assistance Act of 1974. Thus, *Vietnam veteran status* was our last identified minority category.

WHY DO MULTIPLE MINORITIES FACE MULTIPLE CHALLENGES IN THE WORKPLACE?

According to Triandis, Kurowski, and Gelfand (1994), employees accept or reject working with diverse individuals to the extent that there is a perception of similarity between the pertinent groups. Perceived similarity is influenced by the history of conflict between the groups, the amount of cultural distance between the groups, possession of knowledge of the other culture, an understanding of the other culture's language, the experience of equal status interactions, sharing a common social network, and the sharing of superordinate goals.

The importance of perceived similarity can be useful for understanding the factors that help or hinder collaboration among diverse individuals. First, it acknowledges that multiple factors influence the perception of similarity. The more similar individuals perceive themselves to be to one another, the more positive their resulting interactions will be. Conversely, it follows that the more dissimilar an individual is compared to the dominant culture, the more difficult his or her workplace experiences are expected to be.

In the Triandis et al. model, multiple minority status can be considered analogous to cultural distance. The greater the difference between a minority individual's cultural beliefs (such as religion or language) and those of the dominant culture, the less similar he or she is perceived to be by the dominant group. The same is true for minorities who are "different" due to disability, sexual orientation, age, and so on. The greater the differences are between their experiences and those of the nonminority group, the less similar these minorities are perceived to be to the majority group, and the more vulnerable they are to becoming targets of harassment and discrimination.

Personal Stories and Empirical Studies

As of yet, there have been very few empirical studies focusing on multiple minorities in the workplace. A qualitative investigation conducted by Mighty (1997) explored the barriers immigrant women of color experienced in the workplace. Mighty proposed that these individuals experienced "triple jeopardy" because of their minority status membership in three areas: race, gender, and ethnicity. After conducting detailed interviews with fourteen participants, several conclusions were drawn regarding the impact of "triple jeopardy" in the workforce. First, most participants had trouble finding employment. According to the participants, this was not because they lacked the skills or qualifications but because of discrimination due to their race, gender, or immigrant status. Second, many were not satisfied with their salary and/or promotion rate when compared to majority group members. Although by and large the women reported being satisfied with their work, they also felt pressure to excel to make up for their race, gender, and ethnicity. The women also felt that their relationships with white co-workers, though polite, never reached a personal or intimate level of friendship. Furthermore, the participants' lack of trust in the organizations they worked for prevented them from developing a high level of organizational commitment.

A second study conducted by Ford showed that compared to nonminority males, Mexican American females reported higher levels of job stress as well as lower levels of job satisfaction overall. On a similar note, Pak, Dion, and Dion (1991) found that when Chinese college students attending a Canadian university were discriminated against, Chinese women (a double minority group) subsequently reported significantly lower self-esteem in comparison to the men (a single minority group).

In summary, if individuals have multiple characteristics that classify them as minorities, their cultural distance from the dominant group will be even greater. Therefore it might be surmised that as minority status increases (from single minority to double minority to triple minority, etc.), the level of discrimination and harassment will increase in a similar manner. The addition of each level of minority status will likely lead to a corresponding increase in cultural distance, which will in turn put the multiple minority individual in greater danger of harassment and discrimination. Based on this, we offer the following proposition:

Proposition 2

As the number of minority identities increases, the level of workplace harassment and discrimination experienced by the multiple minority will correspondingly increase.

How Important Is Identity Importance?

Another area critical to the investigation of the workplace experiences of minorities concerns *identity importance*. Identity importance is the extent to which individuals value various aspects of their unique identities (for example, race, gender, and sexual orientation). A study by Jaret and Reitzes (1999) measured the importance of racial-ethnic identity for blacks, whites, and multiracials and compared it to other identities, including gender, age, occupation, marital status, and social class. Contrary to the hypothesis that racial-ethnic identity would be most important to black individuals' self-concept, gender was the most important identity for black, white, and multiracial participants. However, blacks did place overall greater importance on their racial-ethnic identity than did whites. Also, black females had the highest ratings of importance for their racial-ethnic identities, whereas white females had the lowest ratings. In fact, black females rated all identities (occupation, age, social class, etc.) as more important to their self-concept than did the other groups.

But how might identity importance influence experiences of harassment and discrimination in the workplace? Perhaps individuals who place greater importance on various aspects of their self-identity, such as their race or gender, also feel less a part of the dominant culture than individuals who place little importance on these personal traits. Those who feel they are part of the out-group may also be more prone to perceiving harassment or discrimination from in-group members.

Individuals who have identical demographic characteristics may attach varying levels of importance to those personal traits. For instance, suppose four different Asian American women work in a given organization. The first woman may believe her gender is one of the most important components of her self-identity. Perhaps the second woman believes her race is the most important facet of her self-identity. The third woman may believe that both her gender and her race are equally important to her self-identity. Finally, the fourth woman may believe neither her race nor gender is of central importance to her self-identity. In this situation, it is hypothesized that the woman who attaches the greatest amount of importance to her dual minority status will also report the highest level of harassment and discrimination, even though all women in this example are double minorities.

We propose that the more important that minority status is to an individual, the higher the likelihood that the individual will experience workplace harassment or discrimination. There are two unique, yet equally important, mechanisms by which this may occur: (1) an increase in the likelihood of *identifying* an incident as harassing, and (2) an increase in the relative *likelihood* of such an incident occurring. First, individuals who attach less importance to their minority identity may not identify objectively harassing or discriminatory behavior as such. For example, a woman may overhear a sexist comment from a co-worker, but if her gender is not a very important part of her self-identity, it may not offend her as much as it may another woman who overhears the same comment but whose gender is of greater importance to her self-identity. Second, identity importance may actually influence the likelihood of harassing incidents. Loden and Rosener (1991) point out that when minority group members express discomfort with the dominant group's values, they are seen as being oversensitive, "rocking the boat," or demanding "special treatment." Therefore, individuals who are very vocal about their minority identities or do not try to "fit in" with the dominant culture may actually expose themselves to more negative workplace experiences.

Consider the "Don't ask, don't tell" policy on sexual orientation in the United States military. As sexual minority identity increases in importance, it will likely be increasingly difficult to comply with this policy. However, individuals who reveal their sexual minority orientation in the military expose themselves to workplace harassment, discrimination, and even discharge from the armed services.

Therefore, it is important to consider not just the absolute level of minority status (single, double, triple, etc.), but also how important each dimension is to the individual in question. Absolute number of minority layers and the relative importance of these dimensions to the individual's self-identity may both contribute to a widening of the distance between perceptions of in-group and out-group members. Therefore, we propose:

Proposition 3

Individuals who attach great levels of importance to minority aspects of their identity will be more likely to report experiences of workplace harassment and discrimination than individuals who attach less importance to their minority status. This increase may be due to an increased propensity to *label* negative interactions as discriminatory or harassing, an increased propensity to be *exposed* to such discrimination or harassment, or a combination of the two.

TESTING THE MODEL'S PROPOSITIONS

In order to test the three propositions outlined above, all faculty and staff at a large public university located in the Pacific Northwest were invited to participate in a comprehensive study of workplace diversity within the university. University faculty and staff were contacted via e-mail regarding the project and were directed to click on a link at the end of the e-mail if they wished to participate in the anonymous online survey. A total of 719 faculty and staff participated in the survey. This represented 18 percent of the approximately 4,000 faculty and staff employees within the university. Although efforts were made to contact as many employees as possible, it is difficult to ascertain how many were actually reached, given the lack of a comprehensive e-mail database of current university employees.

Thirty-four percent of the respondents were male. The vast majority self-reported their ethnicity as white (87.4 percent), which roughly corresponds to the percent of employed whites within the university; 3.5 percent self-identified as Asian or Pacific Islander; 1.4 percent black; 1.2 percent Native American; 1.4 percent Hispanic/Latino; and 4.3 percent chose "other." The majority of respondents reported they were heterosexual (95.8 percent), with 2.3 percent self-reporting as homosexual and 2.0 percent self-identifying as bisexual. Nearly 7 percent of employees reported having a physical disability as defined by the Americans with Disabilities Act. Finally, one third of employees were over forty years of age, meeting the requirements for protection under the Age Discrimination in Employment Act.

Survey Measures

Organizational diversity climate. The Organizational Diversity Climate scale (Probst & Nelson, 2003) diagnoses the organization's diversity climate by assessing individual perceptions of organizational responses to five major types of workplace harassment (age, race, gender, disability, and sexual orientation) perpetrated by two potential sources of harassment (supervisor, co-worker). Employees are presented with ten hypothetical workplace scenarios representing either co-workers or supervisors engaging in harassing or intolerant behaviors. They are then asked to consider what might be the organizational responses to these incidents. Table 8.1 contains a complete set of the scenarios.

As noted earlier, organizational climate can be diagnosed via perceived organizational contingencies between individual behavior and outcomes. Thus, whereas the scenarios themselves provide the examples of harassing or discriminatory behavior, the response scales were written to assess the perceived likely consequences for the alleged harasser and the victim should he or she lodge a complaint about the behavior.

Thus, keeping their organization in mind, respondents were instructed to indicate on a five-point scale (1) how risky it would be for a harassed employee to file a complaint about the supervisor or co-worker, (2) how likely it would be that the complainant would be taken seriously, and (3) the likely consequences for the alleged harasser. Perceptions of risk could range from 1 = "extremely risky: they would almost certainly create problems for themselves" to 5 = "no risk: they would not create problems for themselves." Perceptions of how seriously the complaint would be considered could range from 1 = "almost no chance they would be taken seriously" to 5 = "very good chance they would be taken seriously." Finally, consequences could range from 1 = "probably nothing would be done" to 5 = "there would be a very serious punishment."

Multiple minority status. Multiple minority status could range from 0 (heterosexual, white, Protestant, able-bodied, non-Vietnam veteran, male, below age forty) to 7 (sexual minority, nonwhite, non-Protestant, disabled, Vietnam veteran, female, over age forty). Among participants in this study, six levels of minority status were the highest achieved (a disabled sexual minority, non-Christian male, Vietnam veteran over age forty).

Identity importance. In order to assess identity importance, we asked participants to rate how important each demographic characteristic

Table 8.1
Organizational diversity climate scale scenarios

	Co-worker	Supervisor
Ethnicity/ Race	An employee in your department frequently makes racial and ethnic slurs and refers to minority employees as "token hires" who wouldn't be there without affirmative action programs.	A supervisor in your department makes frequent references to "incompetent minorities who take jobs away from more qualified applicants."
Sexual Orientation	One of your co-workers frequently makes jokes about "gays," "dykes," and "lesbians."	A supervisor in your department frequently says that homosexuality is immoral and that he won't hire or promote any known homosexual if he can help it.
Age	One of the employees in your department frequently makes comments about "old fogies who should retire" because they are "behind the times."	A supervisor in your department indicates that he feels older workers don't have "fresh ideas" to contribute to the department and frequently says that "you can't teach an old dog new tricks."
Disability	A co-worker in your department makes frequent negative comments about disabled employees "playing up their disabilities so they can get special accommodations and privileges."	A supervisor in your department gripes about the Americans with Disabilities Act and says it forces him to make unreasonable accommodations for individuals with "supposed" disabilities.
Gender Harassment (Hulin, Fitzgerald, & Drasgow, 1996)	One of the employees in your department makes frequent remarks about incompetent women doing jobs they are not capable of doing and refers to them as "affirmative action hires" and "bitches with attitudes" in their presence.	A supervisor in your department makes references to "incompetent women trying to do jobs they were never intended to do and taking jobs away from better-qualified workers." He makes all women in the department feel incompetent and unwanted.

(gender, race, age, religion, sexual orientation, veteran status, and physical ability/disability) was to their self-identity using a scale of 1 (not important) to 7 (extremely important). An example item was, "How important is your gender to your self-identity?"

Job gender context. We were also interested in exploring the impact of the gender makeup of the participants' workplace environment (the job-gender context). Therefore, two items were written to assess the dominant gender context of participants' workplace environments. One item asked whether the participant was in a traditional or nontraditional job for his or her gender. The second item asked for the proportion of males to females in the participant's workplace ("mostly men," "more men than women," "more or less the same number of men and women," "more women than men," and "mostly women").

Harassment and discrimination. Several forms of workplace harassment and discrimination were assessed in this study: racioethnic harassment, harassment due to sexual orientation, sexual harassment, age harassment, and harassment due to physical disability. Specifically, a modified version of the Ethnic Harassment Experiences Scale (EHES) (Schneider, Hitlan, & Radhakrishnan, 2000) was used to measure *ethnic and racial harassment.* Participants were asked to rate on a 1 (*never*) to 5 (*very often*) scale how often they had experienced seven specific incidents of racial and/or ethnic harassment (such as "Have any of your colleagues or supervisors made derogatory comments about your race/ethnicity?").

Six items from the Workplace Heterosexist Experiences Questionnaire (WHEQ; Waldo, 1999) were used to assess employees' experiences of *harassment and discrimination based on sexual orientation.* Participants were asked to rate on a five-point scale, ranging from 1 (*never*) to 5 (*very often*), how frequently they experienced incidents of harassment and discrimination based on their sexual orientation (such as "Have any of your colleagues or supervisors made you feel it was necessary for you to 'act straight' [monitor your speech, dress, or mannerisms, etc.]?").

Perceptions of *sexual harassment* were assessed by nine items from the Sexual Experiences Questionnaire (SEQ; Fitzgerald, Gelfand, & Drasgow, 1995). Questions assessed gender harassment (such as "Have any of your colleagues or supervisors told suggestive stories or offensive jokes?"), unwanted sexual attention (such as "Have any of your colleagues or supervisors stared or leered at you in a sexual manner?"), and sexual coercion (such as "Have any of your colleagues or supervisors made you afraid of poor treatment if you didn't cooperate with his/her sexual request?").

Table 8.2
Predictors of workplace harassment and discrimination

Predictor	β	t	$p <$
Organizational diversity climate	−.36	−10.25	.001
Multiple minority status	.14	3.85	.001
Identity importance	.05	1.29	ns
Minority status x identity importance	.07	1.93	.05

Four items were written for this study to assess experiences of *harassment and discrimination based on age*. Participants were asked to rate the frequency of experiences of age-based harassment and discrimination using the five-point scale from 1 (*never*) to 5 (*very often*). Sample items included, "Have any of your colleagues or supervisors called you 'dead wood,' 'old fogie,' or some other slur?" and "Have any of your colleagues or supervisors excluded you from social interactions due to your age?"

Two items were created to assess experiences of *harassment and discrimination based on physical disabilities* (such as "Have any of your colleagues or supervisors made comments about how disabled workers can't do the job properly or don't deserve special accommodations?"). Finally, as an additional harassment/discrimination measure, participants were also asked to indicate yes/no if they had ever been harassed, denied a promotion, or denied a raise due to their race, gender, physical disabilities, sexual orientation, or age.

THE FINDINGS

Testing Proposition 1: Organizational Diversity Climate

Proposition 1 stated that the largest predictor of workplace experiences of discrimination and harassment would be the organizational diversity climate. In order to test this and the other propositions, workplace harassment (as measured by the EHES, WHEQ, SEQ, and the age and disability scales constructed for this study) was regressed onto organizational diversity climate, multiple minority status, identity importance, and the interaction between identity importance and minority status. As can be seen in Table 8.2, organizational diversity climate accounted for the largest amount of variability (13 percent) in reports of workplace harassment and discrimination. Multiple minority

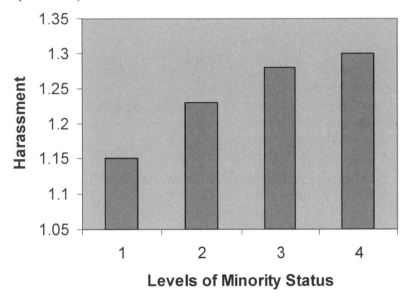

Figure 8.2 Level of reported workplace harassment as a function of minority status

status was also a significant predictor, accounting for 2 percent of the variance. These data suggest that the diversity climate within an organization is the best predictor of employee perceptions of workplace discrimination and harassment, thus supporting Proposition 1.

Similar results were found when analyzing the data from questions that asked specifically whether employees had been harassed, denied a promotion, or denied a pay raise due to their race, gender, physical disability, or age. For each of these three dependent variables, organizational diversity climate was once again the best predictor of the negative workplace experience.

Testing Proposition 2: Multiple Minority Status

As noted above, multiple minority status was significantly related to reports of negative workplace experiences. The more minority groups with which individuals were affiliated, the more likely they were to report experiences of harassment and discrimination.

A follow-up ANOVA was used to compare the reports of harassment/discrimination from single, double, triple, and quadruple minorities. The results of the test were significant, $F(3, 620) = 7.25$, $p < .001$, and suggest that reports of negative workplace interactions steadily increase with increasing layers of minority identity. As illustrated in Figure 8.2, single minorities had a mean harassment/discrimination score of 1.15 (SD = .22); double minorities had a mean score of 1.23 (SD = .28); triple minorities' mean score was 1.28 (SD = .39); and the mean score of quadruple minorities was 1.30 (SD = .24). Thus, support for Proposition 2 was found.

Testing Proposition 3: The Impact of Identity Importance

Proposition 3 predicted that the more important an individual's identity as a minority was, the more likely he or she was to report workplace harassment and discrimination. The analysis presented in Table 8.2 does not suggest such a straightforward conclusion. As can be seen in those results, identity importance itself was not directly related to harassment and discrimination. However, the interaction between identity importance and minority status was significant. In other words, among individuals who did not place much importance on their minority status, multiple minority status was less related to negative workplace experiences. On the other hand, among individuals who reported high levels of identity importance, increasing levels of multiple minority status were more strongly related to increasing reports of negative workplace experiences. Additionally, when employee minority status was low, identity importance was not related to reports of harassment. On the other hand, when there were multiple minority identities, greater identity importance was related to more negative workplace experiences. The form of this interaction can be seen in Figure 8.3.

Similar significant interactions were also found when predicting employee self-reports of workplace harassment, being denied a pay raise, and being denied a promotion. In each case, individuals with high identity importance showed a greater relationship between multiple minority status and these negative workplace outcomes than individuals with low identity importance.

Together, these results provide thought-provoking support for Proposition 3. Minority status is related to workplace experiences of discrimination and harassment, particularly if the minority individuals placed a high level of importance on their minority status. Unfortunately, while intriguing, these data cannot determine whether these results are due to an increase in "sensitivity" on the part of minority individuals or an actual increase in "exposure" to discrimination and harassment.

Other Analyses: The Job Gender Context Matters

There were two different questions used to assess the job gender context in which employees were working. The first assessed whether

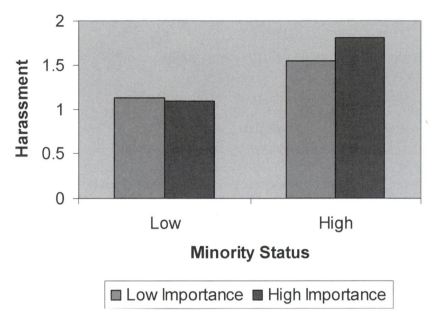

Figure 8.3 The interactive effect of minority status and identity importance

the employee was in a nontraditional position for his or her gender, whereas the second specifically measured the gender composition in the workgroup.

Results consistently suggested that the job-gender context in which employees work has a large impact on their experiences of workplace discrimination and harassment. Employees who indicated that they were in a nontraditional position for their gender were three times more likely to report being harassed at work, two and a half times more likely to be denied a promotion, and four times more likely to report being denied a pay raise. Interestingly, this effect was greater for men in traditionally female positions than women in traditionally male roles. Perhaps this is due to the greater emphasis on and visibility of women's experiences of harassment and discrimination in the workplace.

The second set of analyses centered on the gender composition of the employee's workgroup. We anticipated that females working in a predominantly male job gender context and males working in a predominantly female job gender context would experience higher levels of harassment/discrimination. As expected, we found a significant main effect for job gender context, $F (4, 689) = 5.62, p < .01$, with higher overall levels of harassment/discrimination occurring in environments dominated either by males ($M = 1.26$, $SD = .34$) or females ($M = 1.30$, $SD = .39$) compared to work environments with balanced gender compositions ($M = 1.16$, $SD = .22$).

In addition, an interesting interaction was observed between gender and the job-gender context, $F(4, 689) = 3.45$, $p < .01$. Specifically, men experienced significantly less harassment/discrimination when working in a male job gender context ($M = 1.28$, $SD = .36$) than when working in a female job gender context ($M = 1.42$, $SD = .54$). For females, the exact opposite was true. Women experienced significantly more harassment/discrimination in a male job gender context ($M = 1.24$, $SD = .32$) than in the female job gender context ($M = 1.18$, $SD = .30$). Thus, it appears that both men and women are more likely to report being harassed and discriminated against when they are in a workgroup dominated by members of the opposite sex.

MOVING FORWARD: DEVELOPING TOOLS FOR CHANGE

The goal of this study was to gain a greater understanding of the predictors of workplace harassment and discrimination. In particular, we examined the organizational diversity climate, the multiple minority status of employees, identity importance, and the job-gender context in which employees worked as drivers of these workplace experiences. Overall, the data supported the major propositions developed in this chapter. First, the single biggest and most consistent predictor of workplace harassment and discrimination was the organizational climate for diversity. Second, multiple minorities were subject to greater levels of discrimination and harassment than single minorities. Third, when minorities placed a heavy value on their minority identities, the above relationship was stronger than when their identity importance was lower. Finally, the job gender context was also a significant predictor of workplace experiences, such that employees working in a nontraditional field or in a workgroup dominated by members of the opposite sex were much more likely to face workplace discrimination and harassment. In the sections below, we explore the meaning of these findings and suggest individual and organizational tools for change to combat workplace discrimination and harassment. These tools for change are summarized in the Toolbox for Change.

TOOLS FOR CHANGING THE ORGANIZATIONAL DIVERSITY CLIMATE

Analyses consistently point to the organization's climate for diversity as the best predictor of employee workplace experiences. These findings bode very well for the future of minorities in our workplaces, because an organization's diversity climate is malleable and can be altered, whereas minority status cannot. Our findings suggest that while minority status does play an important role in determining the extent of workplace harassment and discrimination, it has less of an impact than the organizational diversity climate. Therefore, efforts should be focused on creating and maintaining an inclusive and supportive environment for all employees. Diversity-friendly policies and procedures need to be in place, but more importantly, employees need to be made aware of their existence.

Merely stating that an organization must have a positive climate for diversity is easy; however, until recently, diagnosing an organization's climate for diversity has not been. However, with the development of the Organizational Diversity Climate scale (ODC) by Probst and Nelson (2003), organizations have a quick and easy-to-use tool for making such diagnoses. Because the ODC is grounded in perceived organizational contingencies between individual behavior and organizational consequences, scores on the scale can provide practical suggestions for organizations trying to improve their climate for diversity.

Organizations can use scores on the ODC to determine the source of workplace discrimination and harassment—that is, is it co-worker on co-worker harassment or supervisor on subordinate harassment? In addition to identifying which population of workers requires additional diversity training, the three subscales of responses can be used to determine what specific steps an organization must take to improve the climate (for example, lower the risk associated with filing a complaint, disseminate more widely the consequences of harassing behavior, and/or better communicate the seriousness with which complaints will be taken). Finally, results from the ODC can be used to identify which forms of harassment are most prevalent in the organization (ageism, racism, sexism, heterosexism, etc.) and thus assist in determining where the content of future diversity training should focus.

In order to illustrate the interpretations that can be drawn from the ODC, consider the following hypothetical organizational profile in Table 8.3. By computing the means from employees on each of these dimensions, one can diagnose problem areas and make recommendations for organizational improvement. Before proceeding with the

Table 8.3
Hypothetical organizational diversity climate profile: a tool for change

	Source of harassment/discrimination			
	Co-workers		Supervisors	
	2.65		3.90	
		Type of harassment		
Ageism	Sexism	Heterosexism	Racism	Disability
2.10	4.60	4.00	2.13	4.96
	Organizational contingencies			
Risk of reporting harassment	Likelihood of being taken seriously	Consequences for perpetrator		
4.47	4.05	3.25		

Note: Reponses can range from 1 to 5 and are scaled such that *higher numbers* reflect a *more positive* perception of the diversity climate dimension. For example, a 5 on the risk subscale reflects "no risk: complainants would not create problems for themselves."

interpretation, it is important to note that all subscales are scaled such that higher numbers reflect a *more positive diversity climate* on that dimension.

In the example in Table 8.3, co-workers are clearly being seen as more likely to engage in harassing behaviors than supervisors. This suggests that the organization may have done a good job training its supervisory staff but needs additional training for its nonmanagerial employees. In addition, the results of this ODC profile suggest that ageism and racism are the greatest threats to a positive diversity climate. Perceptions of workplace heterosexism, disability-based harassment, and gender harassment are relatively positive (low-occurring), whereas perceptions of ageism and racism are negative (more likely to occur). Finally, employees perceive that there would be little risk in a victim filing a complaint about workplace harassment and feel that there would be a good chance that the organization would take them seriously. However, more could be done to improve employee perceptions regarding the consequences for the perpetrator. In this case, a 3.25 reflects a general feeling that the perpetrator would be "told to stop," but the organization would fall short of giving the employee a formal warning or a very serious punishment.

In summary, by administering the ODC to employees within an organization, organizations can use it as a diagnostic tool to determine who is committing workplace harassment, what types of harassment prevail, and the perceived organizational consequences of such harassment.

IMPROVING THE EXPERIENCES OF MULTIPLE MINORITIES: TOOLS FOR CHANGE

A major strength of this study was the inclusion of a wider array of minority categories than is typically studied. Individuals may feel or be perceived as "different" not just because their race or gender excludes them from the majority group but also for being an older worker, a Vietnam veteran, a member of a minority religious group, or for having an alternative sexual orientation. All of these traits were found to significantly impact how individuals in this study felt about themselves and how they were treated by those around them. In future research, it may be worthwhile to include an even-broader array of minority categories, such as overweight individuals and smokers.

One major implication from this research was the significant relationship between multiple minority status and workplace experiences of harassment and discrimination. As individuals possess increasing layers of diversity, they increasingly perceive themselves as targets of discrimination and harassment. Why is this the case and what can be done about it? It may be that multiple minorities are simply more visible in organizations due to their numerous differences from other employees. Each layer of minority status further distances them from the majority group dominant in the workplace. As theorized by Triandis and colleagues, decreasing perceptions of similarity are expected to be related to increasing levels of perceived distance. This may make multiple minorities more vulnerable to the experience of harassment.

Triandis and colleagues offer multiple methods for countering this perception of distance. Specifically, they recommend that organizations

Stress previous examples of successful cooperation.
Identify similarities and stress commonalities among group members.
Identify advantages of diversity and benefits that can accrue as a result.
Identify and/or create superordinate goals that can unify the workgroup.
(1994, p. 811)

Consider the Impact of Identity Importance

When taken into conjunction with minority status, the level of importance that an employee attaches to his or her multiple identities can play a pivotal role in the workplace experiences of that employee. In this study, we found that harassment and discrimination increased not only as the levels of minority status increased, but also as minority status was identified as more important to the employee's self-identity. As a result of these many "differences" and the importance that employees attached to them, they may *feel* less a part of the dominant culture and they may *be perceived by others* as less a part of the dominant culture.

Although this study revealed that the amount of importance an individual attaches to his or her minority status is a useful predictor of harassment and discrimination, it failed to discover *why*. For instance, is it because individuals who place high importance on their minority status are simply more sensitive in what they consider harassment/discrimination? It may be that because their minority status is so important to them, they are more likely to label comments or behavior directed toward their minority group as harassing or discriminatory than are individuals who place little importance on their minority status.

Conversely, it may also be the case that individuals who place large importance on their minority status are confronted with more harassment and discrimination because they are more vocal about the existence or the importance of their minority status. For example, a woman may be very active in feminist politics and make her co-workers aware of her views. This may make her a target for harassment and discrimination, not simply because she is a female, but because she is vocal about her minority status. It is possible that the harassing co-workers may have "overlooked" her minority status if she did not continually remind them of it with her "militant" (to their way of thinking) stance on women's rights. As noted earlier, research has found that members of the majority group often dismiss outspoken minorities as "oversensitive" or "militant."

Yet a third possibility may be that since multiple minorities are harassed and discriminated against more often than single minorities, this increased harassment/discrimination makes them more aware of their multiple minority status. Since they are constantly being reminded of their multiple minority status, it may become a greater focal point of their self-identity.

A FINAL TOOL FOR CHANGE: RECOGNIZE THAT ANYONE CAN BE A VICTIM OF HARASSMENT AND DISCRIMINATION

A final important finding from this study was the significance of the job gender context in predicting workplace discrimination and harassment. Regardless of whether the minority was (1) a male in a traditionally female position or a female-dominated workgroup or (2) a female in a traditionally male occupation or a male-dominated

Toolbox for Change

Organizational change	Employee change
Diagnose your diversity climate	**Recognize the multiple minority**
Use the ODC as a diagnostic tool for change to assess: Who is committing the harassment. What forms of harassment are prevalent. The risk to victims in reporting harassment. The likelihood of being taken seriously. The consequences for the perpetrator.	Be aware that each of us has multiple identities and group affiliations and that diversity is more than race or gender. Our multiple identities can influence the likelihood that we and others will face workplace discrimination and harassment.
Promote a gender-balanced workforce	**Bridge the gap** Seek to discover areas of similarity between yourself and your co-workers. Participate in organizational diversity efforts and celebrations.
Strive to equalize the proportions of men and women in workgroups. Include men and women in diversity efforts.	

workgroup, the findings were similar: employees working in a nontraditional field or in a workgroup dominated by members of the opposite sex were much more likely to face workplace discrimination and harassment than employees in a gender-balanced workgroup. Thus, regardless of which gender dominates the work environment, the gender in the numerical minority will be a likely target of harassment/discrimination. Previous research has shown that a male job gender context was a predictor of females experiencing sexual harassment (Fitzgerald et al., 1997); however, this study shows that female job gender context is equally important in predicting harassment and discrimination directed at males.

CONCLUSION

There are many factors that influence whether and to what extent employees will be the targets of workplace discrimination or harassment. This chapter outlined several such factors based on a large-scale empirical investigation and recommended multiple tools for change that individuals and their organizations could utilize in the ongoing effort to improve the workplace experiences of all employees.

REFERENCES

Blank, R., & Slipp, S. (1994). *Voices of diversity.* New York: American Management Association.

Cox, T., Jr. (1994). *Cultural diversity in organizations: Theory, research, and practice.* San Francisco: Berrett-Koehler Publishers.

Cox, T., Jr., & Nkomo, S. M. (1990). Invisible men and women: A status report on race as a research variable in organization behavior research. *Journal of Organizational Behavior, 11,* 419–431.

Equal Employment Opportunity Commission. (2002). *Charge statistics: Fiscal year 1992 through fiscal year 2001.* Retrieved September 15, 2003, from www.eeoc.gov/stats/charges.html

Fitzgerald, L. F., Drasgow, F., Hulin, C. L., Gelfand, M. J., & Magley, V. J. (1997). Antecedents and consequences of sexual harassment in organizations: A test of an integrated model. *Journal of Applied Psychology, 82*(4), 578–589.

Fitzgerald, L. F., Gelfand, M. J., & Drasgow, F. (1995). Measuring sexual harassment: Theoretical and psychometric advances. *Basic and Applied Social Psychology, 17,* 425–427.

Hulin, C. L., Fitzgerald, L. F., & Drasgow, F. (1996). Organizational influences on sexual harassment. In M. S. Stockdale (Ed.), *Sexual harassment in the workplace: Perspectives, frontiers, and response strategies* (pp. 127–150). Thousand Oaks, CA: SAGE Publications, Inc.

Hymowitz, C. (1989, February 16). One firm's bids to keep blacks, women. *Wall Street Journal,* p. B1.

Ibarra, H. (1993). Personal networks of women and minorities in management: A conceptual framework. *Academy of Management Review, 18,* 56–87.

Jaret, C., & Reitzes, D. C. (1999). The importance of racial-ethnic identity and social setting for blacks, whites, and multiracials. *Sociological Perspectives, 42*(4), 711–737.

Loden, M., & Rosener, J. B. (1991). *Workforce America: Managing employee diversity as a vital resource.* Burr Ridge, IL: Irwin Professional Publishing.

Meisenheimer, J. R. (1990). Employee absences in 1989: A new look at data from the CPS. *Monthly Labor Review, 113*(8), 28–33.

Mighty, J. E. (1997). Triple jeopardy: Immigrant women of color in the labor force. In P. Prasad & A. Mills (Eds.), *Managing the organizational melting pot: Dilemmas of workplace diversity* (pp. 312–339). Thousand Oaks, CA: SAGE Publications, Inc.

Naylor, J. C., Pritchard, R. D., & Ilgen, D. R. (1980). *A theory of behavior in organizations.* New York: Academic Press.

Offermann, L. R., & Gowing, M. K. (1990). Organizations of the future: Changes and challenges. *American Psychologist, 45,* 95–108.

Pak, A. W., Dion, K. L., & Dion, K. K. (1991). Social-psychological correlates of experienced discrimination: A test of the double jeopardy hypothesis. *International Journal of Intercultural Relations, 15,* 243–254.

Probst, T. M., & Nelson, N. L. (2003, April). *Development and validation of the organizational diversity climate scale.* Paper presented to the 2003 Conference of the Society for Industrial/Organizational Psychology, Orlando, FL.

Schneider, K. T., Hitlan, R. T., & Radhakrishnan, P. (2000). An examination of the nature and correlates of ethnic harassment experiences in multiple contexts. *Journal of Applied Psychology, 85*(1), 3–12.

Smith, T. W. (1984). America's religious mosaic. *American Demographics, 6,* 19–23.

Society for Human Resource Management. (2001). *Impact of diversity initiatives on the bottom line.* Alexandria, VA: Author.

Toossi, M. (2002). A century of change: The U.S. labor force, 1950–2050. *Monthly Labor Review, 125*(5), 15–28.

Triandis, H. C., Kurowski, L. L., & Gelfand, M. J. (1994). Workplace diversity. In H. C. Triandis & M. D. Dunnette (Eds.), *Handbook of industrial and organizational psychology* (2nd ed., Vol. 4, pp. 769–827). Palo Alto, CA: Consulting Psychologists Press.

Waldo, C. R. (1999). Working in a majority context: A structural model of heterosexism as minority stress in the workplace. *Journal of Counseling Psychology, 46*(2), 218–232.

Index

Absenteeism, 194
Acculturation: changes secondary to, 138; conflicts of, 148; definition of, 164; economic issues associated with, 157; ethnic identity and, 149–150, 153–158; language use and, 146; mental health consequences of, 138, 171–172; psychological adaptation to, 152–153; racism and, 148–150; reactions to, 138; situational, 149
Acculturation model, 99
Acculturative stress, 139
Adolescents, 144
Adoptees, 24
Age Discrimination in Employment Act of 1978, 198
Age minority status, 198
Akaka Bill, 73
Allport, Gordon W., vii
Americanization, 167
Anxiety, 54, 168
Asian Americans: Asians versus, 43–44; behaviors, 47–49; bicultural efficacy, 41–42;

cultural sensitivity of, 46–47; cultural values of, 47–49; descriptors of, 45; differential evaluative standards for, 51–52; differential treatment against, 51; educational attainment, 50; group-oriented nature of, 46; job promotion denial, 51; language connections to culture, 44–45; life experiences of, 43; mentoring for, 57–59; prejudice against, 39–42, 49–52; stereotyping of, 45–47; tracking of, 51; unrealistic and unreasonable expectations, 52; whites versus, 47–49; work-related mistreatment of, 51–52
Assimilation: description of, 98, 165–167; of European immigrants, 172; health risk behaviors and, 168; identificational, 166–167; life quality and, 167; race-based differences, 170; stress associated with, 168

About the Series and
the Series Editors

I t is expected that nearly half of the entire U.S. population will be of nonwhite ethnic and racial minorities by the year 2050. With this growing diversity, clinicians, researchers, and, indeed, all Americans need to understand that the Eurocentric psychological views particular to Caucasians may or may not be relevant or adequate to address mental health issues in racial and ethnic minorities. This series addresses those issues, aiming to better understand how these factors affect mental health, and what needs to be done, or done differently, to heal disorders that may arise.

JEAN LAU CHIN is a licensed psychologist and systemwide dean of the California School of Professional Psychology at Alliant International University. She is also president of CEO Services, which offers clinical, educational, and organizational development services emphasizing cultural competence and integrated systems of care. She holds a doctorate from Teacher's College of Columbia University. Dr. Chin's past positions include associate professor of psychiatry at the Center for Minority Training Program, Boston University School of Medicine; regional director of the Massachusetts Behavioral Health Partnership; executive director of the South Cove Community Health Center; and codirector of the Thom Child Guidance Clinic. She has authored, coauthored, or edited books including *Relationships among Asian American Women* (2000), *Community Health Psychology*

(1998), and *Diversity in Psychotherapy: The Politics of Race, Ethnicity and Gender* (1993).

VICTOR DE LA CANCELA is associate clinical professor of medical psychology at the College of Physicians and Surgeons, Columbia University. He is also deputy executive director of Tremont-Crotona Child Development Center, and a clinical psychologist serving with the United States Army Reserve.

JOHN D. ROBINSON is a professor in the Departments of Psychiatry and Surgery at the College of Medicine and Hospital at Howard University. He is a fellow of Divisions 1, 12, 38, 44, 45, 49, 51, and 52 of the American Psychological Association. In 1998, he received a letter of commendation from the president of the United States for teaching excellence. Robinson is a distinguished visiting professor at the Walter Reed Army Medical Center and at the Tripler Army Medical Center. He earned his EdD in counseling psychology at the University of Massachusetts–Amherst, completed a clinical psychology residency at the University of Texas Health Sciences Center at San Antonio, and earned an MPH at Harvard School of Public Health. Robinson worked earlier as chief of interdepartmental programs in the Departments of Psychiatry and Surgery at Howard University, and has also served as dean of the Division of Graduate Studies and Research at the University of the District of Columbia, clinical professor in the Department of Psychiatry at Georgetown University School of Medicine, and clinical attending faculty in the Department of Psychiatry at Harvard University School of Medicine at the Cambridge Hospital.

About the Advisers

JESSICA HENDERSON DANIEL is an assistant professor of psychology in the Department of Psychiatry at Harvard Medical School, and both director of training in psychology and associate director of the LEAH (Leadership Education in Adolescent Health) Training Program in Adolescent Medicine at Children's Hospital of Boston. She is also an adjunct associate professor of psychology in the clinical psychology program at Boston University. Daniel is the past president of the Society for the Psychology of Women, Division 35, APA; and is coeditor of *The Complete Guide to Mental Health for Women* (2003). Her awards include the 1998 A. Clifford Barger Excellence in Mentoring Award from Harvard Medical School; the 2001 Education Distinguished Alumni Award from the University of Illinois; the 2002 Distinguished Contributions to Education and Training Award from APA; and the 2003 Professional Award from the Boston & Vicinity Club, Inc., National Association of Negro Business and Professional Women's Clubs, Inc.

JEFFERY SCOTT MIO is a professor in the Department of Behavioral Sciences at California State Polytechnic University–Pomona, where he also serves as the director of the master of science in psychology program. He received his PhD from the University of Illinois–Chicago in 1984. He taught at California State University–Fullerton in the counseling department from 1984–1986, then taught at Washington State University in the Department of Psychology from 1986 to 1994 before accepting his current position at CSPU–Pomona. His interests are in the teaching of multicultural issues, the development of allies, and how metaphors are used in political persuasion.

NATALIE PORTER is vice provost for academic affairs systemwide at Alliant International University. She is also an associate professor of psychology. She received her PhD from the University of Delaware. Porter's research interests include feminist and anti-racist models of clinical training and supervision, cognitive and emotional developmental changes in individuals abused or traumatized as children, and feminist therapy supervision and ethics.

JOHN D. ROBINSON is a coeditor of *Race and Ethnicity in Psychology*, a Praeger series.

JOSEPH EVERETT TRIMBLE is a professor of psychology at the Center for Cross-Cultural Research at Western Washington University. Trimble was a fellow in the Radcliffe Institute for Advanced Study at Harvard University in 2000 and 2001. He is a research associate for the University of Colorado Health Sciences Center, in the Department of Psychiatry, National Center for American Indian and Alaska Native Mental Health Research. He is also a scholar and adjunct professor of psychology for the Colorado State University Tri-Ethnic Center for Prevention Research. In 1994, he received the Lifetime Achievement Award from the Society for the Psychological Study of Ethnic Minority Issues, Division 45, American Psychological Association. In 2002, he was honored with the Distinguished Psychologist Award from the Washington State Psychological Association. He has authored eighty-two journal articles, chapters, and monographs, as well as authored or edited thirteen books, including the *Handbook of Racial and Ethnic Minority Psychology* (2002).

MELBA J. T. VASQUEZ is in full-time independent practice in Austin, Texas. A past president of APA Divisions 35 (Society for the Psychology of Women) and 17 (Society of Counseling Psychology), she has served in various other leadership positions. She is a fellow of the APA and a diplomate of the ABPP. She publishes in the areas of professional ethics, psychology of women, ethnic minority psychology, and training and supervision. She is coauthor, with Ken Pope, of *Ethics in Counseling and Psychotherapy: A Practical Guide* (1998, 2nd ed.). She is the recipient of several awards including Psychologist of the Year, Texas Psychological Association, 2003; Senior Career Award for Distinguished Contributions to Psychology in the Public Interest, APA, 2002; Janet E. Helms Award for Mentoring and Scholarship,

Columbia University, 2002; John Black Award for Outstanding Achievement in the Practice of Counseling Psychology, Division 17, APA, 2000; and the Distinguished Leader for Women in Psychology Award, Committee of Women Psychology, APA, 2000.

HERBERT Z. WONG has provided management consulting, diversity training, and organizational assessments to over 300 government agencies, businesses, and other organizations. He was the cofounder and president of the National Diversity Conference, Inc., which presented contemporary issues and future directions of workforce diversity. He was a consultant to the President's Commission on Mental Health (1977), the White House Conference for a Drug Free America (1989), and the President's Initiative on Race–White House Office of Science and Technology (2000). In the past twenty-five years, Wong has written extensively on multicultural leadership, cross-cultural communication, and diversity issues. Wong received his PhD in clinical and organizational psychology from the University of Michigan.

About the Contributors

STEPHANIE ROSE BIRD is an assistant professor at the School of the Art Institute of Chicago. She earned her master of fine arts degree in visual arts at the University of California–San Diego.

TIMOTHY DUNNIGAN is an anthropological linguist who teaches in the Department of Anthropology at the University of Minnesota. His primary area of study is the role of cultural semantics in comparative cultural studies. At present, he is working on a dictionary that compares and contrasts how Hmong and English speakers categorize psychological states and processes.

DARRYL FREELAND is associate professor in the Marriage and Family Therapy Program of the California School of Professional Psychology at Alliant International University in San Diego. He received his PhD from the University of Southern California.

MICHAEL GOH is assistant professor with the Counseling and Student Personnel Psychology Program at the University of Minnesota, Minneapolis. His teaching, research, and service are focused on improving access to mental health services for ethnic minority, new immigrant, and international populations as well as being focused on the internationalization of counseling psychology. He was recently appointed a multicultural education fellow at the University of Minnesota. He is a member of the Minnesota Hmong Mental Health Research Group, an interdisciplinary team seeking to develop mental health approaches that are culturally and linguistically appropriate for the Hmong and other Southeast Asian immigrant groups. His research has been presented at regional, national, and international conferences including the American Psychological Association, the American Counseling Association, APA's National Multicultural Conference and Summit, the International Congress of Psychology, and the International Association of Cross-Cultural Psychology. He is coauthor of *Psychology in Singapore: Issues of an Emerging Discipline* (2002) and has published several book chapters and journal articles.

DEBRA M. KAWAHARA is assistant professor in the clinical psychology doctoral program at the California School of Professional Psychology at Alliant International University. Her main interests are multicultural psychology and training, Asian American mental health, and trauma. In addition, she is actively involved in presenting to and training mental health professionals in the delivery of culturally competent services, particularly to ethnic and minority populations. She received her PhD degree (1994) from the California School of Professional Psychology–Los Angeles.

SANDRA MATTAR is associate professor of psychology in the PsyD program at John F. Kennedy University, Graduate School of Professional Psychology, in Orinda, California. She is also an adjunct faculty member in the MA in counseling program at JFKU. Mattar received her psychology degree in Caracas, Venezuela, and her PsyD at the Massachusetts School of Professional Psychology (MSPP). She was a Harvard fellow at the Victims of Violence Program at Cambridge Hospital in Boston. Her main professional work focuses around immigrant families, the psychology of acculturation, ethnic & racial identity, cross-cultural mental health issues, and the psychology of trauma. She has taught courses at University of California Berkeley–Extension and MSPP–Extension. Her publications include the following articles, papers, and chapter: "Depression and Anxiety Among Immigrant Women," "Forging Troubled Waters: The Inclusion of Race and Culture into Teaching and Clinical Practice," "Three Continents, Three Generations: Lessons Learned during My Immigration and Acculturation Process," and "The Self Revisited: A Cross-Cultural Perspective," among others. Mattar speaks four languages and is the daughter of Lebanese immigrants to Venezuela.

NICOLE L. NELSON is a personnel research psychologist at the Federal Aviation Administration Civil Aerospace Medical Institute. She is a principal investigator on the Organizational Assessment Team in the Training and Organizational Research Laboratory. Her current research focuses on organizational effectiveness, performance measurement, and the identification of factors related to human error to enhance performance of aviation-related personnel. Dr. Nelson received her PhD in social/organizational psychology from Washington State University.

TAHIRA M. PROBST is an associate professor of industrial/organizational psychology in the Department of Psychology at Washington State University–Vancouver. Her research interests include issues surrounding workplace diversity, international human resource management, and occupational health psychology. She currently serves on the editorial board of the *Journal of Occupational Health Psychology*, and her research has appeared in outlets such as the *Journal of Applied Psychology, Group and Organization Management, Journal of Occupational and Organizational Psychology, Organizational Behavior and Human Decision Processes*, and *Teaching of Psychology*.

KATHRYN McGRAW SCHUCHMAN is a psychologist in independent practice working with children and adolescents and their families. For thirteen years, she has provided assessment and therapy to children, teens, and young adults. Currently, she specializes in mental health services with refugees and immigrants. Throughout most of her work, Kathryn has been involved in community-based initiatives. She has been chair of the Hmong Mental Health Providers Network, an organization focused on building collaborations and strengthening advocacy among professionals involved in mental health services with Hmong, and is currently developing a nonprofit multicultural center for integrated health. Schuchman is also engaged in cross-cultural research focusing on the mental health concepts, language, indigenous healing practices, and mental health interventions of the Hmong.

MATTHEW J. TAYLOR is an associate professor of psychology and a fellow at the Research Center for Cultural Diversity and Community Renewal at the University of Wisconsin–La Crosse. With a degree in clinical psychology from the University of Missouri–St. Louis, his teaching, research, and clinical interests are eclectic with a core theme of minority mental health. He teaches the courses Cross-Cultural Psychology, Cross-Cultural Development, and Culture and Mental Health. Much of his research has focused on substance abuse and associated problems within minority communities. Other work has examined the use of historical cultural themes in therapeutic scenarios with minority clients. He has practiced clinical cross-cultural psychology at the Indian Health Service (IHS) Hospital in Phoenix, and the American Indian Center of Mid-America in St. Louis. He has also given numerous talks on race, interracial relationships, identity formation, and the impact of American culture on the mental health of minority groups. He is biracial (German-American and black), was adopted at eighteen months by a German-Irish American family, and grew up on the East Coast.

JAYE JANG VAN KIRK is a professor of psychology at San Diego Mesa College. She serves as the Psi Beta vice president for the Western/ Rocky Mountain region and is currently Psi Beta national president-elect. She has interests in psychobiology and in the development of academic potential of students. She has presented sessions on leadership and innovative teaching and was recently invited to speak at the Oxford Round Table at Oxford University, England, on the challenges that ethnic women face in achieving higher education. She received her master's degree in experimental psychology from California State University–Fullerton.

LINNA WANG is assistant professor of marriage and family therapy and coordinator of the Marriage and Family Therapy Program at Alliant International University. She holds a PhD in marriage and family therapy from Brigham Young University, an MBA in strategic management and international business from Alliant, and a BA in English and literature from Shandong University, China.

ANN S. YABUSAKI is a licensed psychologist and has served as faculty, dean, and president of graduate schools of psychology in the San Francisco Bay area. She maintains a private practice and directs the substance abuse treatment program at the Coalition for a Drug-Free Hawaii. She also serves as the principal evaluator for a federal grant to train mental health providers serving Asian and Pacific Island communities.

KENICHI K. YABUSAKI is a private consultant for biochemistry and biomedical diagnostic assay design and development. His doctorate in biochemistry is from the University of Arizona–Tucson. He has held positions as adjunct faculty at John F. Kennedy University and at Rosebridge Graduate School of Integrative Psychology.